SHEPHERDING SOULS

A Handbook for the Pastoral Offices

SHAWN O. STROUT

Copyright © 2024 Shawn O. Strout

All rights reserved. No part of this book may be reproduced, stored in a retrieval system, or transmitted in any form or by any means, electronic or mechanical, including photocopying, recording, or otherwise, without the written permission of the publisher.

Unless otherwise noted, the Scripture quotations are from New Revised Standard Version Bible, copyright © 1989 National Council of the Churches of Christ in the United States of America. Used by permission. All rights reserved worldwide.

Church Publishing
19 East 34th Street
New York, NY 10016
Seabury Books is an imprint of Church Publishing Incorporated.

Cover design by Newgen
Typeset by Nord Compo

ISBN 978-1-64065-659-8 (paperback)
ISBN 978-1-64065-658-1 (eBook)

Library of Congress Control Number: 2024935211

"Saviour, like a shepherd lead us; much we need thy tender care."
—*Hymns for the Young, ca. 1830*

Contents

Acknowledgments vii
Abbreviations ix
Introduction xi

1. Baptism 1
2. Confirmation and Other Rites of Affirmation 40
3. Marriage 77
4. Rites of Reconciliation and Healing 121
5. Ministration at the Time of Death and Burial 169

Appendices
    Appendix A: Baptismal Rites 220
    Appendix B: Rites of Affirmation 222
    Appendix C: Marriage Rites 224
    Appendix D: Rites of Reconciliation 226
    Appendix E: Rites of Public Healing 228
    Appendix F: Rites for Ministration at the Time of Death . . . 230
    Appendix G: Burial 231

Bibliography 233
Index 240

Acknowledgments

Writing a book such as this one requires many people. Thankfully, I have received assistance from many friends and colleagues, for which I am deeply grateful. First and foremost, I thank God for the many gifts I have received. I am also grateful for my students, who continue to inspire me as they prepare to serve God as lay and ordained church leaders in their varied contexts.

I am immensely grateful for the people I call "pastoral consultants," who met with me at various points to offer their perspectives on the practices of the pastoral offices in their communities. Thank you to the Right Reverend John T. W. Harmon, Bishop of Arkansas and former rector of Trinity Parish, Washington, D.C., and the Rev. Richard Wall, rector of St. Paul's Episcopal Church in Washington, D.C. From Virginia Theological Seminary, I extend heartfelt thanks to my colleagues and friends the Rev. Rode Molla, Ph.D., Assistant Professor, the Berryman Family Chair for Children's Spirituality and Nurture; the Rev. Altagracia Pérez-Bullard, Ph.D., Director of Contextual Ministry and Assistant Professor of Practical Theology; and the Rev. John Yieh, Ph.D., the Molly Laird Downs Professor of New Testament.

I also appreciate the assistance of my Faculty Research Seminar members, which included the Rev. James Farwell, Ph.D., Professor of Theology and Liturgy; John Knight, Ph.D., Sprigg Visiting Professor of Philosophical Theology and Ethics and Director of Faculty Research; the Rev. Melody Knowles, Ph.D., Senior Vice President of Academic Affairs and Associate Professor of Old Testament; Dr. Molla, and Dr. Yieh.

Institutionally, I have received incredible support from the Very Rev. Ian S. Markham, Ph.D., Dean and President, and the fantastic staff at the Bishop Payne Library, the best library in the world! I appreciate Maxine King, my research assistant, for taking many of the book's details off my plate. I am also grateful to my editor, Justin Hoffman, for guiding me through this publication process and encouraging me to expand on my original ideas. Finally, I am always grateful to Todd and my parents for their unwavering support.

Abbreviations

BCP	*The Book of Common Prayer* 1979
BCW	*The Book of Common Worship*, 2018
BOW	*The United Methodist Book of Worship*, 1992
ELW	*Evangelical Lutheran Worship*, 2006
ELWPC	*Evangelical Lutheran Worship Pastoral Care*, 2008
OBC	*The Order of Baptism of Children*, Second Typical Edition, 2020
OCM	*The Order of Celebrating Matrimony*, Second Typical Edition, 2016
OCN	*The Order of Confirmation*, Typical Edition, 2016
RITES	*The Rites of the Catholic Church*, 1990

Introduction

From its inception, the Christian church has placed Christ at the center of its worship. The Eucharist, also known as the Lord's Supper, Mass, or the Divine Liturgy, has been the central act of worship for the Christian church for centuries. The Paschal Mystery of Christ, his incarnation, life, passion, death, resurrection, ascension, and second coming, are the central focus of this service. The liturgical year, with its cycles of feasts and fasts, developed as a continuous response to Christ's Paschal Mystery.

In addition to this central focus, the Church has also needed to attend to the events lived by its members. Christians pass through the stages of birth, maturity, marriage, reconciliation, healing, and death. While these human events long predated the advent of the church, other religious traditions also engage with them through their own cultural and theological lenses.

As the church grew, it had to determine how to accompany these human events within its own theological and cultural contexts. That process has been called inculturation or contextualization. Anscar J. Chupungco defines inculturation in relationship to liturgy as "the process whereby pertinent elements of a local culture are integrated into the texts, rites, symbols, and institutions employed by a local church for its worship."[1] All the services of the church engage in inculturation. For the pastoral offices, this process is explicit as they respond to human events with long histories predating Christianity.

Thus, the pastoral offices seek to meet the needs of people in their everyday lives and manifest the myriad ways humans have accompanied these basic needs. This book is a one-stop guide that offers historical context, theological insights, cultural connections, and pastoral perspectives on these services that have met Christians' most profound needs.

Pastoral Offices and Initiatory Rites

The astute reader may question the inclusion of baptism in this volume. Is baptism a pastoral office or an initiatory rite? This question is central to framing how one understands the role of baptism in the church. The answer is that it has operated and still operates as both as do all the pastoral offices.

Undoubtedly, baptism is an initiatory rite, how one becomes a member of the body of Christ, the church. Anthropologists have provided frameworks for how initiatory rituals operate in societies, and Christian baptism falls neatly into that framework, especially when adult baptism is considered the normative model. Theologically, most Christian traditions today understand baptism fundamentally

---

1. Anscar J. Chupungco, "Liturgy and Inculturation," in *Fundamental Liturgy*, II:339.

as an identification with Christ. Thus, it acts as more than an initiation ritual. It is the Christian rite from which all other rites, including the pastoral offices, flow.

Other pastoral offices also fit into this initiatory model. Confirmation and other rites of affirmation allow Christians to be initiated into a mature faith. That might occur in adolescence, but it can also occur in any mature stage of life. Sometimes, these rites are repeated and offer a reinitiation into this mature life of faith.

Marriage is an initiation into a new way of life. Two individuals become one couple. Not only does this change their own lives, but it also changes the lives of their families and friends. They treat them differently as a couple than they did as single individuals. Their communities also understand them to have a new status.

Reconciliation is a form of reinitiation into the church. While the church has normatively understood baptism to be a one-time, permanent event, reconciliation offers Christians a way to reengage with congregational life after sin. At times in history, the church treated penitents almost as excommunicants. Some church leaders even suggested that recourse. However, the church rejected total excommunication for the more liminal experience of a penitent, who could be reaggregated back into the church after due penance.

Anointing for the sick has offered complex forms of initiation. In both its earliest and most current forms, anointing with handlaying was a means by which people who were separated from the church community due to their illness could be reaggregated into the community. During the intervening periods, extreme unction, as it became known, was the beginning of initiation into death.

Burial is an initiation into death. As sickness becomes terminal, the dying enters a liminal state. For Christian theology, that liminal state does not end with death but rather is an initiation into new life through the resurrection. The dead are "commended" to God. They leave this life to enter a new life with Christ.

However, these services—baptism, confirmation, marriage, reconciliation, anointing, and burial—also operate as pastoral offices. Byron Stuhlman defines a pastoral office as "occasional offices concerned with turning points in the personal lives of individual Christians."[2] For baptism, the birth of a child and the desire to raise the child in the Christian faith is one such "turning point." Likewise, an adult's desire to formally enter the Church is a "turning point." Confirmation and other rites of affirmation meet the Christian at the moment of their mature, public affirmation of faith. Marriage is that point when a couple begins a new life together. Reconciliation is a turning from a life of sin to a life of forgiveness and grace. Anointing for healing encounters the sick in their moment of weakness, giving them strength for their journey. Burial offers consolation to the dying and the bereaved.

Tension exists between initiation rites and pastoral offices. This tension is best left taut. Attempts to resolve it in either direction will likely result in skewed

---

2. Byron Stuhlman, *Occasions of Grace: An Historical and Theological Study of the Pastoral Office and Episcopal Services in the Book of Common Prayer*, 6.

understandings and ineffective approaches toward these seminal moments in life. All these services act as both initiatory rites and pastoral offices. Wise pastors will recognize the importance of that dynamic and maintain it.

Outline of the Book

This book is intended to be a handbook for the pastoral offices. It is a one-stop guide for lay and ordained church leaders as they seek to engage congregants in these critical life events. It is not meant to be a comprehensive resource for each of these offices. It is also not meant to be read cover-to-cover. The hope is that it will be a regular resource for pastoral leaders that provides enough information to be helpful and to elicit further questions. Each chapter offers additional resources that can assist the reader in gathering more detailed information if desired.

The chapter sequence in this book may seem self-evident at first glance: baptism, confirmation and other rites of affirmation, marriage, rites of reconciliation and healing, and ministration at the time of death and burial. However, the divisions are not so easily separated. For example, baptism and what would later be known as confirmation were unified rites for the first several centuries of church history. The histories and theologies of reconciliation and healing were so intertwined that attempting to speak of them separately would have created further misunderstanding. Moreover, where is the line between ministration to the sick and the dying? Much overlap exists among these services. Thus, the reader may wish to refer to material in other chapters in addition to the one being directly explored.

Each chapter follows the same outline: historical context, theological insights, cultural connections, pastoral perspectives, discussion questions, and additional resources. Like the chapters, one could read a particular section in isolation to glean the information desired. However, a fuller story is told throughout the chapter. Here, a word or two about each section is in order.

The historical context sections are meant to briefly summarize the story of how these rites developed in the church. The primary focus is on the Western church, although some material exists on Eastern rites. Like the chapter divisions, the historical divisions are somewhat arbitrary. The hope is that the reader will not see these divisions as rigid but suggestive, particularly of significant developments.

The theological insights sections offer an ecumenical perspective. Such an endeavor requires making challenging decisions. The primary sources for these sections were the liturgical materials of the ecclesial traditions discussed. However, other sources are essential when developing doctrine, such as church canons, creeds, confessions, and the works of influential theologians. These sources appear at times, but a complete treatment of them was not possible in the scope of this work.

Another complicating factor is the status these liturgical resources have in their traditions. Some traditions, such as the Roman Catholic Church, Eastern

Orthodox churches, and churches of the Anglican Communion, consider their liturgical resources authorized by their central bodies and prescriptive for use in public worship. However, other traditions, such as the Evangelical Lutheran Church in America, the Presbyterian Church, U.S.A., and the United Methodist Church, have authorized liturgical resources but do not prescribe them. Thus, their actual use in local congregations can vary significantly. Nonetheless, they represent an attempt to find a shared theological voice for these services.

Cultural connections are just that, only connections. The material presented in this book should be understood as examples of how cultures have connected with these rites. They should not be understood as monolithic cultural statements. Cultural communities have myriad differences among them. The hope is that these sections will raise questions for pastors to ask of their congregants through the examples given rather than providing answers. Cultures are richly textured, and wise pastors understand and appreciate their diversity.

Finally, the hope is that the pastoral perspectives will offer food for thought. No book could present every possible pastoral experience. They vary significantly due to context, temperament, experience, and other factors. These sections offer examples that may resemble situations the reader could encounter and, therefore, be prepared. However, having mentors to discuss the complexities of a specific pastoral situation is also helpful.

This book is meant to guide lay and ordained pastoral leaders as they journey with people through the joys and sorrows of their lives. The material will be most helpful if taken as introductory and suggestive rather than definitive and authoritative. May it be a source of challenge, hope, and support.

Social Location

This book seeks to be a resource for a broad audience. However, it was written by a single author with the help of several friends and colleagues.[3] While every attempt has been made to write with this broad audience in mind, the author's social location has undoubtedly affected the outcome. Therefore, explicitly stating that social location would be helpful.

The author identifies as a queer, white, cis-gendered male. He was born in Claremont, New Hampshire, and spent his childhood there. He was baptized in the Roman Catholic Church as an infant and again in the Baptist Church when he was around ten. As a young adult, he was a member of a Unitarian Universalist congregation for about three years, simultaneously studying and practicing Japanese Buddhism. Later, he was confirmed in the Episcopal Church and was ordained in that ecclesial tradition as a deacon in 2012 and as a priest/presbyter in 2013. He resides with his spouse in Alexandria, Virginia, and teaches worship courses at the Virginia Theological Seminary.

---

3. Please see the Acknowledgments above for details.

CHAPTER 1

Baptism

Ecclesial traditions today understand baptism as full initiation into the church. For many traditions, this initiation can occur in infancy at the behest of one's parents. For some traditions, it is only a mature and public affirmation of faith. Nonetheless, all ecclesial traditions recognize it as the entrance into full membership in the church. This chapter seeks to provide historical context, theological insights, pastoral perspectives, and cultural connections regarding baptism.

Historical Context

The New Testament

The history of baptism predates Christianity. Ritual washing has been a part of religious practices since the dawn of humanity. The Hebrew Scriptures are replete with references to washing hands, feet, faces, and bodies as a means of ritual cleansing. Water appears in the very beginning of scripture as Genesis describes, "In the beginning when God created the heavens and the earth, the earth was a formless void and darkness covered the face of the deep, while a wind from God swept over the face of the waters (Gen 1:1-2 NRSV)." From these formless waters sprang forth creation. The Great Flood offers the image of water as a cleansing of the earth. The crossing of the Red Sea is a central image of both repudiation and liberation. Leviticus features numerous commandments on the importance of ritual cleansing. Moreover, the prophets regularly evoke the imagery of water washing away sin.

During the time of Jesus, certain Jewish groups, such as the Essenes and the Pharisees, engaged in repeated baptisms that were linked to ritual cleansing but also took on a new character. They became messianic as a sign, sometimes daily, of preparation for the messiah's coming and eschatological as a hope for that coming.[1]

By the time of the New Testament, the connection between water and ritual cleansing was firmly fixed. All four Gospels share the account of John the Baptizer at the River Jordan "proclaiming a baptism of repentance for the forgiveness

---

1. Maxwell E. Johnson, *The Rites of Christian Initiation*, 8-10. See also the classic work by Everett Ferguson, *Baptism in the Early Church: History, Theology, and Liturgy in the First Five Centuries*, 68-71.

of sins (Mark 1:4)." Like the Essenes, John the Baptizer's message emphasized a different aspect of the water bath. It was not just about ritual cleansing. It was also eschatological and prophetic. By invoking the prophet Isaiah, John seeks to make way for the coming of the Messiah, the "one who is more powerful than I (Mark 1:7)." This Messiah will not just baptize with water but with the Holy Spirit.

However, John's baptism should not be equated with the Essenes' baptism. Apparent differences existed between them. One crucial difference was the frequency. The Essenes and other such groups baptized repeatedly, but John's baptism was once and for all.[2] This unrepeatable character of baptism would become important for the Christian church. Also, the Essenes self-administered baptism, while John was the baptizer. In this way, John acted as an eschatological symbol of God's desire to wash Israel. Christian baptism would share these images of John's baptism rather than those of the Essenes.

It is no small thing that all four Gospels record the baptism of Jesus by John. While the details among the four Gospel accounts differ, one remains the same—the descent of the Holy Spirit on Jesus. This reception of the Holy Spirit marks the difference between "the baptism of John" and "the baptism of Jesus" found in Acts 19. The theological emphasis of baptism changed from ritual cleansing to receiving the Holy Spirit and being identified as an "Anointed One."

The coming of the Holy Spirit on the feast of Pentecost (Acts 2) directly connects with an understanding of Pentecost as a feast of initiation. At the time of the writing of Luke-Acts, Jewish communities celebrated Shavuot or Pentecost as a renewal of the Sinai covenant. It included the welcoming of new converts into the faith. Some research even suggests that the early Christian community may have "Christianized" a liturgical calendar in Jerusalem that marks Pentecost as a day of initiation.[3]

The New Testament does not give exact details of the elements involved in the baptismal rite, very likely because they varied among different communities. Water was an essential ingredient, but little is known about the manner of baptism. Was it aspersion, affusion, immersion, or submersion?[4] Paul's references to baptism as identification with Christ's death and resurrection suggest submersion (Rom 6:3-4). However, early baptismal iconography of Jesus' baptism shows him standing immersed in the water, and archeological evidence of early baptismal pools suggests shallow pools of water that would make submersion difficult.[5]

---

2. Johnson, *The Rites of Christian Initiation*, 10.

3. See Johnson, *The Rites of Christian Initiation*, 23-28 for more details.

4. Aspersion involves sprinkling water over the head of the person being baptized. Affusion is pouring water over the person's head. Immersion is when the baptized person stands in the water, sometimes waist-deep. This method may also involve affusion as the water would then be poured over their head. Submersion means the person's entire body goes under the water. If the water is deep enough, the person may bend their knees and go down into the water facing forward, or, in a shallower pool, they may bend back into the water with assistance from the minister.

5. Johnson, *The Rites of Christian Initiation*, 34.

The words that accompanied the baptismal action are also unclear. Later medieval Scholasticism would require using the Trinitarian formula for a "valid" baptism. Modern ecumenical agreements confirm that expectation. However, the New Testament is ambiguous. Christ commanded his disciples to baptize "in the name of the Father and of the Son and of the Holy Spirit (Matt 28:16-20)." However, Acts acknowledges baptisms in "the name of Jesus." These references are much more likely to reflect theological concerns than actual liturgical practices.

It is also unclear if anointing with oil accompanied the act of washing. Scripture lacks explicit reference to this practice, but it was commonly associated with bathing then. References to being "anointed" or "sealed" with the Holy Spirit (2 Cor 1:22; Eph 1:13; 1 John 2:20) and to having been marked with the "seal on their foreheads" (Rev 7:3) imply a connection. The laying on of hands also appears to be a vital ritual gesture that closely followed the act of washing (Acts 8:14-17 and 19:1-7).

The New Testament is also unclear about the role of infants in baptism. No explicit reference to the baptism of infants exists in the New Testament. Ecclesial communities that emphasize only adult baptism refer to this lack of scriptural evidence to substantiate their practice. However, communities that engage in infant baptism recognize references to the baptism of entire households (Acts 16:15, 18:8, and 1 Cor 1:16). Adult baptism appears to have been the normative practice, with infant baptism being a possible but exceptional option.

Recent scholarship cautions against trying to find a "primitive pattern" for initiation in the New Testament. The evidence suggests a diversity of practices but with a common theme. That theme is a moving away from a repeated ritual cleansing to a once-and-for-all bath (possibly with anointing and handlaying) that involves identification with Christ and the gift of the Holy Spirit.[6]

The Ante-Nicene Period

This diversity of ritual experiences for baptism would continue in the centuries following the New Testament and what would become known as the Ante-Nicene period. No manuscripts containing full rituals remain from this period. Instead, documents known as church orders contain descriptions of what purportedly occurred. Other sources, such as hymns, poetry, epistles, and sermons, provide additional information. However, attempts to generalize this information are unwise.

One such church order was *The Didache* or "The Teaching of the Lord to the Gentiles through the Apostles." Scholars believe it dates back to the late first to the early second century in Syria. The first six chapters of this document contain what appears to be a pre-baptismal catechesis called "The Two Ways."[7]

---

6. Johnson, *The Rites of Christian Initiation*, 37.

7. Johnson, *The Rites of Christian Initiation*, 43-44.

Chapter seven gives the earliest description of a baptismal rite outside of the New Testament.

> 7.1 Regarding baptism. Baptize as follows: after first explaining all these points ... 'Baptize in the name of the Father and of the Son and of the Holy Spirit' [Matt 28.19], in running water. 2. But if you have no running water, baptize in other water; and if you cannot in cold, then in warm. 3. But if you have neither, pour water on the head three times 'in the name of the Father and of the Son and of the Holy Spirit.' 4. Before the baptism, let the baptizer and the candidate for baptism fast, as well as any as are able. Require the candidate to fast one or two days previously.[8]

In the rite that this order describes, the Trinitarian formula appears directly connected with the action of baptism. Water was also a necessary ingredient, with a preference for "running water." Either submersion or immersion was the preferred method of baptism, with affusion being an option only if circumstances dictate. The expectation was pre-baptismal fasting by at least the candidate.

The document does not indicate if participation in the Eucharist immediately follows the act of baptism. Nevertheless, it does prescribe baptism as a prerequisite for communion.

> 9.5 Let no one eat or drink of your thanksgiving [meal] save those who have been baptized in the name of the Lord, since the Lord has said concerning this, "Do not give what is holy to dogs."[9]

What is clear is that there is some period of formation preceding baptism, a response of faith, the rite of baptism, and then participation in the ongoing life of the church.

Justin Martyr (c. 100 – c. 165 CE) was a philosopher and apologist for the Christian faith. In his *First Apology*, he described a baptismal rite to Emperor Antoninus Pius, the intended recipient of his work. Like *The Didache*, he described a period of pre-baptismal catechesis leading to a water bath in which the Trinity was invoked. Justin's description had the baptismal candidates go immediately from the baptism into the eucharistic assembly to be greeted by the exchange of peace.[10]

Tertullian (c. 155 – c. 220 CE) was a Christian writer from North Africa. In his *De Baptismo*, he described a baptismal rite that followed the above pattern with additional details. As mentioned above, a catechumenal period preceded baptism. In Tertullian's description, the Holy Spirit was invoked upon the baptismal waters, and the candidate was washed. Immediately following, the candidate

---

8. E. C. Whitaker and Maxwell E Johnson, *Documents of the Baptismal Liturgy*, 2.
9. Whitaker and Johnson, *Documents of the Baptismal Liturgy*, 2.
10. Whitaker and Johnson, *Documents of the Baptismal Liturgy*, 3.

was anointed with "blessed unction," and hands were imposed with a blessing. Eucharist followed with the reception of "a compound of milk and honey."[11]

One of the most thorough descriptions of the baptismal rite comes from the well-known church order called *The Apostolic Tradition*. Initially, scholars believed that Hippolytus of Rome wrote this document in the third century and, thus, described early Roman practice.[12] Both its descriptions of baptism and the Eucharist became the template for liturgical reforms among several ecclesial traditions. However, later scholarship would show that Hippolytus did not write it; it did not originate in Rome and was a compilation of documents with various dates of origin.[13]

Nonetheless, *The Apostolic Tradition* provides additional important details about the baptismal rite. The catechumens were usually to enter instruction for three years. During that time, they were to pray separately from the congregation and were not to exchange the peace as they had not yet been received by "the faithful." It details the prayers, fasting, and exorcisms catechumens underwent preceding their baptisms. In the baptismal rite, the bishop presided with a deacon having "the oil of exorcism" on the left and another having "the oil of thanksgiving" on the right. The bishop led the candidates through a series of renunciations followed by anointing with the oil of exorcism. Then, the candidates proclaimed their faith in the Trinity, being baptized (presumably submersed or immersed) three times, once with each person of the Trinity. Then, they were anointed with the oil of thanksgiving and received the imposition of hands. Finally, they were led directly into the eucharistic assembly to consume a mixture of honey and milk, a chalice of water, and bread and wine.[14]

Additional documents provide varied details about the rites of baptism performed in their regions and at their times. Some of these descriptions prescribe a certain period for catechesis, and others only mention its occurrence.[15] Some of these rites include pre-baptismal anointings with no post-baptismal anointings.[16] Some of them involve handlaying, while others do not.[17] Some of them describe what might be called a Trinitarian formula,[18] and others include renunciations

---

11. Whitaker and Johnson, *Documents of the Baptismal Liturgy*, 9-11.

12. Most notably, Gregory Dix, ed., *The Treatise on the Apostolic Tradition of St. Hippolytus of Rome, Bishop and Martyr*, xi-xxxvii.

13. Paul F. Bradshaw, *Apostolic Tradition: A New Commentary*, 1-12.

14. Whitaker and Johnson, *Documents of the Baptismal Liturgy*, 5-8.

15. For example, *The Apostolic Tradition* describes a catechumenate of three years, *Documents of the Baptismal Liturgy*, 5. But *The Didache* and Justin Martyr's *First Apology* simply reference that instruction occurs without giving a duration, *Documents of the Baptismal Liturgy*, 2 and 3 respectively.

16. For example, the *Didascalia Apostolorum*, Whitaker and Johnson, *Documents of the Baptismal Liturgy*, 14.

17. *The Apostolic Tradition* and Tertullian's *De Baptismo* mention a post-baptismal handlaying, *Documents of the Baptismal Liturgy*, 8 and 9 respectively. However, *The Didache* and Justin Martyr's *First Apology*, makes no mention of it, *Documents of the Baptismal Liturgy*, 2 and 3 respectively.

18. *The Apostolic Tradition* and Justin Martyr's *First Apology*, in *Documents of the Baptismal Liturgy*, 2 and 3 respectively.

and proclamations of faith.[19] The evidence paints a varied picture of baptismal rites in this period.

Archeology provides additional information about baptismal practice. The earliest Christian "house church" excavated in the city of Dura Europos is believed to have been used for worship between 233 and 256 CE. Figure 1.1 depicts the archeological excavation of this house church. Figure 1.2 shows the floor plan of the building. Section 4 was the main worship area, and Section 6 was the baptistery. Section 5 was a space for teaching. Thus, one could move seamlessly from pre-baptismal catechesis to the baptistery to the eucharistic assembly.

Figure 1.1: Dura Europos, Syria (Alen Ištoković, CC BY 3.0 <https://creativecommons.org/licenses/by/3.0>, via Wikimedia Commons)

While the details of baptismal rites during this time varied, they illuminate a pattern. The candidates were normatively adult converts. Some pre-baptismal catechesis was expected to usually culminate in a series of prayers and fasting immediately before the rite. The water bath typically involved submersion or immersion with other optional forms. Anointings occurred before or after the bath, sometimes with handlaying. Participation in the Eucharist followed.[20]

---

19. *The Apostolic Tradition* includes renunciations of Satan and all his works and then three interrogatories, "Do you believe in God, the Father Almighty ... Christ Jesus, the Son of God ... the holy Spirit and the holy Church and the resurrection of the flesh?" in *Documents of the Baptismal Liturgy*, 7.

20. Johnson, *The Rites of Christian Initiation*, 75-82.

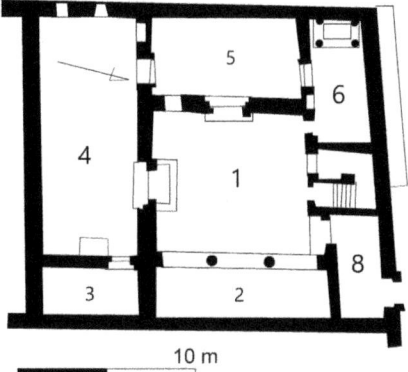

Figure 1.2: Floorplan of Dura Europos (drawn by Udimu, CC BY-SA 3.0 <http://creativecommons.org/licenses/by-sa/3.0/>, via Wikimedia Commons)

This pattern describes a unitive initiation rite with baptism, anointing/handlaying, and Eucharist. One could describe it as "one play in three acts." This unified initiation pattern would persist into the Nicene period but would eventually disintegrate in the West into distinct acts separated by years.

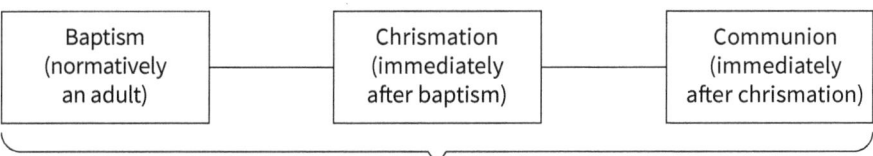

Figure 1.3: Unitive Rite of Initiation

Nicene Period

The Peace of Constantine in 313 CE was one of the most significant events in the church's history. Christianity went from an illegal and often persecuted religion to a legal and imperially sanctioned one. Whether mass conversions accompanied this change in status is a matter of debate.[21] Nonetheless, the legalization of Christianity significantly impacted the role of initiation in the church as seeking membership went from being a clandestine activity to a very public one.

No full liturgical rites from this period are extant. In addition to church orders, other documentation of rites includes the proceedings of church councils and homilies. More evidence exists of a further developed catechumenal period, including a new genre of preaching, the mystagogical homily. Ambrose of Milan, Cyril of Jerusalem, John Chrysostom, and Theodore of Mopsuestia

---

21. For example, see Rodney Stark, *The Rise of Christianity: A Sociologist Reconsiders History*.

are the premier examples of mystagogical preaching. Their sermons to the newly baptized, usually during Eastertide, explained the "mysteries" into which the new Christians had been initiated. These sermons also provide valuable information about the initiatory process.[22]

Another valuable source of information about initiation during this period was the diary of Egeria. She was a woman, perhaps a member of a religious order, who had traveled to Jerusalem. Jerusalem had become a popular pilgrimage site after being restored by Constantine's mother, Helena. Egeria provided detailed accounts of her travels, including the liturgies in which she participated.[23]

The length of pre-baptismal catechesis during this period is hard to determine and appears to have varied significantly. The three-year period mentioned in *The Apostolic Tradition* might have still been in place. However, narratives exist of persons who remained catechumens for many years, deliberately delaying their baptism out of fear of committing a post-baptismal sin that would endanger their salvation. Augustine of Hippo is perhaps the most well-known example of someone who became a catechumen as a child but was not baptized until well into adulthood.[24]

In part because of the variable length of the catechumenate, a more fixed pre-baptismal preparation period developed, which would become known as Lent. When one was ready to move from being a catechumen to a candidate for baptism, one would be "enrolled," and one's status would change to *photizomenoi* ("enlightened ones") in some places or *competentes* ("the elect") in other areas. During forty days of preparation, the *photizomenoi* or *competentes* would undergo a series of scrutinies involving prayer and interrogations about the faith. A rite of *apotaxis* (renunciation) and *syntaxis* (adherence) followed, indicating a "change of ownership" from the devil and the world to God. Pre-baptismal anointings now took on the interpretation of exorcism.

Easter continued to be the favored time for baptisms. The water bath would occur that night, typically by submersion or immersion. Sometimes, it was immediately followed by a post-baptismal anointing done by a deacon for men and a deaconess for women, as baptisms were often in the nude. References exist of clothing the neophytes in a white garment to symbolize their new life in Christ. They were then led to the bishop, or sometimes a presbyter if the bishop was absent, to anoint them with chrism. In the West, handlaying would often accompany the chrismation. In all cases, participation in the Eucharist immediately followed.[25]

The unified initiatory rite remained intact during this period. Architectural developments confirm this practice. With their new legal status, Christians

---

22. For more information, see Edward Yarnold, *The Awe-Inspiring Rites of Initiation: The Origins of the R.C.I.A.*

23. For the most recent scholarship, see Anne McGowan and Paul F. Bradshaw, *The Pilgrimage of Egeria: A New Translation of the* Itinerarium Egeriae *with Introduction and Commentary*.

24. Augustine, *Confessions*, trans. Sarah Ruden.

25. See Johnson, *Rites of Christian Initiation*, 115-200 for more detail.

needed more significant buildings to gather. They chose to utilize the basilica, the architectural style for government buildings, as their expanded public worship spaces. Figure 1.4 depicts the Archbasilica of St. John Lateran, the oldest Christian basilica. It was consecrated in 324 CE and remains in use today. The choice to use basilicas avoided any connection with pagan temples. Many of these basilicas included a baptistery connected to the main building, sometimes with a room where the bishop would perform the chrismation, as seen in Figure 1.5. Thus, one would be baptized, led to chrismation by the bishop, and then brought directly into the basilica's nave for the Eucharist.

Figure 1.4: St. John Lateran, Rome, Italy (MrPanyGoff, CC BY-SA 4.0 <https://creativecommons.org/licenses/by-sa/4.0>, via Wikimedia Commons)

Ambrose of Milan offered an interesting addition to the initiation rites in his area: pedilavium (foot-washing). In his *De Sacramentis*, he described the baptismal rite with similar details as already discussed. However, immediately after the bath, the newly baptized hear the reading from John 13 and then have their feet washed by the "high priest," meaning the bishop. While Ambrose recognized that Rome did not include this action in their baptismal rite, he argued that it should still be considered part of the rite and described it as "a mystery and sanctification."[26]

---

26. Whitaker and Johnson, *Documents of the Baptismal Liturgy*, 180.

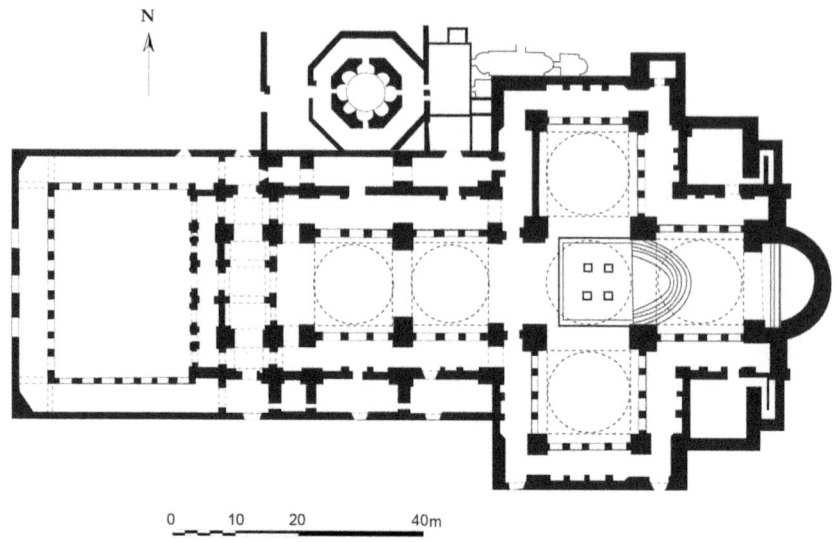

Figure 1.5: Floorplan of St. John Lateran (Marsyas, CC BY 3.0 <https://creativecommons.org/licenses/by/3.0>, via Wikimedia Commons)

While Augustine of Hippo contributed to the descriptions of baptismal rites, his most important influence was theology, which would profoundly impact baptismal theology and practice in the West, arguably until this day. His first significant baptismal teaching arose from the Donatist Controversy. During the persecution of Emperor Diocletian (311 CE), some Christians betrayed their faith by handing over sacred books and objects to the authorities and were known as *traditores*. As they became known, the Donatists believed that these persons, including clergy, must be rebaptized to be accepted back into the church. Furthermore, anyone baptized by a *traditore* would need to be rebaptized as that baptism was not considered "valid" due to the clergyperson's sinful state.[27]

Augustine wrote in his *On Baptism* that the grace of baptism was not dependent on the state of the minister's soul but on Christ's power alone. Thus, rebaptism was not necessary for those baptized by the *traditores*. Nearly all Christians hold this theological understanding of baptism's efficacy. It is the theological foundation for the ecumenical agreement on universal acceptance of baptism.[28]

Augustine's other primary baptismal teaching involved the Pelagian controversy. Pelagianism taught that humanity is born with absolute free will and, therefore, can choose good or evil. Thus, Adam's sin in the Garden of Eden brought about the consequence of death on humanity but did not change human will.

---

27. Serge Lancel, *Saint Augustine*, trans. Antonia Nevill, 164-169.
28. For more details, see Geoffrey Grimshaw Willis, *Saint Augustine and the Donatist Controversy*.

Augustine argued against this point with what would become known as the teaching of "original sin." In his argument, Augustine pointed to pre-baptismal exorcisms for infants and adults. He argued, therefore, that the Church would not practice these exorcisms on infants if they were not the recipients of original sin. He further argued that if an infant were to die unbaptized in the state of original sin, the infant would go to hell but "be involved in the mildest condemnation of all".[29] This teaching would profoundly impact baptismal practice and theology in the West for centuries to come.

The Middle Ages

Two important historical events inform how baptism would change in the West during what would be known as the Middle Ages. Charles the Great, also known as Charlemagne, linked these events. When Pope Gregory III crowned him the next Roman emperor, he acknowledged Charlemagne's consolidation of power in the West and its separation from the East. While the formal Great Schism would not occur for another two hundred years, Charlemagne's coronation as emperor began the process.

Furthermore, Charlemagne attempted to enforce liturgical uniformity in the realm to consolidate power. For centuries before, pilgrims had visited Rome, observed the liturgical practices, and tried to migrate those practices back to their home countries. Of course, with these migrations came changes. For example, most of the Roman liturgies observed were papal liturgies and were not suitable for the needs of regular parishes. Thus, adaptations had to occur. When Charlemagne sent his advisors to Rome to bring back a liturgy for the realm, this earlier migration of texts had already paved their way. Rome never had to enforce liturgical uniformity on the West as it was attempted but never fully accomplished by imperial decree.[30]

The *Gelasian Sacramentary* and *Ordo Romanus XI* are two documents that fully describe the liturgical practice in Rome during this time. Sacramentaries were liturgical books containing most of the material needed by the presider. Ordines were liturgical books containing the rubrics or instructions for the ceremonies. Both documents describe papal liturgies conducted in Rome, often by the "pontiff."

These documents go into much more detail about the rites than the documents mentioned thus far. They also describe some crucial changes that have occurred. The first such change was the now normative practice of infant baptism. "Catechumens" are now infants and are enrolled and "elected" for baptism in the third week of Lent rather than the beginning of Lent. The traditional scrutinies with their accompanying exorcisms were still conducted.

---

29. Augustine, *A Treatise on the Merits and Forgiveness of Sins, and on the Baptism of Infants*, loc. 343 of 2482, Kindle.

30. For further details, see G. Macy, *The Banquet's Wisdom: A Short History of the Theologies of the Lord's Supper*.

The rite of baptism occurred on the Easter Vigil and is described in greater detail. It consisted of several readings and using a (or two at times) Paschal candle(s). The baptism occurred with creedal interrogatories ("Do you believe in God the Father Almighty?"), rather than a formula, to which the sponsors replied, while the infant was triply immersed. After the third immersion, the infant was chrismated by the presbyter and then consignated with handlaying by the bishop.

Interestingly, *Ordo Romanus XI* inserts a symbolically significant action between the chrismation and handlaying. The infant was carried to the throne of the "pontiff," who gave each infant a stole, chrismal cloth, and ten coins. The stole and chrismal cloth were symbolic links to presbyteral ordination and references to the baptismal priesthood. The symbolism of the ten coins may have alluded to a custom involving papal liturgies. The baptismal rites were concluded with the reception of communion by the infants.[31] Thus, the unified initiatory rite remained intact. However, that unification would not last.

As the Middle Ages progressed, a new practice of infant baptism, *quam primum* baptism, became the dominant paradigm. Fueled mainly by the Augustinian understanding of original sin and the concern for high infant mortality rates, this practice sought to baptize infants "as soon as possible" after birth to ensure their eternal salvation.

Figure 1.6: Etching of a midwife doing an emergency baptism on a newborn (Bernard Picart, collection Rijksmuseum)

---

31. Johnson, *The Rites of Christian Initiation*, 222-229.

This concern for the infants' souls and its impact on liturgical practice had several effects. First, baptism became a private affair in the home rather than church. Midwives often performed it as an emergency measure rather than a presbyter or a bishop. The upper half of Figure 1.6 illustrates a baptism performed at home by a priest, and the lower half illustrates a baptism by a midwife also in the home.

Furthermore, this concern shifted the time of baptism to immediately after birth rather than Easter or Pentecost. The link between these great festivals of the liturgical year with their corresponding theologies and baptism was severed. Baptism became a private, family affair rather than an ecclesial event. Thus, the move toward baptism as a pastoral office rather than an initiatory rite began.

The practice of the bishop "confirming" the baptism as a separate rite also developed in the West. Since most baptisms were now emergency baptisms performed by lay people, usually midwives, the bishops desired to ensure they were correctly completed. These "confirmations" would occur a few weeks after the baptism during the bishop's visitation. However, the period between baptism and confirmation would grow significantly over time.

Also, as the theology of the Eucharist moved toward "realism," in which the elements were understood to become the very flesh and blood of Christ, infant communion ceased, and the practice of "first communion" developed, as Figure 1.7 illustrates. Eventually, first communion would precede confirmation in the West such that the order was infant baptism as soon as possible, first communion around seven, and confirmation around twelve or thirteen, as Figure 1.8 illustrates. What had once been a unified rite of Christian initiation disintegrated into three separate rites, resulting in a much more pastoral emphasis.[32]

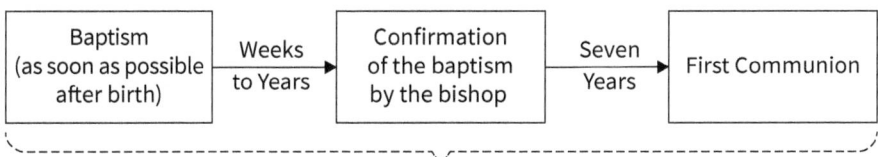

Figure 1.7: Disintegrated Rite of Initiation - Early Middle Ages

Figure 1.8: Disintegrated Rite of Initiation - Later Middle Ages

---

32. J.D.C. Fisher, *Christian Initiation: Baptism in the Medieval West*. Please also see the history section of chapter two for more details on these liturgical developments.

The Reformations

Referring to the sixteenth century in the church's history as the Reformation simplifies a series of reformations across Europe and the British Isles. Four separate reformations occurred in England: the Henrician Reformation, the Edwardian Reformation, the Marian Counter-Reformation, and the Elizabethan Reformation. Significant changes in liturgical practice accompanied these political reformations for the Church of England.[33] That was not always the case elsewhere, but worship and the sacraments, nonetheless, were radically affected by these reformations.

One of the great results of these reformations was dividing the Western church into Roman Catholicism and Protestantism. Almost instantaneously, Protestantism further divided. Initially, the subgroups were Lutheran, Reformed, Anglican, and Anabaptist. Those subgroups were further divided into Methodist/Wesleyan, Separatist or Free Church groups, Quakers, Congregationalists, Unitarians, and many more divisions.

The most significant liturgical concern among these groups was the nature of the Eucharist. Whether and how Christ is present in the Eucharist and its sacrificial character, or lack thereof, were of primary concern.[34] The nature and number of the sacraments were also a point of contention. Some groups, such as the Lutherans, Anglicans, and Reformed, retained a theology of sacraments but limited the number to baptism and the Eucharist (possibly penitence for Luther himself). Other groups no longer used sacramental theology but described the services as "ordinances" that Christians were to obey.

While not all these groups agreed that baptism was a sacrament, they all agreed that it was essential to the life of a Christian. Tracing the history of baptism among all these groups lies well outside the scope of this book.[35] Nonetheless, a couple of significant changes are noteworthy.

First is the rise of the Anabaptist movement. For centuries, the church understood baptism to include infants. Many reformers, including Luther, Zwingli, and Calvin, continued the practice of infant baptism. However, some of the more radical reformers questioned the theology of infant baptism. For example, some suggested that baptism should be delayed until the person is old enough to understand the faith and speak for themselves. Others even suggested that one baptized as an infant should be rebaptized (thus, Ana-"re"-baptist) as an older child or adult.

Anabaptists were persecuted and marginalized by other Protestant groups. They held little socio-political power as the Church of England retained infant

---

33. Christopher Haigh, *English Reformations: Religion, Politics, and Society under the Tudors.*

34. Nathan D. Mitchell, "Reforms, Protestant and Catholic," in *The Oxford History of Christian Worship*, 309.

35. For more detailed information, please see James F. White, *Protestant Worship: Traditions in Transition* and several essays in Wainwright and Westerfield Tucker, eds., *The Oxford History of Christian Worship.*

baptism, and other European cities and states adopted the views of Luther, Zwingli, Calvin, and others who supported infant baptism. Nonetheless, their radical view of baptism led to another significant change, forcing these reformers to clarify their baptismal theologies. For example, Luther retained baptism as a sacrament but emphasized the laity's participation in the priesthood of all believers. Reformed theologians like Zwingli and Calvin emphasized baptism as initiating one into God's covenant or as a sign of one's predestined election. Thomas Cranmer and Anglicanism retained the view of baptismal regeneration.[36]

The practice of baptism also began to shift depending on the ecclesial community. For Anabaptists and others supporting adult baptism, baptismal practice shifted radically. It involved older children or adults who could speak for their faith. It always occurred before the church congregation, maybe not in a church building, but as a public profession of faith.

Lutherans retained infant baptism. Luther taught that infants could be baptized as a sign of God's grace since they could not "earn" it. While Luther was critical of the lack of catechesis surrounding baptism, he retained many pre-baptismal anointings and exorcisms. Uniquely, he added what would become known as his "Flood Prayer." Scholars disagree on whether he originally wrote this prayer or borrowed it from a yet-to-be-discovered medieval source. The imagery linked baptism with two significant events in the Hebrew Scriptures: Noah's flood and the exodus of the people of Israel over the Red Sea. Thomas Cranmer and other reformers would use this prayer in their baptismal rites. Also, Luther emphasized the submersion of the infant in baptism as a potent symbol of dying to one's sin and being raised to new life in Christ.[37]

Most members of the Reformed tradition also retained infant baptism. They emphasized baptism as a sign of membership in God's covenant and often a parallel with the Jewish practice of circumcision. For Ulrich Zwingli, baptism became more of a ceremony, dedicating the infant to God with the hope of future faith. Martin Bucer strengthened this approach by including a pledge by the parents that the child will grow up in the Christian faith. Of course, John Calvin had a robust theology of predestination and election. For him, baptism effectively performed the grace of salvation but only for the elect. For others, it would have no effect. However, since one could not know with certainty if one was a member of the elect, one was still required to be baptized to become a church member.[38]

For Anglicans, the practice was somewhat mixed. As stated in early editions of the prayer book, the desire was for baptisms to occur on Sundays at the primary worship service. However, practice often involved private baptisms outside of the

---

36. White, *Protestant Worship*, 79-89.
37. White, *Protestant Worship*, 41-45. See also Mitchell, "Reforms, Protestant and Catholic," 327.
38. White, *Protestant Worship*, 62-63 and Mitchell, "Reforms, Protestant and Catholic," 327-328.

Sunday service, with only the family attending.[39] In addition, concern for baptismal regeneration from original sin persisted in the Anglican tradition and would lead to *quam primum* or "as soon as possible" baptisms performed by midwives. This dual practice created a theological tension regarding the purpose of baptism that continued to the liturgical renewal movement of the twentieth century.

The Liturgical Renewal Movement

Two essential movements that profoundly impacted baptism were the Liturgical Renewal Movement and the Ecumenical Movement. Both movements had roots in the nineteenth century but came to fruition in the mid-twentieth century. While the movements were distinct and had different aims and methods, they were also intertwined. After all, some of the most significant disagreements from the sixteenth-century reformations centered on different understandings of worship, liturgy, and sacraments. Thus, as Christian traditions began to have more constructive conversations with each other, many of them focused on these primary areas of concern.

Baptism has been a central concern in ecumenical conversations, particularly the mutual acceptance of baptism. Because ecclesial traditions have varied understandings of baptism, complete ecumenical agreement remains a goal but not a reality. Nonetheless, many churches have made multilateral and bilateral agreements on baptism.[40]

As stated above, a significant disagreement on baptism remains between groups supporting infant baptism and groups supporting only adult baptism. However, among those supporting infant baptism, most ecclesial traditions mutually recognize baptism if it is done with water and in the name of the Trinity. This agreement includes Roman Catholics, Old Catholics, Lutherans, Anglicans/Episcopalians, Methodists, and members of the Reformed tradition. It involves the theological understanding that baptism makes one a member of the universal church.

The practice among Oriental and Eastern Orthodox traditions has varied. Some churches in these traditions have rebaptized converts, and some have accepted the baptism of other traditions. Those traditions that rebaptize converts do so out of understanding baptism's indissoluble bond with chrismation and the Eucharist and their implications for ecclesiology. On the other hand, those traditions that accept the baptism of other ecclesial traditions believe the implications for ecclesiology to be similar enough to justify the acceptance.

As one might imagine, mutual acceptance of baptism is complicated among those groups who prefer adult baptism to infant baptism. Many Mennonite churches accept the baptisms of other traditions if performed by immersion.

---

39. G.J Cuming, *A History of Anglican Liturgy*, 59-62.

40. The information in this section relies heavily on Dagmar Heller, *Baptized into Christ: A Guide to the Ecumenical Discussion on Baptism*.

Many Baptist churches will not accept the baptisms of other churches at all. Some will accept them if they are performed by immersion and with a public proclamation of faith by an older child or adult. Many churches, including the Church of the Brethren and Disciples of Christ, recognize the baptisms of other traditions, even infant baptisms. Most Pentecostal churches will accept adult baptism performed in different traditions but not infant baptism.

Another significant baptismal development inspired by the Liturgical Renewal Movement was the restoration of the catechumenate. As mentioned above, the catechumenate originated in the Ante-Nicene period and came to full fruition in the Nicene period. It waned during the Middle Ages when infant baptism became dominant. The Liturgical Renewal Movement sought to reemphasize adult baptism as the normative practice even when infant baptism was permitted and, in doing so, also to restore the use of the catechumenate. The Roman Catholic Church has had the most developed catechumenate with its Rite of Christian Initiation for Adults (RCIA) program. The Episcopal Church and the Evangelical Lutheran Church also have a catechumenal program primarily based on the RCIA.

The final significant development from the Liturgical Renewal Movement was the attempt to reunify the initiatory rites of baptism, confirmation/chrismation, and the Eucharist in some ecclesial communities. Please see chapter two for the history of that process.

Theological Insights[41]

Identification with Christ

Baptism begins with Christ. While this statement may appear simplistic, it marks the beginning of any theological inquiry into baptism. When considering the theology of baptism, the starting place must be the *person* of Jesus Christ. As discussed below, baptism also involves the gift of the Holy Spirit, remission of sins, other fruits, and initiation into the church. Still, these additional theologies flow from the fundamental theology of baptism as identity with Christ.

The New Testament is replete with references to baptism as identity with Christ. Acts 19:1-7 describes the theological and ritual shift among the early followers of Christ from John's baptism to baptism in the name of the Lord Jesus. Paul stated, "John baptized with the baptism of repentance, telling the people to believe in the one who was to come after him, that is, in Jesus (Acts 19:4 NRSV)." Even as a ritual act of repentance, John's baptism pointed to the person of Christ, who was to come after him. The Gospel narratives also reference John's pointing ahead to Christ (Matthew 3:11-12; Mark 1:7-8; Luke 3:16-17;

---

41. Appendix A contains the baptismal rites from the BCP, BCW, BOW, ELW, and OBC in tabular format for easy reference.

and John 1:26-27). Baptism had become about more than ritual cleansing. It was messianic. When baptizing, John foreshadowed the coming of Christ as the Messiah.

Later, Paul reminded the community that baptism no longer sought the Messiah but identified with Jesus Christ. This theme of identity with Christ through baptism runs strong in Paul's letter to the Galatians. In discussing the relationship between law and grace, Paul stated, "...for in Christ Jesus you are all children of God through faith. As many of you as were baptized into Christ have clothed yourselves with Christ. There is no longer Jew or Greek, there is no longer slave or free, there is no longer male and female; for all of you are one in Christ Jesus (Gal 3:26-28)." One becomes a child of God through faith, and baptism is the sign by which this new identity becomes apparent. Paul used the metaphor of being clothed with Christ. From the church's early history to the present day, persons being baptized are often clothed with a white garment to signify their being clothed with Christ.

Baptism not only identifies one with Christ generally but also with Christ's death and resurrection specifically: "Do you not know that all of us who have been baptized into Christ Jesus were baptized into his death? Therefore we have been buried with him by baptism into death, so that, just as Christ was raised from the dead by the glory of the Father, so we too might walk in newness of life (Rom 6:3-4)." The passage continues by stating that this union with Christ's death includes union with his resurrection. Furthermore, because sin and death were defeated through Christ's death and resurrection, they have also been defeated for those who have "died with Christ." Baptism is the sign of this death and subsequent resurrection with Christ. Immersion provides one of the most poignant symbols of this identification with Christ's death and resurrection as the person being baptized symbolically is "buried" in the water and then "rises again" from it.

This identification with Christ in baptism occurs through God's covenant with humanity. Throughout the Hebrew Scriptures, God establishes and re-establishes a covenantal agreement with humanity, beginning with Noah, Abraham, Isaac, Jacob, and Moses. As Paul and other New Testament authors write, Christ becomes the mediator of a new covenant with humanity through his death and resurrection. Therefore, identifying with Christ, particularly with Christ's death and resurrection, incorporates one into this new covenant through Christ's redeeming work. Galatians 3:29 states, "If you belong to Christ, then you are Abraham's offspring, heirs according to the promise."

Christian traditions differ regarding how this baptismal covenant is established. Some traditions describe it as an act of sacramental grace.[42] For other traditions, the power of the Word establishes the covenant, and other traditions make the connection with the covenant explicit.[43]

---

42. OBC 11 and BCP 858.

43. "The Reformed tradition understands baptism to be a sign of God's covenant." BCW, 403.

These distinctions are important as they connect with the broader theological diversity among these traditions. Where they agree is that the covenant begins with God working through Christ. Therefore, baptism cannot be seen as a means by which salvation through Christ is earned. Whether God offered grace at Christ's death and resurrection, and baptism is its sign, or God offers grace at the time of baptism, God initiates grace. Baptism identifies one with Christ and, therefore, with Christ's covenant with God.

The Gift of the Holy Spirit

The book of Acts also connects baptism with the gift of the Holy Spirit. Christ promised the Holy Spirit to his disciples after his ascension (Acts 1:8). John's Gospel describes a more intimate gift as the post-resurrection Christ breathed on his disciples to receive the Holy Spirit (John 20:22). At the festival of Pentecost, Peter preached to the gathered assembly, urging them to "Repent, and be baptized every one of you in the name of Jesus Christ so that your sins may be forgiven; and you will receive the gift of the Holy Spirit (Acts 2:38)." Later in Acts, Paul encountered disciples of Christ who had not received the Holy Spirit. "On hearing this, they were baptized in the name of the Lord Jesus. When Paul had laid his hands on them, the Holy Spirit came upon them (Acts 19:5-6)." In each case, the Holy Spirit was sent as an enlivening gift during Christ's absence from his disciples. Thus, when later disciples identify with Christ through baptism, they also receive the gift of the Holy Spirit.

As discussed in the previous section on historical context, the early church saw no separation between baptism and laying on hands and anointing for the Holy Spirit. They were one unitive rite. Today, liturgical rites have reunited these acts with varying symbols: consignation (the signing of the cross), chrismation (anointing with oil), and handlaying. Different traditions require or offer various combinations of these symbols as options.[44] In all cases, though, these ritual acts occur immediately after the water bath.

All these rites include a theologically significant declaration when the act of consignation or chrismation is included, "[Name of the person], you are sealed by the Holy Spirit in Baptism and marked as Christ's own for ever."[45] This declaration affirms the church's understanding that baptism is unrepeatable. The author of Ephesians uses the Greek verb *sphragizo* when referencing this seal, "In him you also, when you had heard the word of truth, the gospel of your salvation, and had believed in him, were marked with the seal of the promised Holy Spirit; this [or who] is the pledge of our inheritance towards redemption as God's own people, to the praise of his glory (Ephesians 1:13-14)." The noun *sphragis* can be found in the earliest baptismal rites and references this act of being sealed by the Holy Spirit.

---

44. See Appendix A for more details.
45. BCP, 308. The other rites also include nearly the exact language.

The Holy Spirit's agency in this act is notable. While officiants consignate or chrismate the person being baptized, they do not enact the sealing. The consignation/chrismation is a sign of that sealing, which the Holy Spirit performs. Some Christian traditions believe the water bath itself signals the gift of the Holy Spirit.[46] Thus, not all traditions require consignation/chrismation.

Chrismation hearkens back to the Hebrew Scriptures when priests, prophets, and kings were anointed with oil. Christian tradition recognizes that Christ, meaning "Anointed One," fulfilled this threefold office when he was anointed with the Holy Spirit at his baptism (Matt 3:16, Mark 1:10, Luke 3:22, and John 1:32). Thus, the anointing of oil also signifies the baptized person's new identity in Christ as an "Anointed One." In its multivalency, this symbol connects identity with Christ and the gift of the Holy Spirit.

While the fullness of symbols in liturgical rites can communicate theological richness and depth, they are unnecessary. A baptism involving water and the Triune formula[47] is sufficient. At times, misunderstandings have occurred about the timing of the gift of the Holy Spirit. Is the Holy Spirit given at baptism or later at confirmation? Chapter two discusses Confirmation and Other Rites of Affirmation in more detail. Suffice it to say here that the gift of the Holy Spirit necessarily occurs at baptism because it is through the power of the Holy Spirit that the Christian can make a public profession of faith later. The Holy Spirit sanctifies and empowers the Christian in all aspects of discipleship.

Forgiveness of Sins and Other Gifts of Baptism

While nearly all Christian traditions recognize a connection between baptism and the forgiveness of sins, their relationship remains complex. The Nicene and Apostles' Creeds are Christian traditions' most broadly accepted creeds. The Nicene Creed makes the connection between baptism and forgiveness of sins explicit, "I [We] acknowledge one baptism for the forgiveness of sins."[48] However, the nature of that connection is left open; thus, theological questions have arisen.

One theological question is whether baptism conveys the forgiveness of sins or symbolizes it as an act already accomplished through Christ's death and resurrection. If participation in the baptismal rite alone conveys the forgiveness of sins, does that cause baptism to be a work one can accomplish to gain righteousness? Could one claim the forgiveness of sin by one's baptism consequently or even as a right? Therefore, does baptism identify that group as righteous on their

---

46. For example, *The United Methodist Book of Worship* states, "Pouring or sprinkling water upon the candidate's head also signifies God's pouring out of the Holy Spirit." BOW, 123.

47. "I baptize you in the name of the Father, the Son, and the Holy Spirit."

48. BCP 328, and 359; BCW, 84; ELW, 104; and *The United Methodist Hymnal*, 880.

terms, while the lack of baptism identifies the outside group as wicked? On the other hand, if baptism conveys forgiveness of sins, then these questions become pertinent.

If taken out of context, some liturgical texts might suggest baptism conveys the forgiveness of sin.[49] Does God use the water of baptism to bestow the forgiveness of sin? If one were to examine these liturgical rites with the question of the forgiveness of sin being in the foreground, one might mistakenly conclude that they suggest conveyance.

However, it is essential to remember that baptism begins with Christ. Because baptism identifies one with Christ, particularly Christ's death and resurrection, baptism offers forgiveness of sin *due to* that identification with Christ. Some liturgical rites explain this connection between baptism and forgiveness of sin through the person of Jesus Christ more explicitly.[50] Nevertheless, all rites speak of baptism as a union with Christ. Thus, the forgiveness of sin is a consequence of that union.[51] Identification with Christ remains primary.

This understanding of identification with Christ through baptism resulting in forgiveness of sin is essential when discussing original sin. Original sin is the teaching that the sin of Adam in the Garden of Eden resulted not only in the introduction of Adam's mortality to humanity but also in the inheritance of his guilt. Thus, the consequence of sin is not only mortality but also guilt in the eyes of God, regardless of personal sin. Some Christian traditions also teach that original sin has wholly corrupted the very nature of humanity, such that one is incapable of any good thought or deed without the aid of God's grace through Christ.

As discussed in the historical context section above, this understanding of original sin found its most significant support in Augustine of Hippo. In his essay, "On the Merits and Forgiveness of Sins, and on the Baptism of Infants," he connected the practice of infant baptism with original sin.

> The inevitable conclusion from these truths is this, that, as nothing else is affected when infants are baptized except that they are incorporated into the church, in other words, that they are united with the body and members of Christ, unless this benefit has been bestowed upon them, they are manifestly in danger of damnation. Damned, however, they could not be if they really had no sin. Now, since their tender age could not possibly have contracted sin in its own life, it remains for us, even if

---

49. For example, "Heavenly Father, we thank you that by water and the Holy Spirit you have bestowed upon *these* your *servants* the forgiveness of sin . . ." BCP, 308; and "Pour out your Holy Spirit, to bless this gift of water and those who receive it, to wash away their sin . . ." BOW, 137.

50. For example, "In baptism our gracious heavenly Father frees us from sin and death *by joining us to the death and resurrection of our Lord Jesus Christ.*" ELW 227 (emphasis added); and "In baptism God claims us, and seals us to show that we belong to God. God frees us from sin and death, *uniting us with Jesus Christ in his death and resurrection.*" BCW, 407 (emphasis added).

51. For example, see BCP, 306 and BOW, 137.

we are as yet unable to understand, at least to believe that infants inherit original sin.[52]

Thus, Augustine questioned why the church baptized infants if they had no sin since baptism necessarily involved the forgiveness of sin. From this teaching, the practice of *quam primum* ("as soon as possible") baptism prevailed in Western medieval Christendom out of fear that an infant who died unbaptized would be consigned to the *limbus* ("outer edge") of hell. To this day, this fear prevails and has resulted in "emergency baptisms," in which a non-ordained person can administer baptism when the person's life is in imminent danger.

Today, Christian traditions offer varying explanations for the connection between original sin and infant baptism. The rite in the Roman Catholic Church is explicit, "Moreover, the washing with water in the word of life, which is what Baptism is, cleanses human beings of every stain of sin, *both original and personal*, and makes them sharers in the divine nature and in filial adoption." Thus, the General Introduction to the rite instructs that in the case of an emergency anyone, even a non-Christian, may administer the rite with the "requisite intention."[53]

Some rites explain that God's prevenient grace (grace that precedes the act of salvation) is available to everyone, including the unbaptized infant in mortal danger. Thus, emergency baptisms are unnecessary.[54] Other rites lack an explanation but offer instruction that any baptized person may administer baptism in the case of an emergency and suggest care in discerning its appropriate use.[55] Finally, other rites omit an option for emergency baptisms without explanation.[56] Thus, the connection between original sin and baptism remains contested among Western churches, which have inherited Augustine's teaching.

Eastern churches, however, provide an alternative view. Rather than following Augustine's teaching, they follow the instruction of one of his contemporaries, John Chrysostom.

> You have seen how numerous are the gifts of baptism. Although many [people] think that the only gift it confers is the remission of sins, we have counted its honors to the number of ten It is on this account that we baptize even infants, *although they are sinless*, that they may be given the further gifts of sanctification, justice, filial adoption, and inheritance, that they may be [siblings] and members of Christ, and become dwelling places for the Spirit [emphasis added].[57]

---

52. Augustine, *A Treatise on the Merits and Forgiveness of Sins,* loc. 2195 of 2482, Kindle.
53. OBC 12 and 15, respectively, emphasis added.
54. BOW, 126.
55. See BCP, 313 and ELWPC, 115 respectively.
56. For example, BCW of the reformed tradition.
57. John Chrysostom, *Baptismal Instructions*, 57.

Thus, Chrysostom affirms infant baptism, not out of concern for original sin but for the many additional benefits of baptism. These benefits include adoption into the family of God, the sanctification of the Holy Spirit, God's declaration of justice, the inheritance of eternal life, and more.

Following Chrysostom's theology, the Eastern churches understand Adam's sin differently than the Western churches. They recognize that Adam's sin resulted in mortality for all humanity, but it did not pass on his guilt. As Kallistos Ware, a bishop in the Eastern Orthodox Church, explains, "Original sin is not to be interpreted in juridical or quasi-biological terms as if it were some physical 'taint' of guilt, transmitted through sexual intercourse. . . . The doctrine of original sin means rather that we are born into an environment where it is easy to do evil and hard to do good."[58] Thus, an unbaptized infant would not be in danger of damnation because the infant had not sinned.

Infant and Adult Baptism

Since the reformations of the sixteenth century, Christian traditions have disagreed about the proper time to baptize a person. Some traditions, especially those from the Anabaptist tradition, teach that only a person who can make a personal profession of faith should be baptized. This teaching is known as adult baptism or sometimes believers' baptism. Other traditions teach that baptizing infants and young children who cannot make a profession of faith on their own is permissible. This teaching is known as infant baptism.

Historically, Christian traditions that practice only adult baptism recognize baptism as a public profession of faith. Baptism does not convey sacramental grace or signify a union with Christ. Union with Christ, along with the benefits of the remission of sins, justification, sanctification, and other gifts, occurs at the acknowledgment of personal faith. Baptism is when the person acknowledges their faith as a public profession.

Christian traditions that baptize those who cannot answer for themselves believe that the act of baptism either conveys sacramental grace or signifies the pre-existing covenant established by Christ. As already discussed above, baptism bestows the forgiveness of sins and additional gifts on these persons and confirms their participation in the covenant of Christ. These traditions believe these additional benefits support and prepare them for a future public profession of faith.[59]

Traditions that practice infant baptism recognize the necessity of Christian sponsorship to assist in the young child's faith development.[60] They emphasize

---

58. Kallistos Ware, *The Orthodox Way*, 62.

59. For example, "The baptism of believers witnesses to the truth that God's gift of grace calls for our grateful response. The baptism of our young children witnesses to the truth that God claims people in love even before they are able to respond in faith. These two forms of witness are one and the same sacrament." BCW, 404.

60. "As these scriptures make clear, we are not to practice indiscriminate baptism." BOW, 124.

the participation of the parents and sponsors (or godparents) in raising the child in the Christian faith, life, and the entire Christian community. Both infant baptism and adult baptism are communal events that involve lifelong nurturing.

Initiation into and Ministry in the Church

In addition to baptism's many gifts, most Christian traditions teach that baptism also initiates one into the Body of Christ, the church (1 Corinthians 12:13).[61] Therefore, baptism normatively occurs within the church's corporate worship. It is not a private or family affair but an ecclesial event to be witnessed by the community. In addition to the parents' and sponsors' promises, the congregation also promises to support the newly baptized in their life in Christ. This understanding of baptism as an ecclesial affair rather than a private or familial one remains a contemporary renewal. Thus, parents and other sponsors sometimes approach baptism as a family affair. The section below on pastoral perspectives will address some of these challenges. Baptism's ecclesial connection remains a fundamental theology for most Christian traditions.

In addition to initiating one into the church, these Christian traditions also teach that baptism leads one into ministry in the church.[62] Historically, some Christian traditions required confirmation or some other mature profession of faith before one was a full member of the church. The reception of communion might also have been reserved for after such public professions.

However, with the liturgical renewal movement of the twentieth century, most Christian traditions now recognize baptism as full membership in the church and, therefore, as entry into the church's ministries. Even marriage and death are seen as continuations of one's baptism.[63] Thus, the phrase "the ministry of the baptized" has gained great parlance in many Christian traditions today.

As noted above, baptism initiates one into the Body of Christ, the church. Because most Christian traditions affirm the church as "one holy catholic and apostolic," they also recognize baptisms performed in other traditions. Thus, baptism is not baptism into a particular church tradition but into the universal church. This ecumenical agreement around baptismal recognition has been a significant achievement because complete Christian unity remains a future desire rather than a lived reality.

---

61. See BCP, 298; ELW, 225; BCW, 123; and BOW 403-404. Furthermore, while traditions that exclusively practice adult baptism believe that membership in the church occurs at one's personal profession of faith, they still recognize baptism as a sign of that membership.

62. "…baptism signifies the entry of the candidate into the general ministry of all Christians." BOW, 124.

63. "Confirmation, ordinations and consecrations to particular ministries, and all other steps in ministry grow out of what God has done as declared and signified in baptism. The covenant of Christian marriage reflects the Baptismal Covenant. Finally, as declared in the Service of Death and Resurrection, baptism signifies and anticipates death and resurrection to eternal glory." BOW, 123-124.

Cultural Connections

As a rite of initiation, baptism carries with it many cultural connections. Because baptism is primarily about identity as the person being baptized identifies with Christ and Christ's body, the church, baptism holds essential implications, especially for people whose cultures are non-majority Christian. As discussed in the introduction, this section avoids treating cultures monolithically. Examples given in this section should be received as cultural touchpoints rather than cultural representations. They deliberately include cultures from around the world as migration brings all cultures closer. Unfortunately, not all cultures could be represented in the scope of this work. Therefore, church leaders should use this material to prompt further questions when ministering to people formed by cultures other than their own.

Identity and Naming

The central theological theme of baptism is identity with Christ. As discussed above, one becomes "clothed with Christ" through baptism. For many ecclesial traditions, this identity with Christ also confers identity with Christ's body, the church. Even Christian traditions that recognize one's membership in the church through a personal conversion experience or predestined through God's covenant still acknowledge baptism as one's public proclamation of that new identity. This focus on identity can have powerful implications for people formed in cultures in which Christianity is in the minority or cultures impacted by Western colonialism.

The history of the connection between Western colonialism and the spread of Christianity is well documented.[64] This connection between Western colonialism and Christianity profoundly impacted Christianity's reception in non-Western cultures. One of the significant impacts was the giving of "Christian" names at baptism.

In the nineteenth century, western missionaries spread globally and encountered non-Western cultures and religions. To "Christianize" these non-Western cultures, these missionaries imposed Western cultural norms on them, believing them to be identified with Christianity. As a rite of initiation into Christianity, baptism became a focal point for this cultural colonialism.

When a person, either infant or adult, was baptized, they would be given a "Christian" name. These names often came from scripture, e.g., Mary, Paul, Elizabeth, and Samuel, but they could sometimes be Western names. This practice was seen as a way for the newly baptized to shun their former religion and culture, often viewed as pagan and evil. As converts grew, traditions practicing infant baptism would have parents name their child with a Western name. This practice

---

64. For a good summary of this history, see George Tinker, *Missionary Conquest: The Gospel and Native American Cultural Genocide* or David Chidester, *Empire of Religion: Imperialism and Comparative Religion*.

was part of a systemic attempt to annihilate the indigenous cultures of those colonized, known as deculturalization.[65]

Scholars and church leaders began critiquing this practice and other colonialist activities in the late twentieth century. In addition, Christians formed in non-Western cultures began recognizing the influence of colonialism on their cultures and their understanding of Christianity. As one response, they began to reclaim non-Western names as an anti-colonialist practice.

Historically, traditions supporting infant baptism have also connected naming a child at baptism with infant mortality. As discussed above, some cultures practiced *quam primum* ("as soon as possible") baptisms in the home with midwives out of fear for the infant's eternal fate. However, other cultures would wait for a specific interval before seeking baptism for their child. Sometimes, this interval was to determine if the infant would survive. Sometimes, this interval was related to a period of purification for the mother (following the custom of forty days found in scripture). During the period leading up to baptism, the child would remain unnamed to receive their name officially at the rite of baptism. Thus, naming the child was a statement of temporal and eternal life with strong cultural connections. Pronouncing that name at the rite in which they are being incorporated into the body of Christ can connect the newly baptized with Christ and the non-Western culture with Christ. Thus, naming a child can also be a statement of life.

In recent years, some ecclesial traditions have removed the naming of the candidate from the baptismal rite in favor of presenting the baptized person by name. This change in practice could stem from less concern about infant mortality and as an affirmation that one need not be renamed at baptism. However, having the parents affirm the name of the child being baptized could also strengthen the cultural connections with naming and reclaiming cultural identity, especially if the one performing the baptism is of a different culture than the one being baptized.

The influence of deculturalization can be profound. For example, sometimes Christians who live in non-Christian majority cultures consciously choose not to incorporate any cultural elements into their liturgical practices, believing them to be non-Christian. Thus, they may deliberately choose a name for their child with no cultural connection. This decision is a theological choice for these families to reject what they perceive as a non-Christian culture, even if it is their own.

Conversion and Anonymity

Because baptism is fundamentally about identity with Christ and Christ's body, the church, this identification can profoundly impact people in non-Christian majority cultures. In some cultures, family members may perceive

---

65. See Tinker, *Missionary Conquest* and Chidester, *Empire of Religion*.

one's conversion to Christianity as a rejection of their cultural heritage. For cultures practicing ancestral worship, conversion can signify the rejection of the immediate family and the rejection of the ancestors. Family members may wonder, "Who will pray for me when I die?" Thus, conversion can lead to stigmatization and isolation.

Furthermore, the strong connection Christianity has had with colonialism also creates barriers to baptism. To be baptized as a Christian can be perceived as collusion with colonialism. Therefore, conversion involves the rejection of not only religious and social values but also political values.

Therefore, the powerful impact of identity in baptism sometimes can prevent people in non-Christian majority cultures from seeking baptism. While they may have had a personal conversion experience, they choose to delay their baptism out of concern for its social consequences. The public profession of faith involved in baptism carries too high a social cost.

Sacred Spaces

The oldest document outside scripture describing baptismal practice is *The Didache*. This document describes not only a preference for immersion (where the person being baptized stands or sits in the water) or submersion (where the person being baptized goes under the water) as the mode of baptism but also indicates that baptism likely occurred outside in fresh, running water. "7.1 Regarding baptism. Baptize as follows . . . in running water. 2. But if you have no running water, baptize in other water; and if you cannot in cold, then in warm. 3. But if you have neither, pour water on the head three times."[66] As most scholars believe this document came from Syria, it reflects a baptismal practice that could be accommodated outside. As baptismal practice moved to various regions with different climates and cultural practices, its locations varied. Sometimes, it remained outside. Sometimes, it was performed inside the church or in a separate building from the main worship area, a baptistery. This practice was critical when the candidates were unclothed for baptism. As infant baptism became prominent in the West and the sphere of influence moved northward to colder climates, baptismal fonts were placed in the main church building. Figure 1.9 depicts the baptistry at Hagia Sophia.

Today, many churches influenced by northern European cultures continue to locate baptisms within the church building. Even traditions that insist on immersion or submersion as the mode of baptism will install large baptisteries into their church buildings to accommodate an inside baptism. Such practices are likely influenced by the longer seasons of cold weather experienced in northern Europe and the northern regions of North America. Because European culture influences global Christianity, one could mistakenly assume that baptisms typically occur inside a church building.

---

66. Whitaker and Johnson, *Documents of the Baptismal Liturgy*, 2.

Figure 1.9: Overhead photo of the baptistery at the Hagia Sophia (Ansgar Bovet, CC BY 3.0 <https://creativecommons.org/licenses/by/3.0>, via Wikimedia Commons)

However, running water outside can have important cultural meanings for people in or from warmer regions. As a symbol of purification, running water can have exorcistic properties that still water may not symbolize as fully. For some cultures, water has the power to trap evil spirits. For example, the *Mongo* people of Congo believe that water removes all contaminants, including evil spirits, witchcraft, and other pollutants.[67] Therefore, running water for baptisms symbolizes the exorcised evil spirits being trapped and taken away from the baptized persons.

Running water may also symbolize the identification with Christ's death more poignantly in some regions. For example, people living in areas that experience regular and extreme flooding may recognize more fully the dual nature of water as a symbol of death and life. Still water in a baptismal font in the confines of a church building may not express this symbolism as fulsomely.

Of course, using running water outside is only sometimes possible. If running water cannot be used, properly disposing of the lustral water after baptism could be important for people whose cultures recognize it as trapping evil spirits. Also, accommodating the desire for immersion or submersion, even when that practice is not the typical mode for baptism, could strengthen the symbolism of identification with Christ's death, which may be important.

The location of pre-baptismal liturgies can also vary among people formed by different cultures. For example, catechumens might be brought into the forest as a part of the initiation process. Alternatively, the elders of the community might accompany the parents of the baptismal candidate to the church's front door, where the exorcistic rites might occur. Then, the community elders, parents,

---

67. Piet Korse, "Baby Rituals, Ritual Baths, and Baptism – A Case from Congo," in *Life and Death Matters: The Practice of Inculturation in Africa*, 127.

and candidates enter the church for the baptism. Thus, the church building symbolizes one's entrance into the family of God. Also, if chrismation occurs as part of a unified initiatory rite, its location in the church can have important cultural connections.

The use of space is a fundamental component of all ritual activity. It can be especially poignant with initiatory rites, as physical space can symbolize the candidates' journey through the stages of initiation. Having careful conversations about the use of space can allow for deeper cultural connections.

Celebration

Baptism is a joyous occasion. It is a public affirmation of new life in Christ. For many ecclesial traditions, it is also the incorporation of the newly baptized into the body of Christ, the church. It signifies Christ's conquest of sin and death, the victory of the resurrection and eternal life, and the giving of the Holy Spirit.

As the rite has moved from a private, familial affair to an ecclesial affair, baptisms are often performed on Sundays or other major feast days as a part of the corporate rites of the church. Thus, not only can the family celebrate the newly baptized, but so can the entire church. It becomes a community celebration.

While this shift from a private affair to a church affair has deep theological roots, as discussed above, it also has strong cultural connections. In some cultures, a private baptism is viewed with class distinctions. Only the wealthy have private baptisms, while others have communal baptisms. Also, the desire to have baptisms on feast days may extend beyond theological concerns to concerns about attendance. Feast days are often when the greatest number of people would be present to celebrate the baptism. In some cultures, baptisms might be delayed, allowing the family time to gather the resources for the celebration.

Thus, post-baptismal celebrations could vary greatly depending on the cultural factors involved. For example, in cultures where a private family affair prevails, the post-baptismal reception may favor intimacy over the community. However, for cultures with strong communal ties, the post-baptismal celebration could be huge and involve multiple days.

Wise pastors will recognize these cultural differences for the importance of celebration in scheduling the baptism and planning the events surrounding it. Pastors from cultures that differ from those persons seeking baptism and their families can approach this important rite with curiosity rather than pre-conceived notions. Furthermore, as mentioned, pastors should avoid generalizing based on a monolithic view of culture. Each person's story is unique and worthy of time and attention.

Pastoral Perspectives

Thanksgiving for the Birth or Adoption of a Child

For Christian traditions that practice the baptism of infants and small children, one of the most significant pastoral challenges is differentiating between baptism with its complete theology, as discussed above, and parents' desire to celebrate the birth or adoption of a child. The arrival of a child into a family, whether by birth or adoption, is usually a joyous occasion. When infant mortality rates were higher, it also signaled the victory of life over death. Even today, pregnancies can involve complexities, and adoptions can be complicated and lengthy. Thus, parents feel great gratitude when the child finally arrives.

This desire to give thanks for and celebrate the arrival of a new child is legitimate. When parents, grandparents, other family members, and friends wish to gather to offer God thanks for the new child, the church is the appropriate place for that celebration. Such celebrations as part of the worshipping community remind the parents, family, friends, and the congregation of the blessing that new life brings. Rites of thanksgiving for the birth or adoption of a child allow family, friends, and the whole community to express gratitude to God and receive a blessing on behalf of the church. Christian traditions should offer such occasions regularly.

However, such occasions should not be confused with baptism. While baptisms are certainly joyous occasions, they involve much more than expressing gratitude for the birth or adoption of a child. Communities practicing infant baptism must make that distinction clear. Otherwise, the theology of baptism can become diluted, and parents, sponsors, and congregations may agree to promises they cannot keep.

Navigating this distinction requires pastoral skill. Because infant baptism has been considered more of a private or familial affair than an ecclesial one for a long time, parents and sponsors may not understand the full theology of baptism and the promises they will make on behalf of the child. Furthermore, ministers must be aware of the complex family dynamics involved in infant baptism. For example, younger generations may not feel the same need for religious identity as older generations do. Or couples may be interreligious and doubt committing their child to a particular religious tradition. Offering families the rite of thanksgiving for the birth or adoption of a child instead of baptism can be a powerfully pastoral option that allows the family to express their gratitude without committing them and their child to baptismal promises.

Catechesis

Catechesis is essential for baptismal preparation. The Nicene church emphasized catechesis, so many often remained a catechumen until right before death. This approach stemmed from the church's understanding of post-baptismal penitence, as they believed that God would not forgive grave sins committed after baptism. As the church's theology changed and *quam primum* baptisms increased, pre-baptismal catechesis shifted to pre-confirmation catechesis.

Many churches in traditions that practice infant baptism still emphasize pre-confirmation catechesis instead of pre-baptismal catechesis. Nonetheless, pre-baptismal catechesis remains essential and often involves pastoral questions regarding the persons involved, the duration, and the manner of catechesis.

If an older child or adult seeks baptism, they would be the primary person involved in catechesis. Most Christian traditions expect an older child or adult to be sponsored by someone already baptized. This person could be related to the candidate, but a familial relationship is unnecessary since the candidate can respond for themselves in the baptismal rite. If the candidate does not have a family member as a sponsor, selecting a sponsor can become the minister's responsibility.

The selection of a sponsor for a baptismal candidate requires discernment. One of the crucial qualities of a sponsor is a mature Christian faith. It is less important that a sponsor has all the "right answers" to questions a candidate might pose than that the sponsor model mature Christian spirituality. Having a living example of a Spirit-filled faith in the sponsor can deepen the faith in the candidate.

Also, a sponsor should be relatable. For example, having a sponsor who feels that faith is a private affair and is reticent to discuss it could be more of a hindrance than a help to a baptismal candidate. A sponsor needs to feel comfortable discussing faith with others. However, that does not mean a sponsor must be of a similar age, gender, racial/ethnic background, sexual orientation, or any other demographic characteristic. Having a sponsor with different life experiences could help a candidate understand the breadth of the Christian tradition. The willingness to listen and share one's faith journey is the priority in creating the bond between sponsor and candidate.

When a baptismal candidate is an infant or young child, sponsorship can be delicate as it involves the parents, other family members, or friends. Ideally, the parents and other sponsors are themselves mature in the Christian faith. However, the history of infant baptism in a tradition can impact that probability. If the practice of infant baptism in a particular tradition has strong ecclesial ties, parents and sponsors from that tradition are more likely to seek baptism for their young children out of expressing their mature faith journeys. However, if infant baptism historically has been linked more with a baby dedication and seen as a private or familial affair, then challenges can develop. The following section will discuss these challenges in greater detail. Nonetheless, even parents and sponsors with mature faith experience should be involved in pre-baptismal catechesis for their children.

The duration of catechesis can vary widely depending on many factors. Catechesis for older children and adults sometimes involves several months to a year of preparation. Because these candidates will be speaking for themselves in the rite, catechesis should be long enough to allow them a substantive introduction to the Christian faith. Some catechumenal processes begin with the first Sunday in Lent, and others may start as soon as early fall. Of course, if extraordinary circumstances are involved, one may shorten the catechumenal duration or even eliminate it in emergencies.

The practicalities of ministry can also affect the duration of catechesis. Churches with more significant resources in lay and ordained catechists may offer more extensive programs. However, churches with fewer resources should also feel empowered to offer substantive catechumenal programs. The end of the chapter includes further information for all churches seeking a vital catechumenal process regardless of available resources. Investing in a robust catechumenate is well worth the effort involved.

The duration of catechesis for parents and sponsors of infants and young children often can be truncated to a single session with a rehearsal. However, this temptation should be resisted if possible. It is as important for parents and sponsors to understand the promises they are making on behalf of their children as it is for older candidates to make them on their behalf. Since they are making promises to raise the child in the Christian faith, parents of young children may not need the same amount of catechesis as older candidates. Nonetheless, it should involve several sessions where the baptismal rite can be explained and questions can be explored.

The manner of catechesis can take many forms. One of the most robust forms involves formational classes and liturgical involvement. Some Christian traditions offer a catechumenate with specific moments when the catechumens engage liturgically with the congregation. First, they are presented to the community during worship when admitted as catechumens. Then, a few weeks before baptism (sometimes at the beginning of Lent if baptisms are at the Easter Vigil), they sign a book to enroll as candidates for baptism. Then, the baptism itself occurs during a regular worship service.[68]

The advantage of such an integrated approach is that it makes the ecclesial connection explicit to everyone involved. By having the catechumens and candidates come before the congregation before their baptisms, they understand that they are making a public decision, not a private one. For many people in Western society, that is very counter-cultural. Often, faith is a private affair.

---

68. The most extensive example is the "Rite of Christian Initiation of Adults" in RITES, 13-356. Similar but less extensive examples are in BOS, 127-135 and ELW, 232. See also *The Use and Means of Grace*, Proposition 20, 26.

Also, the sponsors recognize that their journey with these catechumens and candidates involves the entire worshipping community. Therefore, if they grew up seeing baptism as a private or family event, this process could help them reflect on their baptism differently.

Finally, the congregation begins to understand that baptism is not just the time to see cute babies but involves a real commitment by those deciding to be baptized. Some traditions even include a liturgical rite for preparing the parents and sponsors of an infant to be baptized.[69] While not as extensive as the catechumenate for older children and adults, this rite can still have many similar benefits.

Whether the catechumenal process involves a liturgical component, care should be taken on the formational portions. To maximize formational opportunities, some churches blend baptismal catechesis with catechesis for rites of affirmation or general Christian formation. Such decisions should be made carefully. Indeed, some formational activities could benefit persons who have already been baptized and, therefore, could be blended. However, some formational activities must be specific to those seeking baptism.

Also, formational activities should understand the pedagogical needs of the participants. Some churches may wish to have different formational activities based on age. Others may choose an intergenerational approach. Candidates for baptism may live with neurodiversity and require tailored strategies to meet those needs. Educational backgrounds can vary. Many factors can impact the pedagogical approach required. Developing a robust but flexible catechumenal process that meets the needs of diverse groups can be challenging.[70]

Challenges with Sponsors

From the church's earliest days, candidates for baptism have had sponsors who journey with them as they prepare for baptism. In addition to providing support, these sponsors model the Christian life for the candidate. Therefore, as noted above, sponsors for older children and adults seeking baptism should be mature in the faith. Ministers should take an active role in selecting sponsors who can be a part of the catechumenal process for older candidates. Since older candidates speak for themselves, there is no obligation for the sponsors to be their parents or family members.

When the candidate for baptism is an infant or young child, additional challenges can arise in sponsorship. One challenge involves parents who may not be regular church attendees. If the parents understand baptism as more of a familial affair than an ecclesial one, they may wait for their first child's birth to return to the church. They often come expecting a celebration of their child's birth without understanding the commitments involved in baptism.

---

69. For example, "Preparation of Parents and Sponsors of Infants and Young Children to be Baptized" in BOS, 141-142; and "Welcome to Baptism" in ELW, 232.

70. Additional resources are provided at the end of the chapter.

This moment is ripe for a pastoral encounter. One approach a minister can take is to schedule a brief meeting with the parents, have a quick rehearsal, baptize the child, and hope to see them at Christmas or Easter at best. While tempting due to the intense pressures of pastoral ministry, this approach misses an opportunity to engage the parents in their Christian journey. After all, they will be making promises on behalf of their child and for themselves that they will raise the child in the Christian faith. Moreover, most baptismal rites also include a pledge made by the congregation to support the child in their Christian journey. How can the congregation offer that support if the parents do not engage with them?

One of the perhaps unforeseen benefits of the secularization of Western society is that baptism and other church rites are less likely to be seen as social obligations. If parents bring their children to church to be baptized when they have not been regular attendees, something has drawn them back. Exploring that spiritual tug can be a fruitful endeavor but requires pastoral care. Shaming parents for their lack of attendance rarely produces a positive result. Exploring the genuine challenges they may face as new parents who, on some level, desire a spiritual life for their child can assist the minister and the congregation in discovering how they can further support young parents. While the pressures of life may nonetheless draw some parents away from regular church attendance, this pastoral moment can still have a lasting effect on their and their children's lives.

Another challenge with sponsors involves grandparents. Due to the changing views on religion and especially religious institutional membership, many new parents today might describe themselves as "nones," i.e., having no religious preference. Alternatively, they may recognize themselves as Christian but do not desire institutional affiliation. However, their parents, the young child's grandparents, feel differently. Ongoing church surveys and other demographic data have shown an increasingly older population in church membership, especially among frequent church attendees. For this older generation, affiliation with the church still holds significant meaning; many want their grandchildren to experience that same meaning.

Therefore, it is not uncommon for a minister to receive a request to baptize a young child not from the parents but from the grandparents. The wise minister handles such requests delicately, as they can involve complex family dynamics. The minister should agree to meet with the grandparents and parents together to avoid triangulation. If the minister discovers that the grandparents are attempting to have the child baptized without the parents' knowledge or against the parents' wishes, the minister would be wise to pastorally explain that such a request cannot be fulfilled without the parents' consent.

Sometimes, grandparents may express their strong desire for the child's baptism and have not considered the parents' wishes or communicated directly with them. In these cases, a joint meeting will be most helpful. Perhaps the minister will discover that the parents have not been attending church regularly but have no ill will against the church and still recognize themselves as members. In this case, the minister can approach the parents as described above.

In another case, the parents may not consider themselves Christian church members but would be fine if their children were baptized. The grandparents might agree to be the sponsors. While this scenario may seem satisfactory, additional probing could produce other challenges. For example, where do the parents and child live relative to the grandparents? If they live far away, how will the grandparents fulfill their vow to support the child in the Christian faith? Will the parents support the child's active involvement in the church as the child grows up? These and other questions are essential in determining whether this scenario is satisfactory.

If one parent actively resists the child being baptized and the other parent actively desires it, the minister will want to proceed cautiously. Pastoral care may warrant attending to the marital dynamics first. How did the couple enter this disagreement on such an important question? Some couples fail to discuss these critical issues before marriage and discover these significant disagreements later. Again, this moment is ripe for pastoral care.

Concern for the consequences of original sin can often motivate grandparents to seek the baptism of their grandchildren even when the parents actively resist it. The pastor can take this opportunity to discuss the various theologies of original sin with these grandparents. Again, pastoral wisdom would caution the minister from directly challenging the grandparents' theological understanding. The concern for the consequences of original sin runs deep in the hearts of those who carry it, and respect for that conviction is essential. Equally, it is crucial to assure the grandparents of God's grace and love in these complex situations.

In today's increasingly globalized world, parents may tell a minister that sponsors for their child's baptism will not be physically present for the liturgical rite. Sometimes, the desired sponsor is entirely unavailable for the ceremony, and sometimes, the selected sponsor can be available virtually using video conferencing technologies. As discussed above regarding grandparents, the minister should first ascertain if the sponsors can fulfill the vows they are taking. Sometimes, parents desire someone to be a sponsor more for their close personal relationship with them than for the person's commitment to raising the child in the Christian faith. The minister can explore this opportunity with the parents and the desired sponsor.

If the minister ascertains that the sponsor desires to be actively involved in the child's Christian faith development, then the minister still needs to attend to the ritual aspects of the request. A completely absent sponsor cannot take the vows in the baptismal rite. One option could be to allow the sponsor that opportunity at a future liturgical gathering when their presence is possible. This occasion could communicate to the family and the congregation the importance of these vows.

Virtual participation in a liturgical rite offers additional challenges. Some Christian traditions, especially more sacramental ones, may not allow virtual participation, especially in a rite as important as baptism. Others may permit it, but logistics could pose problems. Does the space allow good internet connectivity? Will the video conferencing be on someone's phone or tablet? How will the person's participation in the rite be affected? Some creativity could open possibilities.

Ministers may also receive requests for sponsors who explicitly do not claim the Christian faith. A frequent scenario is a baptized Christian who no longer professes the faith, becoming agnostic or atheist or subsequently joining another faith tradition. Another scenario could be someone who was never baptized and is either agnostic, atheist, or an active member of another faith tradition.

However, all Christian traditions require that sponsors for baptism be baptized Christians themselves. As discussed, this requirement recognizes sponsors' critical role in the child's faith development. Furthermore, the sponsors not only make vows regarding the child's growth in the Christian faith, but they also make vows on behalf of the child regarding the faith itself, i.e., the Creed. Therefore, asking someone to make such vows outside their religion or lack thereof is not only disingenuous but also ethically problematic.

One pastoral solution is to suggest that the persons act as witnesses. They can be present for the entire rite. They might also stand with the family when the child is presented for baptism, but they would not participate in the rite by answering questions or making promises. This solution can be equally effective if one of the parents is also of another faith or no faith but supports the child's baptism.

In all these scenarios, the pastor faces an important tension between the heartfelt desire from the parents, or sometimes grandparents, to celebrate the child's birth and the deeply theological purposes for baptism as Christian initiation. The temptation to favor one side of that tension over the other can be significant. However, the wise pastor will seek balance as much as possible.

Baptism near the Time of Death

Pastoral ministry involves accompanying those near, at, and after death. Requests for baptism can come during those times as well. These moments are especially tender ones requiring great pastoral sensitivity.

The timing of the request matters significantly. Sometimes, death is imminent or has already occurred when the request is received. As discussed above, different Christian traditions have differing views on and even rules regulating such emergency baptisms. Some traditions will allow baptized people to perform the rite using water and the Trinitarian formula under these difficult circumstances. On the other hand, some traditions discourage baptism at these times, especially if the request comes out of concern for the consequences of original sin, which the tradition does not uphold.

Nonetheless, the pastor faces a crucial decision between the theological integrity of the rite and pastoral responsiveness to the persons making the request.

This decision need not involve strict polarization: to baptize or not to baptize. The wise pastor permits nuance and grace in these fraught circumstances. For example, if an infant has just died and the mother seeks baptism, the pastor can supplement the rite with prayers recognizing God's grace in such a tragic situation. The pastor might recall the church tradition of "baptism by desire," in which God's grace extends to those who desired baptism (for themselves or on behalf of their young child) but could not enact it.

If death is close but not imminent, the pastor might engage more fully with the person making the request. If the person requests baptism for themselves, the pastor can explore that desire, recognizing that the gifts of baptism can be fruitful no matter the extent of one's life. If the person requests baptism for their young child, the pastor might discuss it. Does it stem from a fear of original sin? If so, how does the pastor's tradition regard original sin? Such opportunities allow the pastor to discuss God's grace, mercy, and love.

One scenario involves significant ethical issues, receiving the request to baptize from a third party. Baptizing an incapacitated older child or adult without consent or a young child without the permission of the parents or guardians is unethical. Unfortunately, the church's history includes such practices, but they are no longer supported. Nonetheless, pastors still receive such requests, sometimes from the adult children of elders of a different or no faith tradition, sometimes from grandparents of infants or other well-meaning individuals. While the pastor can respect the person's theological understanding and great concern, the pastor should never baptize someone without proper consent.

Baptism is an important "turning point" in people's lives. For the candidate, it involves their new life in Christ and membership in the Body of Christ, the church. For their sponsors, baptism often reignites their faith commitment as they walk with their candidate on this journey. Parents and other family members rejoice in the birth of their children but also seek a deepening commitment on their behalf. The congregation witnesses this moment of rebirth, renews their baptismal promises, and agrees to support the new Christians in their faith journey. Baptism impacts all involved and requires pastoral care and discernment for ministers.

Questions for Discussion

1. What did you find surprising from the history of baptism, and how has it reformed your view of it?

2. What aspects of the history of baptism comfort you as you explore this rite?

3. What are your views on the relationship between original sin and baptism?

4. What about the theology of baptism? Does it confuse you or raise additional questions?

5. What is an example of a pastoral practice involving baptism that you have experienced that was not discussed above?

6. How can you keep the tension between baptism as an initiatory rite and baptism as a pastoral office taut?

7. What cultural practices around baptism have you experienced?

8. How have the cultures that have formed you formed your understanding of baptism?

Additional Resources

Bushkofsky, Dennis, Richard W. Rouse, Suzanne Burke. *Go Make Disciples: An Invitation to Baptismal Living: A Handbook to the Catechumenate*. Minneapolis, MN: Augsburg Fortress, 2012.
This book provides a step-by-step process for building a catechumenal program. It is structured in a lesson plan format with suggestions for structuring sessions and additional resources.

Heller, Dagmar. *Baptized into Christ: A Guide to the Ecumenical Discussion on Baptism*. Geneva: World Council of Churches Publications, 2012.
Written from the perspective of the World Council of Churches, this book provides a history of the ecumenical discussions related to baptism and the controversies involved.

Hoffman, Paul E. *Faith Forming Faith: Bringing New Christians to Baptism and Beyond*. Eugene, OR: Cascade Books, 2012.
This book describes one church's experience of creating a year-long catechumenal process. Written for pastors, it provides real-life examples.

Johnson, Maxwell E. *The Rites of Christian Initiation*. Revised edition. Collegeville, MN: Liturgical Press, 2007.
This book provides a detailed and scholarly history of the rites of baptism from the New Testament period to today. It is an excellent resource that could be used for teaching the history of the baptismal rites.

Kavanagh, Aidan. *The Shape of Baptism*. Collegeville, MN: Liturgical press, 1991.
This book also offers an excellent history of the rites of initiation from the New Testament to the reforms of Vatican II.

Whitaker, Edward Charles., Johnson, Maxwell E.. *Documents of the Baptismal Liturgy*. Collegeville, MN: Liturgical Press, 2003.
This book is a reference for primary sources related to the baptismal liturgy. Each section contains a short description of the text, a bibliography of secondary sources, and excerpts from the text focused on the baptismal liturgy.

White, James F. *Protestant Worship: Traditions in Transition*. Louisville, KY: Westminster John Knox Press, 1989.
This book provides a short history of worship in various Protestant traditions. Because of its scope, it provides a short introduction to these histories. A selected bibliography of additional resources is included.

CHAPTER 2

Confirmation and Other Rites of Affirmation

After baptism, occasions can arise for Christians wishing to reaffirm their faith. These occasions are often strongly encouraged or even prescribed, especially for ecclesial traditions practicing infant baptism. For example, some ecclesial traditions require confirmation before one can receive communion. Other traditions have no such requirement but strongly encourage a public profession of faith by one baptized as an infant. Even traditions exclusively practicing adult baptism allow people to reaffirm their faith in Christ.

These occasions for a public, mature affirmation of faith have important pastoral implications for one's faith journey. Especially for traditions practicing infant baptism, they allow Christians to claim the baptismal promises their parents or sponsors made for them. However, the history and theology of confirmation and other rites of affirmation have been intertwined with baptism to such a degree as to create confusion. Is confirmation a continuation of the initiatory rites of baptism? Or is it separate? Most ecclesial traditions today agree they are separate, but that was not always the case. Lingering misunderstandings among parents of older children and adults can also create confusion.

Furthermore, are such rites repeatable? Ecclesial traditions differ in their responses. Those traditions which see these rites as sacraments or sacramental in nature would limit them to one occurrence, with other non-sacramental rites available for repeated affirmations. Other traditions that do not view these rites as sacramental or lack a sacramental theology altogether see no problem with their repetition as needed.

Principally, these rites affirm or reaffirm one's identity in Christ, which began with baptism. While pastorally and culturally, they have affinities with rites of passage, they remain Christological in focus. Nonetheless, the desire to celebrate these maturation rites can create tension with the theological core of the rites, which pastors must navigate wisely.

Historical Context

The history of the rites of affirmation intertwines with baptism, especially during the first fifteen hundred years of Western Christian history. Much of the history provided in chapter one is also relevant to these rites. The history of the baptismal rites' unitive nature and subsequent dissolution in the West is significant. Scholars and theologians have mistakenly interpreted Scripture and liturgical rites as supporting separate rites of affirmation when no separation existed initially. Therefore, this section will reference these anachronistic misinterpretations and provide a more historically accurate interpretation.

At times in the church's history, these rites of affirmation and confirmation have been linked with the reception of the Holy Spirit. Such theological interpretations are highly problematic, especially when these rites are separated from baptismal ones for considerable periods. As will be discussed more fully below, the Holy Spirit is integral to the life of a Christian. Therefore, it is inconceivable that any time could lapse when the Holy Spirit is not present and actively engaged in a Christian's life. Nonetheless, understanding this connection between the rite of confirmation and the Holy Spirit is essential when discussing the history of the rite.

New Testament and Ante-Nicene Period

As discussed in chapter one, the New Testament has no rite of baptism and, therefore, has no rite of confirmation or other rites of affirmation. As a Christian theology of baptism developed, it included the gift of the Holy Spirit. Baptisms, as described in the New Testament, often included anointing (2 Cor 1:22; Eph 1:13; 1 John 2:20) and handlaying (Acts 8:14-17 and 19:1-7). However, describing these actions with the contemporary understanding of confirmation would be anachronistic.[1] Acts 8 describes a group of Samaritans who had been baptized but had not yet received the gift of the Holy Spirit. One might claim this story supports a distinct rite for confirmation, but, as Reginald Fuller explains, "The separation of the laying on of hands [from baptism] in Acts 8 has nothing to do with the western medieval separation of confirmation from baptism but is due rather to Luke's redactional interest in subordinating each successive new stage in the Christian mission to the Jerusalem church and its apostolate."[2] The early church had no concept of confirmation as understood today.

However, the New Testament is replete with public affirmations of faith. Acts chapter two shares the inaugural narrative of the coming of the Holy Spirit

---

1. Edward N. West refers to the New Testament account of handlaying as a "method of confirmation." See Edward N. West, "The Rites of Christian Initiation in the Early Church," in *Confirmation: History, Doctrine, and Practice*, 7.

2. Reginald Fuller, "Christian Initiation in the New Testament," in *Made, Not Born: New Perspectives on Christian Initiation and the Catechumenate*, 14.

in the Lukan tradition, and with that public experience, about three thousand people were baptized and added to the church. These newly formed Christians began to experience persecution. This persecution would engender practices of secrecy, but affirmations of faith were still made in the presence of the church assembly.

The liturgical sources from the Ante-Nicene period include church orders such as *The Didache* and *The Apostolic Tradition* and theological treatises like Tertullian's *De Baptismo*. As referenced in chapter one, these sources describe many combinations of pre-baptismal anointings, post-baptismal anointings, and handlayings. However, understanding any of these practices as equivalent to the modern-day practice of confirmation is anachronistic. Normatively, these practices accompanied baptism as a unitive rite of initiation performed by the bishop, sometimes with a presbyter, for adults[3], as Figure 2.1 depicts.

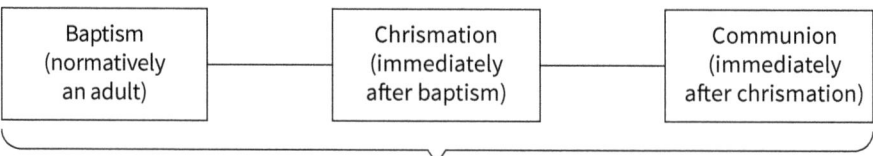

Figure 2.1: Unitive Rite of Initiation

Nicene Period

As the church grew after the legalization of Christianity, the normative practice of the unitive rite of initiation shifted. Bishops could not always perform baptisms as their ministries tended to remain centralized in urban settings. Therefore, ministry to persons living in more rural areas often fell to presbyters. What role should the bishop play if a presbyter has baptized someone? Should the post-baptismal anointing with chrism be left to the bishop? Should handlaying be left to the bishop?

These questions led to papal decrees. For example, Pope Innocent stated in a letter to Decentius (416 CE) that only the bishop should anoint an infant with chrism. However, if a presbyter were to anoint an infant, it should not be on the forehead.[4] Nearly two hundred years later, Pope Gregory I wrote to Januarius that a scandal had arisen, namely, that bishops were prohibiting presbyters from anointing with chrism, and therefore, it should be permitted.[5] Liturgical scholar Gabriele Winkler recognizes that the exact practice done by bishops was indeterminate. The bishop visiting a rural area sought to "confirm" the baptisms done by presbyters. However, it is unclear if that confirmation process involved a first

---

3. See Johnson, *The Rites of Christian Initiation*, 83-114.
4. Whitaker, *Documents of the Baptismal Liturgy*, 206.
5. Whitaker, *Documents of the Baptismal Liturgy*, 206.

anointing with chrism for those unanointed, a second chrismal anointing in addition to the presbyter's, or a handlaying.⁶

Questions began to arise about the theological interpretation of this second episcopal act of confirmation. If baptism bestows on one all the grace needed for the Christian life, why was this subsequent rite necessary? A homily delivered on Pentecost would significantly influence the answer to this question. Scholars agree that the provenance of this homily was Gaul. However, the author and the date have been debated. Dix believed it to be a bishop with the alias of Pseudo-Eusebius of Emesa, written in the later fifth century.⁷ Van Buchem believed it to be written by Faustus of Riez, but Winkler disagrees. She believes it was written by someone else later than the fifth century. Whatever its original authorship and date, it was incorporated into a letter by Pope Melchiades in the ninth century. It was eventually used by the scholastic theologian Peter Lombard in the twelfth century, where it gained influence over the Western church's understanding of confirmation.⁸

The homily states, "In baptism we are born anew for life, after baptism we are confirmed for battle. In baptism we are washed, after baptism we are strengthened."⁹ Thus, it indicates a clear separation between baptism and what would become known as confirmation. If the initiatory rite were primarily unitive in the fifth century, with exceptions for rural ministry, then the separation described in this homily would seem misplaced. However, if Winkler is correct that the homily dates later than the fifth century, it may be theologically explaining the medieval dissolution of the initiatory rite.¹⁰

Before turning to this dissolution of the initiatory rite, one additional historical use of chrism and handlaying is noteworthy. During the fourth century, the church wrestled with the doctrine of the divinity of Christ and the Holy Spirit. In discussing the divinity of the Holy Spirit, theologians such as Irenaeus and the Cappadocians argued that the Father used the Holy Spirit as unction (anointing with oil) for the Son. Thus, anointing with oil became symbolically attached to the doctrine of the divinity of the Holy Spirit.¹¹

When heretics and schismatics sought to be reconciled with the church, the question of their baptisms arose. Was baptism valid if one was baptized by a clergyperson outside of the orthodox faith? As discussed in chapter one, the church,

---

6. Gabriele Winkler, "Confirmation or Chrismation: A Study in Comparative Liturgy," 9-13.

7. Gregory Dix, *The Theology of Confirmation in Relation to Baptism*, 21.

8. Winkler, "Confirmation or Chrismation," 13-15

9. Winkler, "Confirmation or Chrismation," 14. The original Latin text can be found in L. A. Van Buchem, *L'homélie Pseudo-Eusébienne de Pentecôte. L'origine de la* confirmatio *en Gaul Méridionale et l'interprétation de ce rite par Fauste de Riez*, 411.

10. See the Theological Insights section below for further discussion on confirmation as a strengthening of grace.

11. Gerard Austin, *Anointing with the Spirit: The Rite of Confirmation: The Use of Oil and Chrism*, 15.

influenced by the teachings of Augustine, determined that it was. Rebaptism was not necessary.

However, an additional question arose. Had the person received the gift of the Holy Spirit at baptism, or did the person need to be anointed or receive the imposition of hands again? The Council of Laodicea stated that the gift of the Holy Spirit was not given at a baptism outside of the church. Therefore, a post-baptismal anointing was necessary. In fact, the phrase "seal of the gift of the Holy Spirit" found in many baptismal rites today first appears in this act of reconciliation.[12] Leo the Great in the West (440-461 CE) instructed that heretics seeking admission into the church needed "confirmation" through the imposition of hands because they had received "the form of baptism without its power."[13]

Thus, another separation has occurred between baptismal washing and post-baptismal anointing or handlaying. Botte suggests, "From that time on the question could be asked whether this fact did not give rise to the theological reflection which attempted to show that the gift of the Spirit was separable from baptism and that it was necessary to express this fact by a rite which followed the baptism? Such is the hypothesis that I wish to submit to historians and theologians."[14] If Winkler is correct that the Pentecost homily discussed above is dated beyond the fifth century, then that homily could have been one way later theologians attempted to explain these now-separated rites. Furthermore, this evolution of the rite could explain the contemporary practice among traditions with episcopal authority to require episcopal handlaying when receiving someone into that ecclesial tradition.[15]

The Middle Ages

One of the earliest full liturgical rites of the West is *The Gelasian Sacramentary*, dated in the early sixth century. This rite continues the unitive practice of initiation but includes some influential instructions. First, the normative person described is now an infant, not an adult. After the person is dipped three times in the water, the sacramentary instructs, "*Then when the infant has gone up from the font he is signed on the head with chrism by the presbyter, with these words.*" Thus, the presbyter offers the first chrismal anointing. After a prayer, the sacramentary instructs, "*Then the sevenfold Spirit is given to them by the bishop. To seal them, he lays his hand upon them with these words.*" The bishop prays that God would send the Holy Spirit on the newly baptized and endow them with "*the spirit of wisdom and understanding, the spirit of counsel*

---

12. Bernard Botte, "Postbaptismal Anointing in the Ancient Patriarchate of Antioch," in *The Syrian Churches Series*, 6:71.

13. Austin, *Anointing with the Spirit*, 16.

14. Botte, "Postbaptismal Anointing in the Ancient Patriarchate of Antioch," 71.

15. Please see the Theological Insights section below for further discussion.

and might, the spirit of knowledge and godliness, and fill them with the spirit of fear [Isa 11:25] of God." Then, finally, the bishop "*signs them on the forehead with chrism.*"[16]

Thus, all orders of ministry are present: laity, bishop, presbyter, and deacon (with roles in other portions of the rite). The presbyter baptizes and anoints with chrism immediately afterward. The bishop imposes hands on the newly baptized and chrismally anoints them. The rite has remained unitive but now focuses primarily on infants.

However, this unitive rite would dissolve into separate rites: bath, anointing/handlaying, and first communion, as Figure 2.2 depicts. As discussed above, the church's growth was one of the main factors for this dissolution. It became impossible for all the orders to be present at every baptism, and, therefore, as Johnson adroitly states, "various possibilities were open for the celebration of the rites: (1) the rites could be deferred until all of the various orders were present; (2) one minister (i.e., the presbyter) could take the part of another (i.e., the bishop); or (3) the parts of the rite normally performed by the absent minister (i.e., the bishop) could be omitted until he was able to be present."[17]

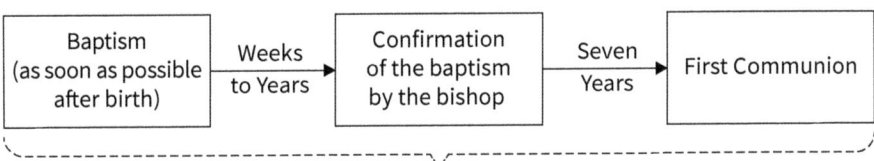

Figure 2.2: Disintegrated Rite of Initiation - Early Middle Ages

As time progressed, two paths became evident. In the East, bishops permitted presbyters to anoint the newly baptized with chrism consecrated by a bishop—these newly baptized persons, whether infant or adult, were permitted to receive communion immediately afterward. Thus, the East has maintained the unitive rite of initiation.

Evidence suggests that initially, the Western church progressed similarly. Gallican sacramentaries from the seventh and eighth centuries included only one post-baptismal anointing completed by either the presbyter or the bishop. Liturgical scholar Leonell Mitchell stated succinctly, "In sum, none of the Gallican sacramentaries includes a rite of episcopal confirmation, nor have we any evidence requiring us to assume that such a rite was customarily added to the extant baptismal rites, nor that the administration of the single Gallican post-baptismal anointing was confined to bishops."[18] So, even as late as the eighth century, the

---

16. Whitaker, *Documents of the Baptismal Liturgy*, 235, italics in original.
17. Johnson, *The Rites of Christian Initiation*, 247.
18. Leonel L. Mitchell, *Baptismal Anointing*, 125.

unitive rite of initiation was intact if performed more frequently by a presbyter than a bishop.[19]

Eventually, the Western church took a different path. One of the factors influencing this different path was the development of *quam primum* baptism. As discussed more thoroughly in chapter one, *quam primum* (or "as soon as possible") baptisms became normative in the West due to Augustine's teaching of original sin. Combined with a great fear of infant mortality, Augustine's teaching on original sin caused baptisms to move from the church done by a bishop or presbyter to the private home, often done by a midwife immediately after birth. By the fourteenth century, local church councils required parents to bring their child to a clergyperson for baptism by eight days old, regardless of the season of the year. Thus, the time between birth and baptism shrank significantly.[20]

A further development was the flip-flopping of communion and confirmation. The unitive rite of the early church consisted of the water bath (sometimes with pre-baptismal anointings), at least one post-baptismal anointing, often with handlaying, and then immediate entry into the eucharistic assembly to receive communion. Even when infants became the predominant baptismal candidates, infant communion continued.

However, as eucharistic realism increased in the ninth and tenth centuries and further focused in the eleventh century, the church grew concerned about infants receiving the host, now perceived as the actual flesh of Christ, who could not swallow it. Initially, infant communion continued but only with wine. The priest might dip a finger into the chalice and commune the infant with a drop of wine.[21]

Eventually, the concern about eucharistic realism would expand such that the laity was no longer administered the chalice. Thus, infants would not be communicated at all. By the Lateran Council (1215), which enjoined all Christians to receive communion by the "age of discretion," infant communion had ceased as the council makes no mention of it for those under the "age of discretion."[22] This practice would become known as first communion.

How did confirmation end up following first communion? Fisher suggests that the origins of this transposition occurred in the eighth century with the Carolingian reforms.[23] Charlemagne attempted to unify his empire through liturgical conformity with Rome. Alcuin became the principal architect of this conformity. Roman liturgical rites were imported into Gaul. As mentioned above, Gallican rites previously had only one post-baptismal anointing completed by the

---

19. See Joseph L. Levesque, "The Theology of Postbaptismal Rites in the Seventh and Eighth Century Gallican Church," 39-43.
20. J.D.C. Fisher, *Christian Initiation: Baptism in the Medieval West*, 111-112.
21. Fisher, *Christian Initiation*, 101-104.
22. Fisher, *Christian Initiation*, 104.
23. Fisher, *Christian Initiation*, 57-67.

presbyter. However, the Roman rites insisted on an episcopal post-baptismal anointing. The later Gallican rites under Alcuin's influence added this episcopal post-baptismal anointing *after* the bath, the presbyteral anointing, and communion. As already discussed, bishops grew increasingly unable to be present for baptisms. Thus, the time between the bath, presbyteral anointing, and reception of communion and the episcopal anointing grew. Initially, it was only a week or so. Eventually, it became years.

By the thirteenth century, the unitive initiatory rite had dissolved into three distinct rites separated by years with a reordering of the rites. What had been bath-anointing/handlaying-communion in a single service became bath-communion-anointing/handlaying separated by years. Confirmation occurred after first communion, often by several years, which occurred after baptism by several years.[24]

Thus, scholastic theologians such as Peter Lombard and Thomas Aquinas would eventually describe confirmation as a distinct sacrament from baptism. Using the Pentecost sermon from the fifth century or later, they claimed that this distinct sacrament provides additional grace from baptism meant to strengthen one for battle. Aquinas would go on to say that baptism provided grace for one's salvation, and confirmation provided grace for one to battle with the enemies of the faith. Thus, baptism took on an even more private and individualistic character, while confirmation became the public rite of the mature Christian.[25]

The Reformations

One hundred years before the continental and English reformations, John Wycliffe, a predecessor to Protestantism, wrote about confirmation in his *Trialogue*. He opposed the necessity of confirmation, "I do not see that this sacrament is generally necessary for the salvation of the faithful, nor that those pretending to confirm children confirm them regularly, nor that this sacrament should be reserved especially to the bishops of Caesar." While he preliminarily described confirmation as a sacrament, he goes on to suggest that it is "the action of the devil," which would call into question its sacramentality.[26]

Martin Luther rejected confirmation as a sacrament because his sacramental theology necessitated a biblical mandate from Christ. Since confirmation lacked that dominical command, Luther felt it could not be considered a sacrament.[27] However, Luther believed confirmation could continue as a means of examining

---

24. Fisher, *Christian Initiation*, 125-127.

25. Austin, *The Rite of Confirmation*, 26-27. See also Peter Turner, *Sources of Confirmation from the Fathers through the Reformers*, 40-42.

26. Turner, *Sources of Confirmation*, 43.

27. Turner, *Sources of Confirmation*, 43.

the faith of children who had been baptized as infants and then reared in the faith. He even stated that this examination could be followed by a pastor who "lays hands on [the children], and confirms them."[28] However, Luther composed no rites of confirmation.

Andreas Osiander, a German Lutheran theologian and reformer, is believed to be the principal architect of the *Brandenburg-Nuremburg Church Order* of 1533. While this church order contains no rite of confirmation, it does describe the expectations for full membership in the church.

> When the people present themselves, the ministers shall discreetly ask them, as they have opportunity, whether they know the ten commandments, the creed and the Lord's prayer, whether they have a right understanding of the holy sacrament and know what it will profit them if they receive it worthily, but, more particularly, whether they have hatred or enmity towards any man, for nothing is more opposed to this holy sacrament than disunity.[29]

At this time, it was the Lutheran practice that a public profession of faith should precede the reception of communion. Thus, "holy sacrament" refers to the Lord's Supper, not confirmation. The means of preparation are noteworthy. The people were to attest to their knowledge of the Ten Commandments, the Creed, and the Lord's Prayer. Thus, knowledge became the prerequisite for full church membership and receiving communion.

Martin Bucer (1491-1551) was a Protestant reformer who came to Strasburg after being excommunicated from the Roman Catholic Church. No evidence exists of a rite of confirmation written by him. However, a Strasburg Order of Confirmation appears to be influenced by him, if not his work. It describes how baptized children were to be presented to the church to be "received and confirmed." The pastor addresses the children, indicating how they have been prepared by studying the Ten Commandments, the Creed, and the Lord's Prayer. Then, the children are to publicly answer the first six questions of Luther's Small Catechism and the Ten Commandments. At the end of their examination, the pastor admonishes them to continue to learn and live a good Christian life. The rite ends with the pastor extending a hand over the children and praying for God's blessing.[30]

In England, Henry VIII defended confirmation as a sacrament. In his *Assertio Septem Sacramentorum* (Defense of the Seven Sacraments), he argues against Luther's view.

---

28. J.D.C. Fisher, *Christian Initiation: The Reformation Period*, 171-172.

29. Fisher, *Christian Initiation*, 173.

30. Fisher, *Christian Initiation: The Reformation Period*, 174-178. Current Lutheran thought recognizes Luther's Small and Large Catechisms as commentary on the baptismal process in which the Ten Commandments, Creeds, Lord's Prayer, Sacraments, and Absolution play the central role.

I am astonished therefore what has come into Luther's mind that he should maintain that confirmation is to be regarded as only a rite and a ceremony, and deny that it should be regarded as a true sacrament; for not only by the testimony of the holy doctors and by the faith of the whole church, but also in the clearest passages of holy scripture it is shown by the visible sign of the hand of the bishops to confer not only grace but also the Spirit of grace himself. Therefore let Luther cease to despise the sacrament of confirmation, which the dignity of the minister and the authority of the church and the usefulness of the sacrament itself commend.[31]

However, this view would change with time. By 1536, Henry issued the *Ten Articles*, listing only baptism, penance, and the Eucharist as sacraments. The following year, a Convocation was convened to discuss the missing four sacraments in which the bishops disagreed about their status.[32] The *Bishops' Book*, issued the following year, described confirmation as a sacrament. Like its medieval precursors, it described this sacrament as providing gifts of the Holy Spirit that fortify one for spiritual battle.[33]

With Henry's death and his son Edward's reign begun, reformed theology took a stronger foothold in England. The 1549 Book of Common Prayer included a rite of confirmation. The rite begins with a catechism for children. The following instruction states that the godparents of the children are to bring them to the bishop when the children "can say in theyr mother tong, the articles of the faith, the lordes prayer, and the ten commaundementes: And can also aunswere to suche questions of this shorte Cathechisme, as the Busshop (or suche as he shall appoynte) shall by his discrecion appose them in." The following prayer by the bishop asks God to send the Holy Spirit on them and to give them the sevenfold gifts. The bishop then signs them on the forehead with unction and lays hands on them. The final instruction states, "And there shal none be admitted to the holye communion: until suche time as he be confirmed."[34]

The 1559 Book of Common Prayer took a more reformed approach in its confirmation rite. The signing of the cross with unction was omitted. Instead, the bishop was to lay hands on each child and pray, "DEFENDE, O Lorde, this childe with thy heavenly grace, that he may continue thine for ever, and daiely encrease in thy holy spirite more and more, untill he come unto thy everlastyng kyngdome. Amen." Furthermore, the final instruction changed notably, "*And there shal none be admitted to the holy Communion, until suche tyme as he can saye the*

---

31. Fisher, *Christian Initiation: The Reformation Period*, 20.

32. Fisher, *Christian Initiation: The Reformation Period*, 208-220.; and Charles Lloyd and Andrew Raines, eds., *Formularies of Faith: Confessional Documents Issued by Henry VII and Thomas Cranmer*, 1-17.

33. Fisher, *Christian Initiation: The Reformation Period*, 221-222; and Lloyd and Raines, *Formularies of Faith*, 37-195.

34. Brian Cummings, ed., *The Book of Common Prayer: The Texts of 1549, 1559, and 1662*, 58-63.

Catechisme, and bee confirmed."[35] It applied a further emphasis on instruction and recitation as entry to communion. This expectation that children be cognitively prepared for communion would carry into the twentieth century.

John Calvin (1509-1564) wrote vehemently against confirmation as a sacrament. In his *Institutes of the Christian Religion*, he quotes Augustine, who said that the word must be added to the element for it to become a sacrament. Calvin states that the word is absent since Scripture says nothing about confirmation. All that remains is the "oil, that is, a thick and greasy liquid, but nothing more," thus not a sacrament.[36] In his later work responding to the Council of Trent, Calvin's criticism becomes more direct.

> I hasten ... to declare that I am certainly not of the number of those who think that Confirmation, as observed under the Roman Papacy, is an idle ceremony, inasmuch as I regard it as one of the most deadly wiles of Satan. Let us remember that this pretended sacrament is nowhere recommended in scripture, either under this name or with this ritual, or this signification.[37]

He believed the rite of confirmation did injustice to baptism as it suggests that one needs an added grace beyond baptism to live the Christian life fruitfully. Nonetheless, he considered a public rite in which one baptized as an infant can affirm the faith as necessary. However, he provided no such rite in Geneva.[38]

Other reformers took a similar tack. John Knox, Ulrich Zwingli, and Philipp Melancthon denied confirmation as a sacrament and provided no rite of confirmation.[39] Because the Anabaptists insisted that one should be mature enough to profess one's faith to be baptized, no need for confirmation existed. Nonetheless, English Baptists initially added imposition of hands after the bath but did not retain this practice.[40]

The Roman Catholic Church responded to the reformers in what has sometimes been referred to as the Counter-Reformation or the Catholic Reformation. Pope Paul III convoked the Council of Trent in 1545 to address what were considered to be the "heresies" of the Protestant Reformation. The council consisted of twenty-five sessions, concluding in 1563. The approach taken by the council was to issue condemnatory propositions against the perceived errors of the reformers. The council did not name particular reformers or expound on Roman

---

35. Cummings, *The Book of Common Prayer*, 155-156.

36. John Calvin, *Institutes of the Christian* Religion, IV.19.5 (626). See Fisher, *Christian Initiation: The Reformation Period*, 254.

37. John Calvin, *Tracts and Treatises in Defense of the Reformed Faith*, 3:183.

38. Fisher, *Christian Initiation: The Reformation Period*, 260.

39. Fisher, *Christian Initiation: The Reformation Period*, 260; also, Turner, *Sources of Confirmation*, 44-45.

40. D. H. Tripp, "The Radical Reformation," in *The Study of Liturgy*, 167.

Catholic teaching. The council frequently referred to the reformers' teachings in an unnuanced manner.[41]

The council issued thirteen propositions "On the Sacraments in General," fourteen "On Baptism," and three "On Confirmation." Canon One from "On Confirmation" defended confirmation as a sacrament. Canon Two condemned anyone who taught that confirmation was merely a profession of faith and prohibited the use of chrism. Canon Three defended the bishop as the "ordinary minister of holy confirmation."[42]

The post-Tridentine liturgical books continued to uphold the separation of the initiatory rites (baptism, first communion, and confirmation) from medieval practice. While infants were the primary candidates for baptism and older children were the primary candidates for first communion and confirmation, exceptions did exist. The *Catechism of the Council of Trent for Parish Priests* referred to adult baptism and even the possibility of infant confirmation.[43]

The Liturgical Renewal Movement

As discussed in chapter one, the liturgical renewal movement of the twentieth century focused extensively on the renewal of baptism as an ecclesial affair rather than a private, familial one. In addition, some ecclesial traditions in the West sought to reunify the baptismal rite that had been disintegrated during the medieval period by reviving the postbaptismal rites of handlaying and anointing (usually optional) and infant communion.[44]

In that reunification work, questions about the nature of confirmation arose. What was confirmation meant to be? Was it a completion of the baptismal rite? Or was it a public, mature affirmation of faith? Of course, ecclesial traditions approached this question from different perspectives, given their distinctive understandings of baptism and confirmation.[45]

The Second Vatican Council (1962-1965) sought to reform the initiatory rites of the Roman Catholic Church. It asked for a revision of the rite for infant baptism with *Ordo Baptismi Parvulorum* (*Rite of Baptism for Children*) being promulgated in 1969. *Ordo Confirmationis* (*Rite of Confirmation*), promulgated in 1971. These revised rites made a stronger connection to baptismal promises as directed by the Council. However, the most significant change in Roman

---

41. Johnson, *The Rites of Christian Initiation*, 362-363.

42. Norman P. Tanner, ed., "Canons on the sacrament of confirmation," *Council of Trent*, Session 7, 3:3, in *Decrees of the Ecumenical Councils*, 2:686.

43. For adult baptism, Catholic Church and Theodore Alois Buckley, *The Catechism of the Council of Trent*, 176-177; and for the possibility of infant confirmation, "after baptism, the sacrament of confirmation may indeed be administered to all; but, that until children shall have attained the use of reason, its administration is inexpedient," 205.

44. Since the initiatory rite in Eastern Orthodox churches never disintegrated, no reunification was necessary.

45. The Theological Insights section will address these questions more thoroughly.

Catholic initiatory practices occurred in *Ordo Initiationis Christianae Adultorum* (*Rite of Christian Initiation of Adults*, RCIA), promulgated in 1972. This rite sought to restore the ancient unity of baptism, chrismation/confirmation, and communion in a single liturgical act following a detailed period of catechesis.[46] However, because infant baptism remains the predominant mode of baptism in the Roman Catholic Church, the practice of the initiatory rites remains separated in most cases.

From the sixteenth century onward, Lutheran traditions developed several approaches to confirmation. In Arthur Repp's seminal work on the history of confirmation in the Lutheran tradition, he identified six types of confirmation practiced in Lutheran churches. The first four types were practiced in the sixteenth century, with the final two developing afterward. The catechetical type of confirmation emphasized instruction to prepare one to receive communion. The hierarchical type included an affirmation of faith and a vow of obedience to the church. The sacramental type involved some form of conferral of the Holy Spirit and completion of baptism. The traditional type included many pre-Reformation characteristics, such as handlaying and episcopal administration. It was a rare form. The pietistic type of confirmation, developed in the early seventeenth century, involved conversion and renewal of baptismal promises and introduced a subjective element to the rite. Finally, the rationalistic type of confirmation, developed in the eighteenth and nineteenth centuries, emphasized the completion of baptism with certain rights that one obtained, such as the reception of communion, marriage, and baptismal sponsorship.[47]

As part of the liturgical renewal movement of the mid-twentieth century across ecclesial traditions, Lutheran traditions in America formed the Inter-Lutheran Commission on Worship (ILCW) in 1967. This commission initiated liturgical reform among these traditions, including baptism and affirmation of the baptismal covenant or confirmation. It resulted in the publication of the *Lutheran Book of Worship*, which was authorized for use among many Lutheran traditions in North America and was the predecessor to *Evangelical Lutheran Worship* (ELW) of what would become the Evangelical Lutheran Church in America (ELCA).[48]

In developing the baptismal rite, the ILCW agreed to a postbaptismal handlaying and optional anointing with oil. However, these post-baptismal rites were criticized as suggesting that they confer the Holy Spirit rather than the bath itself. The Commission affirmed "that the Holy Spirit is the gift of baptism, rather than some subsequent event."[49] In 1977 and 1978, several Lutheran denominational

---

46. Johnson, *The Rites of Christian Initiation*, 375. For more details on the reformed rite of confirmation, see Austin, *The Rite of Confirmation*, 41-59.

47. Arthur C. Repp, *Confirmation in the Lutheran Church*, 21-84; also, Jeffrey A. Truscott, *The Reform of Baptism and Confirmation in American Lutheranism*, 128-129.

48. Truscott, *The Reform of Baptism and Confirmation in American Lutheranism*, 19-20.

49. Truscott, *The Reform of Baptism and Confirmation in American Lutheranism*, 109.

bodies approved using the *Lutheran Book of Worship* with the postbaptismal rites, but the Lutheran Church Missouri Synod did not.[50]

Like many traditions from the reformations, North American Lutheranism considered confirmation as "a rite of initiation into the eucharistic fellowship of the church, based on the attainment of greater knowledge of Scripture and Luther's Small Catechism by the catechumens/candidates."[51] Thus, unlike the Roman Catholic Church, which had reordered rites from bath-handlaying/anointing-communion as one unitive rite of baptism to baptism-first communion-confirmation as separate rites, some Lutherans (and Anglicans, as seen below) retained the original order of baptism-confirmation-communion but as separate rites, as Figure 2.3 depicts.

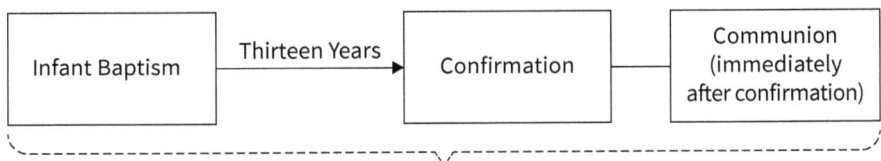

Figure 2.3: Disintegrated Rite of Initiation - Protestant

However, with the publication of LBW, the reunification of the water bath and handlaying with optional anointing occurred. What would this mean for confirmation and communion? In 1964, three Lutheran traditions formed the Joint Commission on the Theology and Practice of Confirmation to study this question.[52] In its 1970 report, the Commission defined confirmation as "a pastoral and educational ministry of the church which helps the baptized child through Word and Sacrament to identify more deeply with the Christian community and participate more fully in its mission."[53] The report continues that communion should not be viewed as "a means of strengthening, rather than as a goal toward which the entire confirmation process points."[54] Thus, it recommended allowing children to receive "first communion" by fifth grade.[55] Interestingly, the Commission recommended that the order of baptism-confirmation-communion now be flipped similarly to that of the Roman Catholic Church, as Figure 2.4 depicts.

---

50. Truscott, *The Reform of Baptism and Confirmation in American Lutheranism*, 116.

51. Truscott, *The Reform of Baptism and Confirmation in American Lutheranism*, 136.

52. Truscott, *The Reform of Baptism and Confirmation in American Lutheranism*, 138.

53. "The Report of the Joint Commission on the Theology and Practice of Confirmation," (Lutheran Church in America, The American Lutheran Church, and The Lutheran Church-Missouri Synod), 39.

54. "The Report of the Joint Commission on the Theology and Practice of Confirmation," 44.

55. "The Report of the Joint Commission on the Theology and Practice of Confirmation," 46.

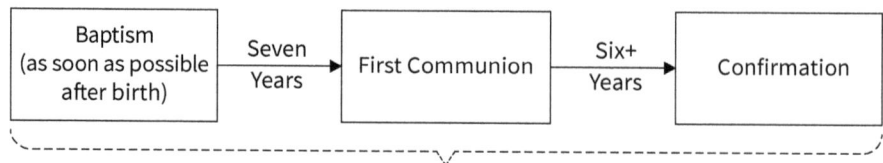

Figure 2.4: Disintegrated Rite of Initiation - Later Middle Ages

During 1971-1975, the Commission modified its thinking on first communion and confirmation and formed a subcommittee to discuss the matter further. The subcommittee articulated four principles that would become important for Lutheran understanding of rites of affirmation, which Truscott succinctly summarizes.

> First, persons baptized in infancy with a rite that clearly expresses the gift of the Holy Spirit, should in later years affirm baptismal promises before an assembled congregation. Second, baptized persons who have lapsed should return to active membership in the church by an affirmation of baptism rite that includes appropriate intercessory prayers. Third, communing members of other churches (denominations) should also mark transfer of membership into a Lutheran congregation with an affirmation of baptism rite. . . . Fourth, no rite should be interposed between baptism and first communion, even though the latter may take place long after the former.[56]

The subcommittee subsequently composed a "Rite of the Affirmation of the Baptismal Covenant," which sought to incorporate these four principles. Thus, they produced neither a distinct first communion rite nor a confirmation rite. Congregations could use the "Rite of the Affirmation of the Baptismal Covenant" for confirmation, reception of members from another denomination, or reaffirmation of faith.

The Episcopal Church underwent a similar process of intense study and discussion around the rite of confirmation but with a slightly different result. For nearly three centuries, confirmation made little impact on Anglican thinking and theology. However, the nineteenth century brought a renewal of the rite. Like the Lutheran rites, the Anglican rite of confirmation includes a prayer for the bestowal of the sevenfold gifts of the Holy Spirit and a mature affirmation of faith. Theologians debated whether confirmation was the completion of the initiatory rite begun in baptism or a mature, public affirmation of faith.[57]

---

56. Truscott, *The Reform of Baptism and Confirmation in American Lutheranism*, 149-150. See also "The Use and Means of Grace," Principles 18 and 30, 24 and 34 for the ELCA's current thinking on confirmation.

57. Ruth A. Meyers, *Continuing the Reformation: Re-Visioning Baptism in the Episcopal Church*, 67-78.

The practice of receiving members from other denominations into the Episcopal Church varied and created confusion. At times, bishops would use the confirmation rite to receive such members, but this practice was not uniform. In 1937, the House of Bishops agreed that persons confirmed in the Roman Catholic Church, the Eastern Orthodox Church, the Old Catholic Church, and the Reformed Episcopal Church could receive communion in the Episcopal Church without being reconfirmed. However, practices continued to vary, and confusion continued to reign.[58]

The 1928 American revision of the Book of Common Prayer contained an instruction following the confirmation rite: *"And there shall none be admitted to the Holy Communion, until such time as he be confirmed, or be ready and desirous to be confirmed."*[59] During these discussions about the nature of confirmation, this rubric caused controversy on two fronts. First, a disagreement arose about whether unconfirmed but baptized Christians should be permitted to receive communion in the Episcopal Church. This disagreement took on significant implications for ecumenical relationships. The other disagreement centered on communion for children prior to confirmation.[60]

As the Episcopal Church moved toward comprehensive prayer book revision, a series of *Prayer Book Studies* were published as intermediaries, experimental rites, and educational aids. *Prayer Book Studies 18: On Baptism and Confirmation* made a landmark statement, "The basic principle of this proposal is the reunion of Baptism, Confirmation, and Communion into a single continuous service, as it was in the primitive Church."[61] The drafting committee rejected developing a rite of first communion but agreed to an "Admission to Holy Communion" rite to receive baptized members of other churches into the Episcopal Church. After some debate, an instruction was added that baptized but unconfirmed persons may receive the imposition of hands at this service. Furthermore, a reaffirmation of faith rite was also rejected. Eventually, "A Form of Commitment to Christian Service" was added to the Pastoral Offices section, thus separating it from initiation.[62]

The reaction to *Prayer Book Studies 18* from the church was mixed. On the one hand, the desire to recognize baptism as full membership in the church and thus eliminate the need for confirmation before communion received significant support. The 1970 General Convention approved admitting baptized children to communion before confirmation.[63]

---

58. Meyers, *Continuing the Reformation*, 78-82.

59. *The Book of Common Prayer and Administration of the Sacraments and Other Rites and Ceremonies of the Church*, 1928 Edition, 299.

60. Meyers, *Continuing the Reformation*, 87-101.

61. *Prayer Book Studies 18: On Baptism and Confirmation*, 19.

62. *Prayer Book Studies 18: On Baptism and Confirmation*, 139-147.

63. Meyers, *Continuing the Reformation*, 147-156.

However, the attempt to eliminate confirmation as a separate rite from baptism did not fare well. In 1971, the House of Bishops published "A Statement on Holy Baptism and Its Relation to Confirmation," in which they affirmed that baptism is full initiation into the church and reception of the gift of the Holy Spirit. They stated that confirmation should not be "regarded as a procedure of admission to the Holy Communion; nor is it 'joining the Church.'" However, they believed a distinct rite of confirmation with episcopal handlaying was "a public, mature, decision for Christ."[64]

The Standing Liturgical Commission responded by producing *Prayer Book Studies 26*. The postbaptismal actions of imposition of hands, signing of the cross, and optional chrismation remained. It also included a rite initially entitled "Form for the Affirmation of Baptismal Vows," which would have paralleled the development of the Lutheran traditions. However, that title would be edited several times and ultimately rejected. Furthermore, the desire for distinct rites for Confirmation, Reception, and Reaffirmation took sway. In the end, a compromise was reached. The baptismal rite included the option for confirmation, reception, or reaffirmation, and a separate rite entitled "Confirmation with forms for Reception and for the Reaffirmation of Baptismal Vows" was included in the Pastoral Offices section.[65] However, one could argue that this compromise further confused the theology of confirmation and other rites of affirmation in the Episcopal Church.

In Methodism, confirmation was a late addition. John Wesley never proposed a rite of confirmation and suggested that the experience of the indwelling of the Holy Spirit was a form of confirmation.[66] This emphasis on a subjective experience rather than a sacramental one would accord with the pietistic view of confirmation in Lutheranism described above. Methodism's insistence on infant baptism and a personal confession of faith created theological tension, especially regarding church membership. To be a full member of the church, one had to be baptized and publicly profess one's faith. Baptism initiated one, adult or infant, into the invisible church, but initiation into the visible denomination required a profession of faith. Thus, for children, catechesis was also required.[67]

In the mid to late-nineteenth century, American Methodists sought a rite to receive members into the church. The Methodist Episcopal Church produced a "Form for Receiving Persons into the Church After Probation" in 1864, and the Methodist Episcopal Church, South followed suit in 1870 with a "Form of the Reception and Recognition of Church-Members." Among other promises, the candidates reaffirmed their faith in the baptismal covenant and received the "right hand of fellowship" as the concluding ritual action. Informally, Methodists

---

64. Meyers, *Continuing the Reformation*, 163. For the text of the statement, see 265-266.
65. Meyers, *Continuing the Reformation*, 172-186.
66. Ole E. Borgen, *John Wesley on the Sacraments: A Theological Study*, 170 n204.
67. Karen B. Westerfield Tucker, *American Methodist Worship*, 112.

began to refer to this ritual as confirmation even though no such official nomenclature existed.[68]

In 1932, the Methodist Episcopal Church published an "Order for Receiving Persons into the Church." This order included an imposition of hands accompanied by a blessing, "The Lord defend thee with his heavenly grace and by his Spirit confirm thee in the faith and fellowship of all true disciples of Jesus Christ."[69] Again, while not officially titled confirmation, church literature commonly referred to it as such. In 1965, the Methodist Church published an "Order of Confirmation and Reception into the Church," seeking to restore baptism as the sign of membership with confirmation as a renewal of baptismal promises and a pledge toward active engagement in the church. By the end of the twentieth century, Methodism had not resolved the tension between infant baptism and full church membership.[70]

American Presbyterianism followed a similar course to American Methodism. Like many other reformers, John Calvin soundly rejected the Roman Catholic doctrine of confirmation, but he did speak well of a liturgical rite in which children would be presented to the church for a public profession of faith following catechesis. This mixed message was further confounded by the heritage of American Presbyterians from English Puritans and Scottish Presbyterians. Due to their historical and political tensions with the Church of England, these groups sought to distance themselves by rejecting confirmation.[71]

Because Presbyterians viewed baptism as a sign of being a member of the covenant community, no further rites were necessary for church membership. However, admission to the Lord's Supper required catechetical preparation. Two schools of thought emerged around this prerequisite. The more traditional group viewed proper catechesis as sufficient. Another group, influenced by the Great Awakenings, believed one must undergo a spiritual awakening before being admitted to the table.[72]

When the first General Assembly of the American Presbyterian Church met in 1789, they adopted the *Westminster Directory for Worship*. A new chapter entitled "Of the Admission of Persons to Sealing-Ordinances" was added to this directory. This chapter merely directed pastors to instruct baptized children and then to let them know at maturity that they could come to the Lord's Table. However, the criteria for admission were "knowledge and piety," a compromise between the school seeking only catechesis and the school seeking a spiritual awakening.[73]

---

68. Westerfield Tucker, *American Methodist Worship*, 113.
69. As quoted in Westerfield Tucker, *American Methodist Worship*, 115.
70. Westerfield Tucker, *American Methodist Worship*, 115-116.
71. Richard Robert Osmer, *Confirmation: Presbyterian Practices in Ecumenical Perspective*, 113.
72. Osmer, *Confirmation: Presbyterian Practices in Ecumenical Perspective*, 123-126.
73. Osmer, *Confirmation: Presbyterian Practices in Ecumenical Perspective*, 126-127.

In the late nineteenth century, the liturgical renewal and ecumenical movements affected American Presbyterianism by encouraging the study of the pre-Puritan Reformed liturgical heritage. This study led to the development of the first *Book of Common Worship* in 1906, which included a service entitled "The Order for the Confirmation of Baptismal Vows." This service involved the candidates making a public profession of their baptismal vows. However, a 1932 revision of the *Book of Common Worship* changed the service title to "Reception to the Lord's Supper" and removed all references to confirmation. However, the third revision in 1946 would restore the title and language but emphasized its purpose to profess the faith after adequate catechesis.[74]

In 1961, alterations were made to *The Directory of Worship* accompanying the union of the Presbyterian Church (USA) and the United Presbyterian Church in the U.S.A. (UPCUSA). The section on confirmation clearly articulated that the rite was not a completion of baptism but a public profession of faith as a personal response to God's grace. This definition stood in line with Presbyterian thinking since 1906.[75]

However, that thinking would change with the publication of *The Worshipbook: Services* in 1970. This resource included confirmation as two services for "The Commissioning of Baptized Members" and the other for the reception of new members. Rather than language about affirming one's baptismal covenant, this service included language about commissioning for ministry. Also, around this time, the UPCUSA voted to admit children to communion, recognizing that baptism signified full membership in the church.[76]

When the UPCUSA and the southern church reunited to form the Presbyterian Church of the United States of America (PCUSA) in 1983, they continued revising the *Book of Common Worship*. They published that revision in 1993. In it, they describe baptism as full initiation into the church involving three actions: washing, anointing, and celebrating the Eucharist. Thus, they changed the name of confirmation to "Reaffirmation of the Baptismal Covenant for Those Making a Public Profession of Faith."[77]

The history of confirmation and other rites of affirmation is complex. After the unitive rite of initiation disintegrated in the West, the church struggled to identify the purpose and theology for confirmation. One significant ecumenical agreement emerged. Baptism is full initiation into the church and, therefore, does not need completion in any subsequent rite. Another agreement appears to have emerged more implicitly through practice than explicitly stated. For traditions practicing infant baptism, some opportunity for a mature, public affirmation of faith is necessary. However, what that proclamation entails differs significantly both among and within ecclesial traditions.

---

74. Osmer, *Confirmation: Presbyterian Practices in Ecumenical Perspective*, 141-142, 149.

75. Osmer, *Confirmation: Presbyterian Practices in Ecumenical Perspective*, 150.

76. Osmer, *Confirmation: Presbyterian Practices in Ecumenical Perspective*, 151.

77. Osmer, *Confirmation: Presbyterian Practices in Ecumenical Perspective*, 157.

Theological Insights[78]

Some have described confirmation as a rite in search of a theology. The history of confirmation and other rites of affirmation in the West reveals a complexity beyond that of other pastoral offices. The disintegration of the initiatory rite required the Western church to adapt its theology of initiation generally and of confirmation particularly. These adaptations resulted in the emergence of several theologies.

This section focuses on some essential theologies associated with confirmation and other rites of affirmation. While it will discuss particular theological themes, these themes will inevitably overlap. Furthermore, these themes evolved, as discussed above. This section seeks to speak to these themes in contemporary practice with reference to historical interpretations when necessary. Furthermore, ecclesial traditions differ significantly on these themes both among and within themselves. Thus, a certain theological nimbleness will be beneficial.

The Holy Spirit

Chrismation and confirmation are closely related to the Holy Spirit. However, the nature of that relationship varies among ecclesial traditions and even within a tradition. Since liturgies use symbolic language, which operates on multiple levels of meaning, these varieties are expected even within a tradition. However, differing theologies of grace, salvation, sanctification, and the Holy Spirit among the traditions also contribute to these interpretations.

Some traditions speak of the "gift of the Holy Spirit."[79] This phrase indicates that the one being chrismated or confirmed receives the person of the Holy Spirit, as no descriptions of the "gift" follow. This phrase usually appears at the chrismation immediately following the baptismal water bath.[80] It suggests that the person has encountered the Holy Spirit for the first time at that moment. However, such an interpretation is problematic. Scripture indicates that the Holy Spirit is involved in evangelism before baptism (John 16:8-11 and 1 John 4:2-6). Even in the case of infant baptism, the Holy Spirit prompts Christian parents to bring their children to the rite. The Holy Spirit has been involved with humanity since creation (Genesis 1:2). Thus, neither chrismation immediately after baptism nor confirmation later is one's first encounter with the Holy Spirit.

---

78. Appendix B contains the rites of affirmation from the BCP, BCW, BOW, ELW, and OCN in tabular format for easy reference.

79. For the Eastern Orthodox traditions, see Stefanos Alexopoulos and Maxwell E. Johnson, *Introduction to Eastern Christian Liturgies*, 28-30. For Roman Catholicism, see OCN, 21 and 29. For the Episcopal Church, United Methodist Church, Evangelical Lutheran Church in America, and Presbyterian Church, USA, see Appendix B.

80. Only the Roman Catholic Church includes this phrase at confirmation, which occurs significantly later than infant baptism.

Another keyword provides clarity—"seal." Some rites speak of being "sealed with the Gift of the Holy Spirit."[81] Other rites indicate that the person is "sealed by the Holy Spirit."[82] In either case, this seal does not suggest one's first encounter with the Holy Spirit. Instead, it suggests a renewed relationship with the Holy Spirit through sealing.

This sealing hearkens back to Ephesians 1:13-14, "In him you also, when you had heard the word of truth, the gospel of your salvation, and had believed in him, were marked with the seal of the promised Holy Spirit; this is the pledge of our inheritance towards redemption as God's own people, to the praise of his glory." With this sealing, the relationship with the Holy Spirit becomes fixed. The phrase "and marked as Christ's own forever" often accompanies this sealing. The newly chrismated or confirmed person enters a relationship with the Triune God that will endure through eternity.

Since most ecclesial traditions today offer this sealing at the time of baptism, what further relationship does the later act of confirmation have with the Holy Spirit?[83] Liturgical rites express two theologies. The first theology often involves strengthening by the Holy Spirit and may also involve "gifts of the Holy Spirit." This interpretation hearkens back to the medieval view that confirmation offers grace as a defense and protection against the world's temptations and draws on the Johannine image of the Holy Spirit as the Paraclete, the "one who walks alongside." As the wiles of the devil and vicissitudes of life barrage the Christian with temptations, the Holy Spirit offers guidance, protection, and defense.

This strengthening of the Holy Spirit often includes commissioning for ministry. Because confirmation often follows catechesis, the expectation is that one is now prepared for ministry in the church. Some people have described confirmation as the "ordination of the laity," but this description creates theological problems as it divides the laity into two groups: confirmed and unconfirmed. If any rite is the "ordination of the laity," it is baptism, not confirmation.[84]

The second theology of confirmation associated with the Holy Spirit involves the gifts of the Holy Spirit. Sometimes, these gifts are enumerated as the "sevenfold gifts of the Holy Spirit," which include wisdom, understanding,

---

81. OCN, 29; and the Byzantine Rite in Alexopoulos and Johnson, *Introduction to Eastern Christian Liturgies*, 29.

82. See Appendix B.

83. Among the major Christian traditions today, only the Roman Catholic Church describes confirmation as a "completion of baptismal grace;" *Catechism of the Catholic Church*, sec.1285. In the Rite of Christian Initiation of Adults, confirmation occurs immediately after baptism; RITES, 333. A priest may administer emergency confirmation for an unconfirmed Christian in mortal danger, *Catechism of the Catholic Church*, sec. 1314.

84. For examples of baptism as ordination, see Aidan Kavanagh, "Unfinished and Unbegun Revisited: The Rite of Christian Initiation of Adults." In *Living Water, Sealing Spirit*, 269; and John Zizioulas, "Ordination—A Sacrament? An Orthodox Reply," in *The Plurality of Ministries*, 36.

counsel, fortitude, knowledge, piety, and fear of the Lord (Isaiah 11:2-3).[85] Again, one must be careful not to suggest that one receives these gifts for the first time at confirmation, as they are essential for all baptized Christians. Furthermore, one also wants to avoid suggesting that the gifts are strengthened only at confirmation, as growing in these gifts is a lifelong endeavor for all Christians. The original idea behind this theology may have involved confirmation as a maturation rite. If the typical age of a confirmand was seven or thirteen, these sevenfold gifts could now be used more maturely. However, confirmation may occur later in life, and one may have used the gifts of the Holy Spirit already.

Thus, theologies that tie confirmation, as a rite occurring substantially after baptism, with the Holy Spirit, either as the person or as the gifts, are problematic. The Holy Spirit and the Holy Spirit's gifts must be available to the Christian immediately. Otherwise, sanctification will be delayed until this later rite.

Initiation

With the liturgical renewal movement, ecclesial traditions in the West stated that baptism is initiation into the Body of Christ, the church.[86] While this statement may appear straightforward, it contains nuanced meanings depending on the ecclesiology (theology of the church) involved. Since different ecclesial traditions have varied ecclesiologies, their understanding of initiation will also differ.

One of the major divisions in ecclesiology involves the nature of the church. Is the church an invisible, mystical body or a visible institution? Some theologians have coined the terms "invisible church" and "visible church" to describe this distinction. The "invisible church" often refers to the church as the Body of Christ, also known as the universal or catholic church.[87] The "visible church" refers to the institutions of the church. Since the sixteenth-century reformations, the visible church has often meant various denominations or traditions.[88]

This distinction became important with the liturgical and ecumenical movements' desire to recognize a common baptism. Most Christian traditions acknowledge baptisms in the name of the Trinity using water regardless of the tradition in which it was performed. In doing so, they affirm that baptism initiates into the "invisible," universal or catholic church.[89]

---

85. See Appendix B.
86. See *Catechism of the Catholic Church*, 1213; BCP 298; ELW, 225; BOW, 131; and BCW, 407.
87. Not to be confused with the Catholic Church or Roman Catholic Church.
88. Admittedly, this description, in its brevity, lacks nuance. For detailed information on ecclesiology, including of various traditions, see Paul Avis, ed., *The Oxford Handbook of Ecclesiology*.
89. See chapter one for more details on common baptism. Not all ecclesial traditions recognize the distinction between the "visible" and "invisible" church but still acknowledge a common baptism.

These traditions also recognize that receiving someone into a particular denomination, tradition, or local congregation requires some liturgical acknowledgment. However, the exact form used differs among and within ecclesial traditions. Some traditions or ministers within a tradition will re-chrismate a baptized Christian wishing to join that tradition.[90] Other traditions have a liturgical form of reception or use a more generic form of reaffirmation of baptism.[91] However, inconsistencies exist about which persons from which traditions must also be confirmed, re-confirmed, receive the imposition of hands, or be welcomed into the congregation.[92]

A similar conundrum involves adults and older children baptized as infants in Western traditions. While these traditions recognize baptism as initiation into the church as the Body of Christ, they often expect some catechesis to occur and then some liturgical form as a public affirmation of faith. What is the person's ecclesial status between baptism and this public affirmation of faith? Is the person a full member of the local congregation with all the rights and responsibilities that entails? Or is there an implied, if not explicit, distinction between those Christians who have publicly affirmed their faith and those who have not? Again, ecclesial traditions differ in their practices.

For ecclesial traditions with episcopal authority, the role of the bishop can be crucial. The bishop symbolizes the unity of the church. Therefore, having the bishop perform these rites connects them with this desired unity. Not all traditions expect the bishop to perform them, and even for those that do, circumstances may occur where the bishop is absent. Nonetheless, in these traditions, the desire is often to have the bishop be present either personally or symbolically by episcopally consecrated chrism.

Receiving Communion

Historically, the church has recognized that initiation by baptism precedes the reception of communion.[93] Adults and older children baptized and chrismated or confirmed within the same service immediately receive communion within the rite. These persons have typically received pre-baptismal catechesis, made a public profession of faith in their baptism, and are ready to receive communion.

---

90. See John H. Erickson, "Divergencies in Pastoral Practice in the Reception of Converts," in *Orthodox Perspectives on Pastoral Praxis*, 149-177.

91. RITES, 275; see also Appendix B.

92. Since these inconsistencies often occur within a tradition, ministers should speak to their supervising authority for assistance in choosing the correct liturgical form.

93. Some ecclesial traditions practice communion without baptism, also known as communion before baptism or open table. For example, in the Episcopal Church, see Richard Fabian, "First the Table, then the Font."; Stephen Edmonson, "Opening the Table: The Body of Christ and God's Prodigal Grace," 214; and Sara Miles, *Take This Bread*. In the United Methodist Church, see Mark Stamm, *Let Every Soul be Jesus' Guest*. In the Evangelical Lutheran Church in America, see Evangelical Lutheran Church in America, "Table and Font: Who is Welcome?"

However, two groups pose additional theological challenges: baptized infants and members of another tradition. For baptized infants, the determining factors involve the "age of discretion" and catechesis. In 1 Corinthians 11:27-29, Paul writes, "Whoever, therefore, eats the bread or drinks the cup of the Lord in an unworthy manner will be answerable for the body and blood of the Lord. Examine yourselves, and only then eat of the bread and drink of the cup. For all who eat and drink without discerning the body, eat and drink judgement against themselves." This instruction requires that one be old enough and have received enough catechesis to examine oneself. Thus, ecclesial traditions that do not typically practice infant communion would refer to this instruction. Communion requires baptism and the ability to examine oneself and confess sin before receiving.[94]

Other traditions practicing infant communion argue that the grace of baptism is sufficient. The baptized infant can receive communion because they are in a state of grace and are full church members. No examination of sin is necessary. They recognize the necessity of catechesis and confession of sin but do not see those activities as prerequisites for receiving communion in the case of young children.

Another group that poses theological challenges to receiving communion before confirmation are members of another ecclesial tradition. Traditions that believe there is little distinction between the "invisible church" and the "visible church" often require chrismation or confirmation before communion. One must be a full member of the church, typically understood as that ecclesial tradition, before receiving communion.

However, this interpretation creates tension with baptismal reciprocity. If baptisms in other ecclesial traditions are accepted, then no further form of initiation should be necessary. This desire to re-chrismate places baptized, and sometimes even confirmed, Christians from another tradition in a similar state of limbo as people baptized as infants. Are they full members of the church or not?

The unitive rite of initiation understood baptism, chrismation, and communion to be a single act of initiation. One became a full member of the church at that time. A theological clarity existed that the dissolution of the unitive rite in the West and the separation of ecclesial traditions has occluded. The liturgical renewal and ecumenical movements of the twentieth and twenty-first centuries have sought to bring greater clarity to these critical issues. These discussions have produced significant results, but further conversation remains necessary.

---

94. Albeit current biblical scholarship understands Paul's imperative to the Corinthians to be a corporate command, not an individual injunction, in that the entire assembly was to examine themselves, particularly their treatment of the poor and marginalized, before receiving communion.

Reaffirming Faith

The desire can arise in the life of any Christian to reaffirm one's faith. Theologically, it is fitting that such reaffirmations occur within the context of the church and are associated with baptism. Because the church teaches that baptism is permanent, rebaptism and reconfirmation are not necessary and, typically, not permitted.[95] Nonetheless, associating reaffirmations of faith with baptism draws on the connection to baptism as a primary symbol of grace and reinforces the permanence of baptism.

Some ecclesial traditions have attempted to move away from confirmation as a once-for-all, separated service from baptism.[96] They recognize that the need to affirm or reaffirm one's faith can occur at various times. Perhaps one might call the first occurrence "confirmation" and others "reaffirmation," but the underlying theology remains the same. These services are opportunities for Christians to connect with their baptismal promises and make a public affirmation of faith.

Reaffirmations also invoke the Holy Spirit. They acknowledge that the Holy Spirit has begun working in the candidate's life and ask for the work to be strengthened. This strengthening of the Holy Spirit fortifies the candidate for discipleship in Christ and service for the church. Thus, the purpose is not just to be a "good Christian" (i.e., sanctification) but for mission and evangelism. The Holy Spirit empowers all Christians for mission and evangelism throughout their lifetimes.

The theologies of confirmation and other rites of affirmation are as convoluted as their history. Much of this confusion results from the dissolution of the unitive initiatory rite and the separation of ecclesial traditions. Simple answers remain elusive. Pastors will need to consider the theological tradition of their ecclesial traditions and likely consult with supervising clergy in some cases.

Cultural Connections

This section seeks to offer pastors cultural touchpoints that can assist them in asking further questions. Wise pastors will avoid treating cultures monolithically, recognizing the great diversity among and within them. This section's intent is not to encourage "liturgical tourism" but rather to illustrate the complexities involved and prompt further questions.

---

95. As discussed in the previous section, ecclesial traditions differ on accepting the confirmations of other traditions. Thus, for those traditions that confirm members of other traditions even when they have already been confirmed in that tradition, they would argue that the person had never been properly confirmed rather than being reconfirmed.

96. ELW has no confirmation rite, only Affirmation of Baptism, ELW 234; BOW and BCW combine confirmation and reaffirmation in a single service, BOW, 139-140 and BCW, 420-423.

Celebrating First Communion and Confirmation

As discussed above, the Roman Catholic Church continues to celebrate separate rites of initiation for children—infant baptism, first communion at the "age of discretion," and confirmation, as depicted in Figure 2.5. As the *Catechism of the Catholic Church* states, "Baptism, the Eucharist, and the sacrament of Confirmation together constitute the 'sacrament of Christian initiation,' whose unity must be safeguarded. It must be explained to the faithful that the reception of the sacrament of Confirmation is necessary for the completion of baptismal grace."[97] Thus, celebrating first communion and confirmation is a priority for people formed in cultures influenced by Roman Catholicism.

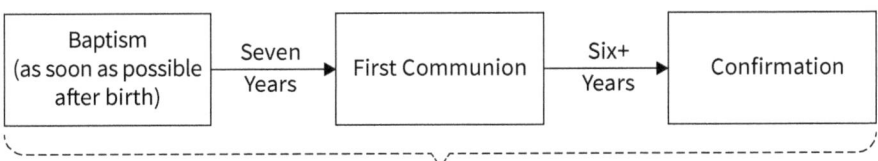

Figure 2.5: Disintegrated Rite of Initiation - Later Middle Ages

Like baptism, celebrating first communion and confirmation can become more of a familial affair than an ecclesial one. Extravagant celebrations are common, involving large family gatherings. A great deal of expense can go into these celebrations, sometimes requiring them to be delayed until funds are available.[98]

In some cultures and ecclesial traditions, one must pay for the rite of confirmation. Congregations may even post the fees for confirmation. In addition, the length of catechesis can vary greatly. Some congregations may require an entire year, while others require only a few weeks. Sometimes, family members will "shop around" for a church offering confirmation without charging a fee and involving the least amount of catechesis. Congregations may respond positively to these efforts, resulting in large numbers of people receiving sacramental rites but relatively few faithfully participating members. This practice can encourage families to view the Christian life more in terms of particular sacramental moments rather than a fuller life experience.[99]

These strong cultural and familial ties to first communion and confirmation can challenge ecclesial traditions that have returned to a unitive initiatory rite. How does a pastor honor the theology of a unitive rite of initiation while meeting their parishioners' cultural and pastoral needs? One potential solution has been

---

97. *Catechism of the Catholic Church*, 1285.

98. Tom Callard and Anthony Guillén, "Confirmation and Sacraments in Latino Ministries," in *Signed, Sealed, Delivered*, 80-81.

99. Callard and Guillén, "Confirmation and Sacraments in Latino Ministries," 81-85.

celebrating a "Solemn Communion" rather than a first communion. This rite offers the family a special moment while maintaining the ecclesiology that all baptized persons are full church members.[100]

Confirmation and Puberty Rites of Passage

Anthropologists have identified rites of passage among all cultural groups. These rites of passage can involve life stages such as birth, puberty, marriage, and death. Arnold van Gennep's classic work *Rites of Passage* describes three stages: separation, transition, and reintegration, as depicted in Figure 2.6.[101]

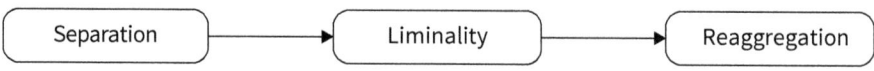

Figure 2.6: Van Gennep's Stages of Initiation Rites

An example of a rite of passage among the VaMwenye people of Zimbabwe is circumcision. Unlike the Jewish practice of circumcising a boy in the first eight days from birth, the VaMwenye people circumcise their boys entering puberty. The boys leave their communities to go to the bush or the mountains. For several days, they are secluded and taught the responsibilities of adulthood. Then, after being circumcised, they return to their communities as full-grown men.[102] This pattern follows Van Gennep's three stages of separation, transition, and reintegration.

The *quinceañera* is another example of a rite of passage. This rite originated in Mexican culture and involved young girls leaving their friends at the age of fifteen [separation] to receive training on being an adult woman [transition]. When they returned from the training [reintegration], their families would hold a large celebration for them. While originating in Mexican culture, the practice has spread among many Latine cultures regardless of their origin. Among Roman Catholics, the priest may offer a blessing.[103] Other ecclesial traditions have developed a pastoral rite for the occasion.[104]

What about confirmation? Is it a rite of passage similar to those rites described above? One could argue that it is. A child, often around the age of puberty, leaves their friends [separation] to be taught how to be a mature Christian [transition] and then returns as a full member of the church [reintegration].

---

100. See Pastoral Perspectives below for more details on children and communion.

101. Arnold van Gennep, *The Rites of Passage*, 44.

102. John Chitakure, *African Traditional Religion Encounters Christianity*, 41-44.

103. James Empereur and Eduardo Fernández, *La Vida Sacra: Contemporary Hispanic Sacramental Theology*, 112.

104. For example, in The Episcopal Church, see *The Book of Occasional Services 2022*, 185-190.

This view of confirmation often leads to calling it "graduation from church school." The congregation, along with parents, can greatly emphasize confirmation. This overemphasis on confirmation can lead to adolescents leaving the church after completing the requisite classes and rituals. They only return to church when they have children to repeat the cycle.

Rites of passage are important moments and should be marked as such by the church. However, confirmation and other rites of affirmation should not be confused with a rite of passage. Confirmation can and should happen at any age when one desires to affirm their baptismal promises. Furthermore, in some ecclesial communities, other rites affirming one's baptismal promises repeatedly occur as desired. Sharon Ely Pearson adroitly states, "No matter what chronological age one is when confirmed ... it is a milestone event reaffirming a commitment to Christ, not a new status within the community."[105]

Conversion, Colonialism, and Dual Identities

The impact of colonialism on non-Western cultures has created an experience of dual identities in which converts often feel a tension between their indigenous cultures and religions and the culture and religion of Westernized Christianity. This tension often expresses itself in their identity. For example, is one an African Christian or a Christian African? This tension can also be experienced ecumenically within Christianity when one ecclesial tradition holds much greater cultural dominance than others.

As discussed in chapter one, baptism has played a role in conversions and the spread of colonialism. Similarly, confirmation has contributed. One example is the Anglican Church of Kenya. The *Gikuyu* tribe of Kenya has three levels of social organization: family (*mbari* or *nyomba*), clan (*moherega*), and an age-grading system (*riika*). The *riika* is formed when *Gikuyu* girls and boys undergo the *irua* ceremony, which involves a prolonged set of puberty rites culminating in circumcision.[106]

In the late nineteenth century, the Church Missionary Society in England sent missionaries to Kenya. Due to their ignorance of Kenyan cultural practices, these missionaries demonized the indigenous rites of passage and attempted to replace them with the Anglican rite of confirmation instead. Kenneth Ofula says, "This represented a proliferation of Thomas Cramner's ideology of confirmation as a rite of passage and a fetishisation of the 1549 Catechism."[107] The catechism and the resulting rite of confirmation became a tool for colonialism.

---

105. Sharon Ely Pearson, "Rites of Passage," in *Signed, Sealed, Delivered*, 130.

106. Kenneth Ofula, "'The River Between': Negotiating Dual Identities in the Anglican Churches of Kenya," 99-101.

107. Ofula, "'The River Between,'" 104. For the catechism, see Cummings, *The Book of Common Prayer*, 59-61.

Nonetheless, concern about the practice of adolescent circumcision, especially female circumcision, began in the 1920s. Initially, missionaries declared the practice unchristian, and the Labour Party went so far as to make it illegal in 1929. The condemnation continued into the post-colonial period.[108]

While the practice of female circumcision was condemned, other portions of the *irua* rite contained significant cultural benefits in preparing young boys and girls for adulthood. In a case study with the Marakwet people of Kenya, Muhia Karianjahi developed a "Christianized" version of the *irua* practice called Rites of Passage Experiences (ROPES). It involved a year-long program of weekly and monthly meetings with peers and counselors, culminating in a week-long retreat where their parents join them for a graduation celebration. This program was offered alongside confirmation, and many people would register for both programs.[109]

Another example of the role of conversion, colonialism, and dual identities is among the Santal Catholics. The Santals comprise the largest homogenous scheduled tribe in India. Due to missionary efforts by the Jesuits in the 1930s, conversions to Roman Catholicism outpaced conversions to Protestantism, even though the latter was the initial missionary group in the mid-nineteenth century. Like many Christian converts in non-Christian cultures, Santal Catholic converts experience a dual identity.[110]

For example, the Santal culture expects young men to undergo an initiation rite known as *caco chatiar*. Selva Raj describes this ceremony.

> Celebrated in early adolescence, the caco chatiar is a tribal initiation rite mandatory for all Santal young men. On the appointed day, the midwife who assisted at his birth bathes the candidate, after which young women anoint him with oil and turmeric. The village moral guardian (jog manjhi) then recites the tribal lore to the initiate, beginning with the creation myths, the origins of the tribe, and its wanderings and present habitat. The community attending the ceremony is offered rice beer. At this time, the jogmanjhi declares that, by partaking in rice beer fellowship, the village society offers its collective approval for the induction of the candidate into Santal society.[111]

This initiation rite has both social and religious dimensions to it. Many Santal Catholics claim that when they participate in the rite, they are doing so only for its cultural dimensions and substitute the Catholic rite of confirmation for its religious dimensions. However, fieldwork suggests that the distinction is less

---

108. Ofula, "'The River Between,'" 106-107.
109. Ofula, "'The River Between,'" 107-108.
110. Selva J. Raj, "The Santal Sacred Grove and Catholic Inculturation," 6-7.
111. Raj, "The Santal Sacred Grove and Catholic Inculturation," 6.

pronounced. Santal Catholics must participate in both groups' social and religious rituals. They often must choose between being Catholic Santals or Santal Catholics.[112]

This tension between religious and cultural dual identities can also be felt ecumenically. For example, confirmation plays a vital role among Lutherans in Ethiopia. Christians wishing to transfer from the Ethiopian Orthodox Tewahedo Church to the Ethiopian Evangelical Church Mekane Yesus would participate in confirmation classes. These classes would include instruction on the history and theology of Lutheranism, including Luther's Small and Large Catechisms, and life skills. Because the Ethiopian Orthodox Church plays a prominent role in Ethiopian culture, these Lutheran "converts" can experience a similar dual identity as described above. They feel a tension between the theology and practices of the Lutheran church and the desire to retain Orthodox traditions, which have a vital cultural component. For example, Lutheran "converts" will often request to have their babies baptized at forty days for a male or eighty days for a female, which is an Ethiopian Orthodox tradition, even though the Lutheran church has no such prescriptions.[113]

Because the history of confirmation involves initiation and mature affirmation, it has also had intertwined cultural elements. At times, confirmation has incorporated cultural elements concerning conversion and initiation. At other times, it has incorporated cultural elements corresponding with rites of passage. Both the history of confirmation and these cultural elements have created theological tension. On the one hand, pastors may desire to assert the theological unity of baptism, confirmation, and communion. However, on the other hand, these rites, as separate events, also play an essential role in the cultural lives of congregants. Wise pastors will attempt to navigate this tension with balance rather than with extremes.

Pastoral Perspectives

Confirmation, reception, and other rites of affirmation have had an entangled history, confusing theologies, and challenging cultural connections. One temptation pastors face is to emphasize any of these areas over the others. For example, a pastor might emphasize the tradition of confirmation as the graduation of a catechetical program. Another pastor may emphasize the theology of baptism as full initiation. Another pastor might consider the cultural needs of the parishioners of the highest importance. However, balancing all three aspects will yield the most significant fruit. To do so, pastors must be inquisitive, flexible, and creative.

---

112. Raj, "The Santal Sacred Grove and Catholic Inculturation," 7.
113. Rode Molla, personal communication, April 3, 2023.

Communion before Confirmation

One area in which the tradition of confirmation and the cultural need for a rite of passage often clashes with the theology of an integrated initiatory rite is communion before confirmation. As noted above, confirmation was a prerequisite for communion for many ecclesial traditions before the late twentieth century. Thus, children would not receive communion until they were confirmed. In some ecclesial traditions, first communion (typically following first confession) at the "age of discretion" was the prerequisite.

When many ecclesial traditions sought to reunify their initiatory rites and emphasize baptism over confirmation as full initiation into the church, they faced the issue of children receiving communion before confirmation. These traditions teach that no other rite beyond baptism is necessary for anyone of any age to receive communion. However, parents raised when confirmation was a prerequisite for communion want their children to receive confirmation before communion. How does a pastor navigate this tension wisely?

First, a pastor can instruct the parents and the congregation on the history of confirmation. Frequently, people mistakenly believe this change in liturgical practice is a contemporary invention rather than having deep roots in the church's history. Explaining the history of confirmation and how it became separated from baptism can assist people in understanding the importance of reunifying the rites.

In addition to its history, explaining the theology of confirmation can be illuminating. Because of its strong attachment to catechesis, confirmation has often been considered an achievement earned rather than a grace received. Even ecclesial traditions that do not confer any sacramental character to confirmation should avoid this graduation mentality. Helping congregants, especially parents, understand confirmation as thanksgiving for the grace received to affirm one's faith can assist them in avoiding the belief that confirmation grants one a particular status in the church.

Some ecclesial traditions have replaced the one-time rite of confirmation with a repeatable rite of affirmation of baptismal vows. These traditions can explain how all Christians of any age and at any point in their life may need to reaffirm their faith. This repetition can avoid the temptation to see the rite as an achievement to be gained. Even ecclesial traditions that have retained a one-time rite of confirmation can still emphasize that a Christian may take the first step through confirmation of many such steps of faith affirmation.

Some parents may come from a culture where first communion holds great importance. It is wise for pastors to understand that the desire for their child to celebrate a first communion may have strong cultural and familial ties. Therefore, explaining the history and theology of a reunified rite of initiation may be inadequate to address the pastoral needs of this family.

An alternative to first communion could be "solemn communion."[114] "Solemn communion" can be especially appropriate in a congregation that may have a mix of views on communing young children. It avoids suggesting that one must wait for a specific age before receiving communion while also providing a celebratory event for those for whom marking this moment is important. The pastor can provide catechesis about the Eucharist and invite all children to participate regardless if this service will be the first one in which they receive communion. Emphasizing that communion is a gift from grace rather than an achievement one has earned for being good or thoroughly instructed will be just as crucial as confirmation.

Time for Confirmation

Historically, the age at which confirmation classes would begin was twelve. A recent study entitled "The Confirmation Project" indicated that this trend continues.[115] This age corresponds to the view of confirmation as a rite of passage preparing children for adult membership in the church.

However, some people have questioned this approach. Is an early adolescent ready to make such a commitment? Should the confirmation age be delayed until early adulthood, perhaps after undergraduate education? Since early adolescence often marks the beginning of abstract questioning, is it the appropriate time to make such a commitment? Would young adulthood be a better choice?[116]

When parents and congregations view confirmation as a one-stop event, the pressure to find the "right time" for confirmation is more significant. However, if confirmation is seen as a step along the journey, a lifelong approach to catechesis could be the model. Lisa Kimball, Vice President for Lifelong Learning at Virginia Theological Seminary, uses the metaphor of a base camp: "What if we were to think of confirmation as an established base camp on the Christian journey? Base camps are critical to safe climbs or treks in challenging terrain. Base camps are not the beginning of an adventurer's journey, no more than confirmation is a beginning."[117] A base camp is not a one-stop place but rather a haven to which and from which an adventurer goes.

If confirmation is viewed as part of a lifelong process of Christian formation rather than a graduation, it becomes intergenerational. Children, adolescents, and adults of all ages can participate in catechesis. As Erin Hatzung states, "In this

---

114. This idea was shared with the author in personal communication with Altagracia Pérez-Bullard on April 3, 2023.

115. Katherine M. Douglass, "Findings from The Confirmation Project," 11.

116. Pearson, "Rites of Passage," 123-130 and Bloy House, "Claiming the Vision: Baptismal Identity in the Episcopal Church."

117. Lisa Kimball, "Building Base Camps," in *Signed, Sealed, Delivered*, 131.

way, confirmation is a lifelong journey where confirmands are knit into a lifelong confirming community."[118] Such an approach mimics the catechetical approach to baptism described in chapter one.

Catechesis for Confirmation

Preparation for confirmation has not had a good history. Catechisms from the reformations were strongly didactic, with questions and answers usually involving the Ten Commandments, Creed, and Lord's Prayer.[119] Children preparing for confirmation were expected to memorize the responses by rote and often recite them to a bishop or other leading figure in front of the public assembly.

This approach privileges a purely didactic means of instruction and learning rather than a more holistic approach. It also sets up confirmation to be the graduation ceremony for having successfully memorized all the requisite information. Can one imagine taking such an approach with other forms of catechesis? For example, should an adult Bible study consist only of memorizing information about the Bible?

Involving a more holistic approach to catechesis for confirmation allows participants to appreciate fully the life of faith. This approach can include didactic instruction, as it is important for Christians to learn aspects of the church's life. For example, confirmation classes often include instruction on the history of the church, the ecclesial tradition, and critical doctrines. How that material is presented should be pedagogically appropriate for the ages involved.

However, it is essential to go beyond content instruction. For example, a unit on spiritual practices can be vital for a maturing Christian to experience. Spiritual practices, such as creating prayer beads or participating in centering prayer, can engage learners in ways that didactic learning will not. Service-oriented activities can also help the participants experience the importance of mission in the Christian life.

Frequently, congregations will combine catechesis for baptism, confirmation, reception, and reaffirmation of faith. Such an approach has advantages. It allows more participants to meet and learn from each other. Smaller-resourced congregations can pool their efforts, allowing even seasoned members to relearn some of the basics of the faith.

However, this approach also comes with challenges. Preparing people for baptism and confirmation simultaneously can lead to their conflation in the eyes of the participants and the congregation. Also, expecting mature Christians

---

118. Erin Swenson Hatzung, "Reimagining Confirmation Ministry as a Lifelong Practice," 86.

119. For examples, see Luther's Small Catechism, Robert Kolb and Timothy J. Wengert, eds., *The Book of Concord: The Confessions of the Evangelical Lutheran Church*, 347-379; the Shorter Catechism from *The Westminster Standards, Book of Confessions*, 269-280; and Catechism for Children, Cummings, *The Book of Common Prayer*, 59-61.

from another tradition seeking reception into the church to undergo the same catechesis as participants seeking baptism or confirmation can imply that reception is a form of conversion. For example, it is not uncommon to hear people refer to someone from one Christian ecclesial tradition as a "convert" to their tradition. This imprecision confuses ecumenism with evangelism. One possibility can be to have specific plenary sessions when all participants are involved and then certain specified sessions for baptism, confirmation, reception, and reaffirmation.

Having a mentor (or godparent) for baptism is required in most ecclesial traditions. It often is not required in confirmation, reception, or affirmations of faith. Nonetheless, it could be beneficial. Using the terms sponsor or godparent might cause unnecessary confusion with baptism, but using terms such as "guide" or "shepherd" allows one to see the person as someone coming alongside them in this new journey. Like baptism, having guides or shepherds permits other congregation members to participate in catechesis.

Purpose of Confirmation

As discussed, the theology of confirmation has been less clear over its history than for other sacraments or liturgical rites. Is confirmation the completion of initiation? Is it a graduation from catechesis? Is it a public affirmation of faith? Is it commissioning for ministry? Is it a welcome into the congregation? It has been all these things at one time or another and frequently simultaneously.

While a liturgical rite can have multiple purposes, it can be confusing for congregants when it appears to be at cross-purposes with another rite, in this case, baptism. However, confirmation has also been confused with reception and reaffirmations of faith. Clarity about the purpose of confirmation assists congregants in living more fully in it.

Most ecclesial traditions have clarified that confirmation is not the completion of initiation. However, many congregants still believe it is, and many congregations still act as if it is. For example, requiring confirmation before serving in a leadership position gives the impression that one is not wholly a Christian until confirmed. Such practices can lead congregants into thinking that two levels of Christians exist in the church: unconfirmed and confirmed.

Some congregations also act as if confirmation is graduation from catechesis. While most pastors desire lifelong formation for their congregants, they can also unknowingly contribute to this perception of confirmation. If confirmation classes receive the most attention in a congregation's catechetical program, they will likely appear as a goal one must achieve. However, if confirmation classes are among various other catechetical opportunities, they are more likely to appear as necessary but no more important than any other catechesis.

For some congregations, confirmation is the only time members publicly affirm their faith. This practice places too much weight on confirmation. Providing opportunities for regular reaffirmations of faith allows congregations to see public affirmations of faith as a regular Christian practice rather than a special event reserved only for a specific time. Regular communal renewals of baptismal vows can powerfully illustrate the importance of one's baptism as a lifelong journey. The Easter Vigil is particularly suited for such moments. If even in smaller groups, offering opportunities for public testimonies can also support a spiritual practice of proclaiming one's faith regularly. Confirmation can be a wonderfully joyous occasion for public affirmations of faith, but it should not be the only time for these occasions.

Some people have suggested that confirmation is commissioning for ministry. It has sometimes been called "the ordination of the laity." A regular practice among some congregations is to have participants in confirmation classes spend their last session learning about the congregation's ministries and then selecting the ones they feel called to serve. Service inside and outside the church is an integral part of Christian discipleship. However, it should not begin with confirmation. It begins with baptism.

One could argue that confirmation could act to commission children and youth into ministry. Again, that practice suggests that children and youth are incapable of ministry before confirmation or only in a limited manner. Confirmation becomes when they "truly" begin to minister in the congregation. As Ruth Meyers sagely states, "Yet an emphasis on confirmation as *the* distinctive rite that now sends them into the world in mission diminishes and distorts the Spirit's work in children and teenagers throughout the course of their development."[120] This perspective does not preclude confirmation as a time when one reaffirms one's commitment to ministry in the church, but it need not be *the* moment when that happens.

Congregations have also used confirmation to welcome new members into the congregation. This practice can confuse both the people seeking membership in the congregation and the current members. Pastors often must discern if the person must be confirmed or received depending on their previous ecclesial tradition. This practice is often inconsistent among ecclesial traditions and within them. It can cause great confusion and make people feel that their previous membership in the church was insufficient. Pastors should discuss with their leadership how to handle the reception of new members. Clarity, as much as possible, will be most pastorally beneficial.

So, what, then, is the purpose of confirmation? Perhaps determining the purpose for confirmation is less important than understanding it as a moment in a Christian's entire journey. If it becomes *the* moment, it can all too quickly lead to a decline in participation afterward. However, abolishing it altogether may be unwise given confirmation's strong traditional and cultural roots.

---

120. Ruth Meyers, "Fresh Thoughts on Confirmation," 328.

Instead, confirmation can be a critical moment, but *a* moment among many moments in which a Christian remembers baptismal promises, the gift of the Holy Spirit, and renews a commitment to Christian discipleship and service.

Questions for Discussion

1. What do you think was lost in the historical separation of what was later called confirmation from baptism and communion? Was anything gained?

2. Where does your tradition fall on the spectrum of viewing confirmation and other rites of affirmation more as unique sacraments or repeated affirmations?

3. Do you see anything from another tradition's practice of confirmation and other rites of affirmation that your church could learn from?

4. What cultural practices around confirmation and other rites of affirmation have you experienced?

5. How might your practice of confirmation and other rites of affirmation preserve a balance between understanding it as catechetical graduation, ecclesial initiation, and cultural practice?

6. What can practitioners do to ensure confirmation remains a critical moment on a journey rather than the destination itself?

Additional Resources

Austin, Gerard. *Anointing With the Spirit: The Rite of Confirmation.* Collegeville, MN: The Liturgical Press, 1986.
Written by a distinguished Roman Catholic liturgical scholar, this book discusses the relevant Catholic history of confirmation and Vatical II developments in practice and theology.

Confirmation: Engaging Lutheran Foundations and Practices. Minneapolis, MN: Augsburg Fortress, 1999.
Written by different professors at seminaries of the Evangelical Lutheran Church in America, this book introduces the theology and practice of confirmation from a contemporary Lutheran perspective.

The Confirmation Project. www.theconfirmationproject.com
This grant has studied confirmation practices among the African Methodist Episcopal Church, The Episcopal Church, the Evangelical Lutheran Church in America, the Presbyterian Church in the USA, and the United Methodist Church. The Resources section includes helpful information on their research.

Cultivating Teen Faith: Insights from the Confirmation Project. Edited by Richard Osmer and Katherine M. Douglass. Grand Rapids: Eerdmans, 2018.
This book is a book-length report from a three-year study of confirmation programs in thousands of congregations across five different American protestant denominations. It gives special attention to what factors make contemporary confirmation programs successful. A webpage from the Confirmation project also contains many helpful confirmation workbooks and programs from different denominations, and can be found here: https://www.theconfirmationproject.com/resources/.

Johnson, Maxwell E.. *The Rites of Christian Initiation.* Revised edition. Collegeville, MN: Liturgical Press, 2007.
This book is focused on more than just confirmation; it is a very good scholarly introduction to the history of the full rites of Christian initiation. It primarily details how what later came to be called confirmation existed before its eventual separation from the other rites of initiation.

Signed, Sealed, Delivered: Theologies of Confirmation for the 21st Century. Compiled by Sharon Ely Pearson. New York: Morehouse Publishing, 2014.
This book provides diverse voices from theologians and practitioners in the Episcopal Church on contemporary practices of confirmation and suggestions. It helpfully includes theological and practical reflections and an annotated bibliography of confirmation resources.

Turner, Peter. *Sources of Confirmation from the Fathers through the Reformers.* Collegeville, MN: The Liturgical Press, 1993.
This book includes a wide selection of translations of primary sources from figures of the early Church through the 17th century, reflecting on the theology of confirmation. It would be a beneficial resource for understanding different pre-modern understandings of confirmation.

CHAPTER 3

Marriage

Marriage predates the Christian tradition by centuries. All cultures and religious traditions have some form of marital customs and traditions. Thus, Christianity cannot claim marriage as unique to its tradition. Instead, marriage entered Christianity through societal norms and continues to be influenced by those diverse norms. Nevertheless, Christian theologies of marriage have emerged over time. These theologies have sometimes adopted cultural norms and sometimes have countered them. Furthermore, the theological differences among ecclesial traditions have also influenced marriage.

Like other pastoral offices, Christian marriage follows Ven Gennep's rites of initiation with separation, transition/liminality, and reintegration.[1] During the betrothal period, the couple separates from friends and family to enter a new liminal status. At different times and in different cultures, the status of a betrothal can nearly equal marriage in its responsibilities and expectations for the couple. Then, of course, the wedding ceremony marks the couple's reintegration into the community but with a new status as a married couple.

Historical Context

New Testament to Nicene Period

Like all the pastoral offices, no marriage liturgy exists in the New Testament. Instead, Christ and the apostles teach and preach within the cultural milieu of first-century Palestine, including Jewish and Roman influences. Table 3.1 lists the similarities and differences between these two cultural influences.
These Roman and Jewish cultural influences will continue through the history of marriage. Future liturgies will emphasize different aspects of them.

The Jewish influences come primarily from the Talmudic and post-Talmudic periods. The deuterocanonical book Tobit describes a marriage between Tobias and Sarah, which included many of the cultural influences described above. It included a *yadah*-prayer that praises God as creator and forthrightly states that marriage's purpose is to avoid lust. Later, it included a blessing from

---

1. Van Gennep, *The Rites of Passage*, 44.

Roman Society	Jewish Society
Betrothal	*Betrothal*
Exchange of promises	By money, contract, or cohabitation
Gift of ring and pledges by groom	Betrothal berakah
Kiss	
Marriage	*Marriage*
	All-day fast by bride and groom
Dressing of bride at her home crown of myrtle or orange veil (*flammeum*)	Dressing of bride and groom both in crowns of myrtle bride in veil
Presentation of the bride to groom	
Consultation of the oracles	
Contract (*tabulae matrimoniales*)	
Exchange of consents, joining hands	
Sacrifice and wedding feast	
Procession of all to groom's house	Procession of bride and attendants to house of groom
	Contract (*ketubah*) written at threshold
	Wedding feast with seven *berakoth*

Table 3.1. Stages and Rites of Marriage in Roman and Jewish Societies from Byron Stuhlman, *Occasions of Grace*, 73. Printed by permission of the publisher.

Sarah's father, Raguel, asking God that they might experience fecundity in their marriage. This blessing will appear again in medieval Christian texts.[2]

Later Talmudic texts provided more details as a clear demarcation between betrothal and marriage developed. Maidens would dance on the Day of Atonement in search of husbands. When ready to be married, the couple fasted and confessed their sins. The bride and groom frequently wore myrtle crowns and may have worn a veil as they processed to the groom's house. The contract was written down at the threshold, marking the legality of the marriage. Then, a festive meal ensued. At the end of the meal, the groom offered the *sheva berakoth*, Seven Blessings.[3]

While it is impossible to describe the marriage rite of early Christians from the New Testament alone, it is possible to outline it. These Christians likely continued in the Jewish practices of the day both before and after their expulsion from the synagogues. The Gospels and Epistles suggest that betrothal was a serious commitment almost as binding as marriage. Eventually, the couple would

---

2. Kenneth Stevenson, *Nuptial Blessing: A Study of Christian Marriage Rites*, 6.
3. Stevenson, *Nuptial Blessing*, 7.

enter into a formal agreement with a wedding feast to follow. Very likely, some form of blessing akin to the Seven Blessings followed the celebratory meal.[4]

The teachings of Jesus and the apostles that reference marriage fall into two large categories: metaphors and household codes. The New Testament's use of marital metaphors typically describes the anticipation of the kingdom of God and the messiah. For example, Jesus is referred to as the bridegroom, who is to come for his bride (Matt 9:15, Mark 2:19, and Luke 5:34). In the parable of the wise and foolish virgins, the virgins await the coming of the bridegroom, i.e., the messiah (Matt 24:1-13). One of the most iconic marriage passages in the Gospels, which finds its way into later lectionaries, is the wedding feast at Cana (John 2:1-11). While this passage will be used later to justify marriage as a sacrament, it does not feature the wedding ceremony. The miracle occurred after the ceremony during the feast when no wine was left to serve, with Christ replenishing the wine from the water for purification. This narrative begins the series of messianic signs in John.

Jesus' teachings on celibacy (Matt 19:10-12), adultery (Matt 5:28), divorce (Matt 19:9 and Mark 10:10-12), and remarriage (Matt 22:23-33, Mark 12: 18-27, and Luke 20:27-40) should be read eschatologically. Rather than setting down a code of conduct, Christ asked his disciples to be ready for his return. Paul took a similar tact in his writing on celibacy, monogamy, divorce, and remarriage (1 Cor 7), in which his greatest concern was that the church remained ready for Christ's return.

The apostle Paul continued the metaphor of Christ as the bridegroom, but now the church was the betrothed with the wedding to happen when Christ returns (2 Cor 11:2). The author of Ephesians, possibly writing in the name of Paul, blended the metaphorical imagery of Christ and the church with the household code when stating, "Wives, be subject to your husbands as you are to the Lord. For the husband is the head of the wife just as Christ is the head of the church, the body of which he is the Saviour. Just as the church is subject to Christ, so also wives ought to be, in everything, to their husbands (Eph 5:22-23)." Here, the influence of Roman society came into play with the household code. These household codes had their roots in the Greek philosophers, who developed detailed lists of the ethical actions members of a household should take toward those in authority, including parents, children, spouses, and servants.[5] This passage appears in medieval lectionaries but tends to be avoided in contemporary ones.

As for other books of the New Testament, the Pastoral Epistles speak of the requirement that church leaders be monogamous and take care of the affairs of their households (1 Tim 3:4-12; 5:4,10, and Titus 1:6; 2:3-5). The Book of Revelations provides additional marital imagery with the Lamb (Christ) as the bridegroom at the wedding banquet (Rev 19:1-10).

Moving into the sub-apostolic period, Ignatius of Antioch (c. 35 – c. 107 CE) offered the first non-Biblical quotation about marriage, which became popular among later theologians, "But it becomes both men and women who marry, to form

---

4. Stevenson, *Nuptial Blessing*, 12-13.
5. Raymond Brown, *An Introduction to the New Testament*, 608.

their union with the approval of the bishop, that their marriage may be according to God, and not after their own lust. Let all things be done to the honour of God."[6] This quotation signals two important factors regarding Christian marriage.

First, couples at that time did not necessarily understand marriage to be a church affair. The fact that Ignatius had to exhort couples planning to get married to go to their bishop for approval indicates that such a practice was not yet normative. Of course, the church had no legal standing with the Roman Empire at this point in history. Furthermore, marriage was considered a private or familial affair, not a public one. By requiring a couple to go to the bishop, the church sought to endorse their marriage as Christian.

Second, Ignatius offered a theological rationale for marriage. Marriage was meant to point one toward God rather than being a fulfillment of one's lust. This desire to avoid lust or passion would continue to be a predominant purpose for marriage throughout its history. Other purposes would eventually be articulated and gain precedence. Nonetheless, the desire for godliness through the avoidance of lust was an influential theological theme for marriage.

Tertullian (c. 160 – c. 225 CE) wrote extensively about marriage, and his writings provided some clues to marital practice at that time, at least in his region of North Africa. It included the veiling of virgins after betrothal, which is sealed with a kiss, and the giving of the right hand, which was a Roman practice. However, Tertullian argued that giving crowns, another Roman practice, was idolatrous. The marriage rite might also include giving a ring at the betrothal. Marriages were to be performed by bishops in front of a congregation, often ending with a nuptial blessing or a nuptial Mass. The purpose of marriage was to forestall lust, and the blessing of marriage was childbearing.

Tertullian also described the couple in egalitarian terms. They are to support each other equally in the faith. They are to fast together, pray together, and worship together. They are to instruct, encourage, and strengthen each other. They are to become "two in one flesh."[7]

During the fourth century, further clarity about Christian marriage rituals developed. John Chrysostom (c. 347 – 407 CE) provided the most abundant descriptions of these rites. They involved a betrothal period culminating in a feast that could last several days. In a disputed work, he compared the marriage at Cana with marriage during his time, suggesting that Christ is present through the priest. A ring was sometimes used. Chrysostom also defended the practice of crowning as a symbol of the couple's victory over lust.[8] Figure 3.1 illustrates a crown that might have been used then and is still used in Eastern Christian weddings today. A ring was sometimes involved.

Augustine provided the most significant theological developments for marriage in the West. His references to marriage were extensive and scattered throughout his

---

6. Ignatius, *Ad Polycarpum* in *The Ante-Nicene Fathers*, 1:95.

7. Stevenson, *Nuptial Blessing*, 16-17.

8. Stevenson, *Nuptial Blessing*, 23-24.

Figure 3.1: Orthodox wedding crowns (Finnish Heritage Agency, CC BY 4.0 https://creativecommons.org/licenses/by/4.0/, via Wikimedia Commons)

writings, but Kenneth Stevenson provides a helpful summary. First, Augustine spoke of marriage not merely as a *vinculum* ("link," or "joining") but as a *sacramentum*. However, Augustine used *sacramentum* to mean "a sacred obligation," not one of the seven sacraments that later scholastic theologians would develop. He often spoke of three purposes for marriage: *fides* (fidelity), *proles* (offspring), and *sacramentum* (sacred obligation). These three purposes for marriage would return numerous times in subsequent Western theologies of marriage.[9]

Secondly, Augustine referred to the *tabulae matrimoniales* frequently in his writings. The *tabulae matrimoniales* were contracts read aloud at weddings and signed by witnesses and the bishop.[10] Augustine often cited the *tabulae matrimoniales* in his theological arguments. For example, he referred to them when he argued against the Manichaeans that sexual intercourse for procreation was good. Sexual intercourse was a fulfillment of the contract made between the husband and wife. Understanding that couples would not limit sexual intimacy to procreative acts, he developed the idea of *venialis culpa* (venial sins) for these non-procreative sexual acts. He also referred to the *tabulae matrimoniales* when he taught about the subordination of

---

9. Stevenson, *Nuptial Blessing*, 29.
10. Stevenson, *Nuptial Blessing*, 30.

wives to their husbands. However, it is not clear that the *tabulae matrimoniales* contained an explicit provision for the subordination of wives to their husbands as it did for procreation as the purpose of marriage. Finally, Augustine also used *tabulae matrimoniales* in discussing the marital covenant between Christ and the church.[11]

Stevenson's third summarization of Augustine's writing on marriages involves his references to Genesis 1:28, in which God blessed Adam and Eve and commanded them to "be fruitful and multiply."[12] Coupled with his references to procreation from the *tabulae matrimoniales*, Augustine argued in favor of marital sexual intimacy with the purpose of fecundity. The modern reader must understand that his opponents decried any form of sexual intimacy regardless of the marital state or its purpose. Thus, Augustine took the more liberal position.

Finally, Augustine referred to a few more details of what may have been the marriage liturgy. Once, he mentioned the bridal veil. He also referred to a wedding procession to the entry way of a building, maybe the church, and forbade unruly wedding parties.[13] While Augustine provided some more important liturgical details, his significant contribution was theological.

While the church had been exhorting couples to go to their bishop for a blessing of their marriage, it intensified its involvement in marriage during the fourth century. Now, the church wanted couples to come to the church as part of the marriage ritual. The domestic rites continued, but a new element, the blessing at the church, was added.

Kenneth Stevenson describes this mix of marital rites as different strata. "Stratum 1" was the nuptial Mass, and "stratum 2" was the domestic rites, such as the blessing of the rings and the bedchamber. Later, in the twelfth century, a new rite of consent developed in the Western church, which he describes as "stratum 3."[14] In most cases, the Eastern churches do not include consent in their marriage rites. This absence does not mean that mutual consent was not important in Eastern churches but rather that it was not the legal framework for marriage that it became in the West.

Liturgical sources during this period approached these three strata differently. Sometimes, they rearranged them in a different order. Sometimes, they combined them into a single liturgical service or separated them into distinct services. Nonetheless, these three strata of domestic rites, nuptial blessing, and consent persisted through the medieval and reformation periods into contemporary rites in the Western church.

In discussing the liturgical texts during this period, it is essential to note that they often represented the liturgies of ecclesiastical centers such as Rome or Constantinople and did not necessarily represent what local parishes utilized. This representation is especially accurate when it comes to marriage, given the tension that existed between domestic rites and ecclesiastical blessing.

---

11. David G. Hunter, "Augustine and the Making of Marriage in Roman North Africa," 73-84.
12. Stevenson, *Nuptial Blessing*, 30.
13. Stevenson, *Nuptial Blessing*, 30.
14. Kenneth W. Stevenson, *To Join Together: The Rite of Marriage*, 27-28.

Marriage in the East

Before discussing marriage in the medieval Western church, looking at marriage in Eastern churches will be beneficial. The history of Christian marriage in Eastern churches began similarly to that of Western churches, with the two parts of betrothal and marriage. Many Jewish and Roman customs, including crowning, joining of hands, rings, and the common cup, also became Christianized in the East. Like the West, marriage in the East was originally three separate stages: the betrothal, which could last an indeterminate time, the marriage, and then seven or eight days later, the ritualized removal of the crowns.[15]

The earliest evidence of a marriage liturgy in the East is in the Byzantine tradition, with the wedding of Emperor Maurice to Constantina in 582. It included a betrothal rite with the wedding eight days later that included the joining of hands, the crowning of the couple, and communion. In 741, imperial legislation made church marriages valid, and then, during the reign of Emperor Leo VI (886-912 CE), they became obligatory.[16]

The earliest liturgical book of the Byzantine tradition is from the eighth century and includes a "Prayer for Betrothal" and a "Prayer for Wedding." The prayer of the common cup came before communion, indicating that it was not eucharistic. Another manuscript dating to the early eleventh century identified marriage as "Crowning," clarifying that communion is from the presanctified gifts and that the prayer of the common cup now followed it.

The advent of the printing press in the sixteenth century stabilized the rite. The marriage liturgy no longer included the Eucharist. It involved a series of prayers, litanies, and readings, along with the crowning and the reception of the common cup. The betrothal continued to include exchanging rings, which was now done right before the crowning service. The lifting of the crowns appears at the end of the service rather than several days later. So, the separated rites had been united into a single rite.[17]

Other Eastern traditions follow a similar pattern as the Byzantine tradition, with some notable exceptions. For example, the Armenian tradition included a "Canon of Making the Exchange of Crosses" instead of the exchange of rings in the Byzantine tradition. It also included the blessing of betrothal gifts, the blessing of robes, and the joining of hands. However, more modern rites included some apparent Western influences, such as the veiling of the bride and, especially, a threefold interrogation confirming the consent of both parties. The removal of the crowns now occurred at the end of the service rather than as a separate service.[18]

---

15. Alexopoulos and Johnson, *Introduction to Eastern Christian Liturgies*, 214-215.
16. Alexopoulos and Johnson, *Introduction to Eastern Christian Liturgies*, 222.
17. Alexopoulos and Johnson, *Introduction to Eastern Christian Liturgies*, 223-226.
18. Alexopoulos and Johnson, *Introduction to Eastern Christian Liturgies*, 215-222.

The Coptic tradition included a unique element of Eastern traditions—anointing the couple with oil. This anointing occurred before the crowning. This use of oil theologically links marriage with baptism, coronation, and healing.

The Ethiopian rite is similar to the Coptic rite except that the Coptic rite imagines marriage occurring within the Eucharist. Because Ethiopian custom views the Eucharist so highly, most people choose to be married civilly rather than through the church. In 2001, the Ethiopian Church published an English translation of an abridged form of the marriage rites, which does not include the Eucharist. This rite may have been a pastoral attempt to encourage people to be married in the church.[19]

The East Syrian rite is perhaps the most elaborate of them all. It includes all the elements discussed thus far. It has retained the separate threefold stages, with the betrothal rite occurring in the home and the marriage rite occurring in the church. The final stage returns to the home, but this time, it is for the blessing of the bridal chamber rather than the removal of the crowns.

The West Syrian rite includes Christianized Hindu customs of Thali and Saree. The Thali is a gold heart with a cross embossed on it, which the groom ties around the neck of the bride as Figure 3.2 depicts. The Saree is a veil, with which the groom covers the head of the bride while a hymn exalting the cross is sung.[20]

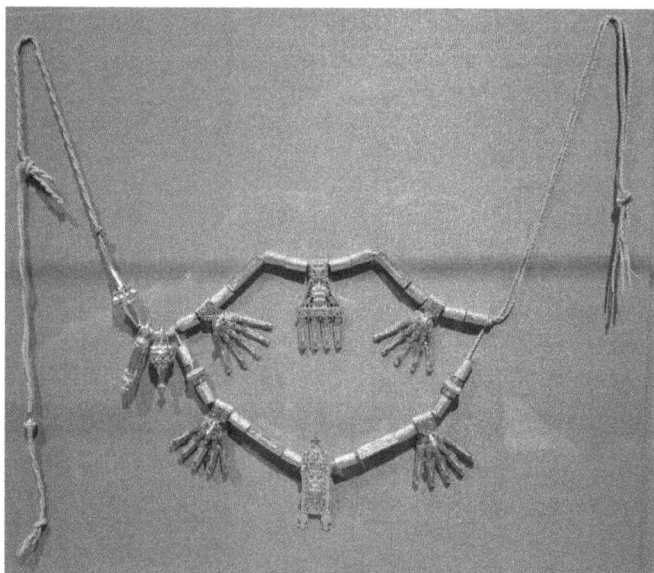

Figure 3.2: Thali wedding necklace (Honolulu Museum of Art, Public Domain Dedication - CC0; https://garystockbridge617.getarchive.net/amp/media/kali-tiru-marriage-necklace-tamil-nadu-india-19th-early-20th-century-gold-and-52db9f)

---

19. Alexopoulos and Johnson, *Introduction to Eastern Christian Liturgies*, 226-234.
20. Alexopoulos and Johnson, *Introduction to Eastern Christian Liturgies*, 234-245.

Alexopoulos and Johnson summarize these Eastern rites with four common themes. First, the fundamental theological theme for marriage is the imagery of Christ's marital bond with the church from Ephesians 5. Second, Christ blesses the couple as the celebrant as he blessed the wedding at Cana with his presence. Third, God incorporates the couple into salvation history, like couples from the Old Testament. Finally, the central rite of the marriage liturgy quickly becomes the crowning, which symbolizes the joy of marriage and the couple's participation in the kingdom of God.[21]

Before leaving the rites of the Eastern churches, a brief note about the Byzantine Rite of *Adelphopoiesis* ("making brothers") is important. This rite gave legal, social, and religious recognition to what would today be known as a "domestic partnership" between two men. The prayers and readings for this rite differ from those for crowning, and the central liturgical act is placing their hands on the gospel book rather than exchanging rings or crowning.[22]

This rite gained attention when James Boswell cited it in his *Same-Sex Unions in Premodern Europe* as an example of a same-sex equivalent to the rite of crowning.[23] However, Stuhlman notes two crucial exceptions that would argue against this rite being a precursor to modern-day same-sex unions. First, the blessings and prayers only speak of a spiritual bond, not a physical one between the two people. On the other hand, the crowning rites speak of both a spiritual and a physical bond. Also, neither canon nor civil law would have exempted persons united by this rite from the penalty for homosexual intimacy. Thus, Stuhlman adroitly concludes, "If the contemporary church adopts a rite for same-sex unions, the rite of *adelphopoiesis* provides a problematic precedent: one purpose of such a rite today should surely be to provide an appropriate context for sexual intimacy."[24]

The Medieval West

The earliest liturgical text referencing marriage in the West comes from what is known as the Veronese or Leonine Sacramentary. This collection of liturgical material is not a true sacramentary but a collection of prayers. Initially, it was attributed to Leo the Great, but scholars believe it contains more informal texts, probably of Roman origin, and compiled in the early sixth century.[25]

This collection contains no liturgical rites for marriage but prayers for the Eucharist containing solemn blessings of the marriage. The marriage itself was likely completed at home beforehand, and thus, this material would be an example of Stevenson's "stratum 1" for an ecclesial blessing. The title of this section of prayers is "Here Begins the Nuptial Veiling," referencing the Roman custom of veiling as illustrated in

---

21. Alexopoulos and Johnson, *Introduction to Eastern Christian Liturgies*, 249.
22. Stuhlman, *Occasions of Grace*, 86-89.
23. John Boswell, *Same-Sex Unions in Premodern Europe*, 207-209 and 231-234.
24. Stuhlman, *Occasions of Grace*, 89.
25. Mark Searle and Kenneth W. Stevenson, eds., *Documents of the Marriage Liturgy*, 40.

Figure 3.3. While not explicitly stated, the implication is that the priest veils only the bride because all the prayers are for the bride. They represent the paternalistic view of women as made not in the image of God but in the image of man, who is made in the image of God. The "ideal bride" will be subservient to her husband as she was to her father, sexually faithful to her husband, and bear children for him.[26]

Figure 3.3: New Liturgical Movement (https://www.newliturgicalmovement.org/2019/02/the-velatio-nuptialis-ancient-and.html) and Schola Sainte-Cécile (https://schola-sainte-cecile.com/2014/07/11/un-antique-usage-la-velatio-nuptialis-ou-le-mariage-au-poele/)

The Gelasian Sacramentary dates as far back as the early eighth century. It contains prayers from the Franco-Germanic area that were Romanized. It does not contain a marriage liturgy but prayers and blessings for the Eucharist. Like the Verona material, it primarily focuses on the bride. However, the postcommunion blessing refers to both the bride and the groom. Searle and Stevenson suggest it may have been inserted by a Frankish scribe uncomfortable with the Roman focus on only the bride.[27]

The Gregorian Sacramentary is a true sacramentary with all the material for the priest to preside at the Eucharist. However, it also does not contain an actual marriage liturgy, only the prayers for the nuptial Mass, which may indicate that the marriage still occurred at home as part of the domestic rites to be blessed later in the church.

---

26. Searle and Stevenson, *Documents of the Marriage Liturgy*, 41.

27. Searle and Stevenson, *Documents of the Marriage Liturgy*, 50.

The earliest material in this sacramentary dates as far back as the eighth century, even though it is meant to be the liturgy of Gregory the Great from two centuries earlier. The Gregorian Sacramentary includes material from the Verona Sacramentary.[28]

Like the Verona Sacramentary, the Gregorian Sacramentary focuses solely on the bride needing special prayers and blessings due to her inferior state. In addition to providing social stability, a new purpose for the fruitfulness of marriage is "to increase the adoptive children of God," i.e., through baptism. Thus, the purpose of marriage is not just the avoidance of lust but also the encouragement of procreation for the growth of the church. This focus on procreation would continue into contemporary marriage rites in the Roman Catholic Church.

A new aspect of the Gregorian Sacramentary is a prayer regarding original sin. This prayer indicated that the holiness of marriage survived the advent of original sin and the Flood, "O God, through you a woman is joined to her husband and society is chiefly ordered by that blessing which was neither lost by original sin nor washed away in the flood."[29] The Gregorian Sacramentary would have a significant influence on later rites.

The Bobbio Missal from the eighth century contains material from the non-Roman liturgies of Gaul. It includes an example of a stratum two domestic ritual, a "Blessing of the Marriage Chamber for Those Marrying." It does not include a marriage liturgy or an ecclesiastical blessing. However, it does include a "Prayer over Those who Marry for the Second Time."[30]

The Pontifical of Egbert, a tenth-century English pontifical, contains additional domestic rites but, again, no nuptial Mass. It has several general prayers for the marriage and the couple. It also contains a "Blessing of the Wedding Chamber," "Blessing of the Ring [notice singular]," and a "Blessing of the Bed."[31]

The Benedictional of Robert of Jumièges, although likely from Robert, Archbishop of Rouen at the beginning of the eleventh century, contains both a nuptial Mass and domestic rites. It titles the nuptial Mass as "Mass for the Blessing of a Bride," and the material comes from the Gregorian Sacramentary. It also includes "Blessings over the Young People," which includes a blessing for the couple and a blessing of the ring. It also references Tobit.[32]

Visigothic, or Old Spanish, liturgical rites resisted the Romanization occurring in other parts of the continent. The *Liber Ordinum*, a collection of these rites dating from the eleventh century, contains domestic and ecclesiastical blessings. It has an "Order for the Blessing the Wedding Chamber," followed by an "Order for Those Marrying" in the context of Vespers, not the Eucharist. Then, it has an "Order of the Arrhas." The arrhas were gifts given to the bride. This practice originated in the ancient practice of giving a dowry. That practice intermingled

---

28. Searle and Stevenson, *Documents of the Marriage Liturgy*, 45.
29. Searle and Stevenson, *Documents of the Marriage Liturgy*, 46 and 48, respectively.
30. Searle and Stevenson, *Documents of the Marriage Liturgy*, 101-102.
31. Searle and Stevenson, *Documents of the Marriage Liturgy*, 103-106.
32. Searle and Stevenson, *Documents of the Marriage Liturgy*, 107-112.

with the Roman practice of providing the bride with gifts to sustain her should she become a widow. In this rite, it is a blessing of rings, plural now. Then, the nuptial Mass follows. After Mass, the priest is to veil both the bride and groom with a pall or sheet, placing a cord of white and purple on top of it. This collection also contains prayers for one person marrying for the first time and the other marrying for a second time, as well as "Another Order for Second Marriages."[33]

The eleventh and twelfth centuries involved a good deal of ecclesial reform. One aspect of this reform was the desire to make the wedding rites more public. At this time, Stevenson's third stratum about consent enters as a public declaration of consent becomes essential. Scholastic theologians such as Peter Lombard taught that the consent of the couple marked the "efficient cause of marriage."[34]

The Bury St. Edmunds Missal, dated 1125-1135 CE, contains all three of Stevenson's strata: nuptial Mass, domestic rites, and rite of consent. It combines all three elements into a single service and rearranges the order. It is an example of the Anglo-Norman synthesis.[35]

The liturgy began with the blessing of the rings, which now occurred at the church door rather than in the home, making it public. Then, the priest asked the couple to give their consent. The bridal gifts were offered. The person who gave away the bride would step forward to give her to the man. The priest and the bridegroom placed the ring first on the thumb of the bride, reciting "In the name of the Father," then the index finger, reciting "and of the Son," and then finally on the middle finger, reciting, "and of the Holy Spirit. Amen." The bridegroom says to the bride, "With this ring I thee wed, this gold and silver I thee give, with my body I thee worship, and with this dowry I thee endow." After receiving all these items, the bride fell to her husband's feet. The priest offered final prayers and led the couple into the church. The couple entered the church and stood before the altar. The priest recited several additional prayers. Then, the Mass began. After the Peace of the Lord, the couple exchanged a kiss. After the Mass, the priest blessed the couple, blessed the cup, referencing the wedding at Cana, and then blessed the marriage, presumably sometime later.[36]

The Sarum Manual of Salisbury Cathedral was widely used throughout England and beyond. It represents a medieval marriage liturgy immediately preceding the English reformations. It is very similar in structure to the Bury St. Edmunds Missal. The final banns, dowry, and rings were given at the church door. The priest asked for the couple's consent. Then, the groom offered the ring, blessed by the priest. However, in this service, the groom began with the bride's index finger and ended with her fourth finger (now known as the "ring finger") because "there is a vein which runs to the heart." Also, "the clink of coins signifies interior love which is always to be fresh between them."

---

33. Searle and Stevenson, *Documents of the Marriage Liturgy*, 120-134.
34. Searle and Stevenson, *Documents of the Marriage Liturgy*, 148-149.
35. Stevenson, *To Join Together*, 39.
36. Searle and Stevenson, *Documents of the Marriage Liturgy*, 149-155.

Another unique feature of this service is that the banns, the consent, and the exchange of rings were all said in the vernacular. The couple entered the church with further prayers. The nuptial Mass continued with the blessing of bread, wine, and cup, referencing the wedding at Cana at the end. The following night, the priest would go to their home to bless the marriage bed.[37]

The Sarum Manual was influential by introducing marital vows into the rite for the first time. Previous marital rites included only questions on consent. The Sarum Manual added vows to these questions.[38] Later rites of the reformation, particularly Cranmer's Book of Common Prayer, would retain the use of vows. They would become nearly ubiquitous in Western marital rites.

The medieval rites of the Western church illustrate this tension between domestic rituals and ecclesial blessing. By the end of the period, this tension resolved with an integrated, public liturgy in which all three strata—nuptial Mass, domestic rites, and liturgy of consent—occurred. However, by this time, the betrothal period had faded into the background in preference for the public rites. Also, the attention remained primarily on the bride. The earlier rites contained much more explicitly paternalistic material. However, the vestiges of this material remained with the giving away of the bride, the dowry, and specific prayers.

The medieval period also involved further development of the theology of marriage. As discussed above, Augustine taught that one of the three purposes of marriage was to be a *sacramentum*. However, Augustine did not provide a systematic sacramental theology, and it would be anachronistic to suggest that he conceived of marriage as a sacrament in the same way that later scholastic theologians, such as Hugh of St. Victor, Peter Lombard, and Thomas Aquinas would. During the twelfth and thirteenth centuries, these scholastic theologians confirmed marriage as one of the seven sacraments.[39]

By raising marriage to sacramental status, these theologians argued that it was no longer just a contract between two people under natural or social laws. It was now subject to the law of the church. Because the love between a husband and wife symbolized the love between Christ and the church, which is an unbreakable bond, they taught that the bond between husband and wife was also unbreakable. Furthermore, as a sacrament, marriage would now fall under the canonical authority of the church.[40]

Even though marriage fell under the spiritual jurisdiction of the church, a priest was not necessary. The couple were the ministers of the sacrament. The only requirement was their consent, which could occur in a service in their home

---

37. Searle and Stevenson, *Documents of the Marriage Liturgy*, 163-178.

38. Stevenson, *To Join Together*, 240.

39. Hugh of Saint Victor, *On the Sacraments of the Christian Faith: (De Sacramentis)*, 324-369; Peter Lombard, *The Sentences: Book 4: On the Doctrine of Signs*, 157-233; Thomas Aquinas, *Summa Theologica*, qq. 42-68, 3:2715-2825.

40. John Witte, Jr., *From Sacrament to Contract: Marriage, Religion, and Law in the Western Tradition*, 26.

without a priest or in the church with a priest. The Fourth Lateran Council (1215 CE) would strongly encourage a couple to seek the consent of their parents, publish their banns, invite witnesses, and have the marriage blessed by a priest, but none of these customs were required.[41]

As a sacrament, marriage conferred grace as long as no obstacle was placed in its way. This sacramental grace transformed the couple, just like baptism transformed the Christian. While baptism erased original sin, marriage erased sexual sin. Furthermore, as a sacrament, marriage was indissoluble. Therefore, divorce was impossible. The only means of ending a marriage was death or annulment if an impediment was discovered that would have rendered the marriage non-sacramental. This change in status radically altered the relationship between marriage and the church.[42]

The Reformations

Marriage was an important topic among both the English and Continental reformers. The fundamental criterion for a sacrament in the eyes of the reformers was its institution by Christ. Since marriage predated Christ by centuries, he did not institute it. Therefore, the reformers quickly agreed that it was not a sacrament.

When the Western church determined that marriage was a sacrament, it made a theological statement and a canonical one. Since the church administers the sacraments, it could now hold greater authority over marriage. The reformers viewed the church's jurisdiction over marriage as highly problematic. While they believed the church had a role in blessing marital unions, they did not believe it should have jurisdiction over them.

As the influence of the reformers grew, political changes occurred. Governments separated themselves from papal authority and, therefore, the jurisdiction of the Roman Catholic Church. As these separations increased, the civil governments increasingly enacted Marriage Acts to gain juridical control of marriage.[43]

While the reformers did not consider marriage a sacrament, they still needed to develop rites. Martin Luther's 1529 "Order of Marriage for Common Pastors" is simple and biblical. He removed many of the medieval ceremonials and prayers. He continued the practice of publishing the banns of marriage. The couple offered consent at the church door, exchanged rings without blessing, and joined hands. The priest then declared them married. They processed into the church to the altar, where the priest read Genesis 2:18, 21-24, and other passages. After the readings, the priest extended his hands over the couple, offered a simple prayer, which included references to Genesis 2 and Ephesians 5, and concluded

---

41. Witte, *From Sacrament to Contract*, 26-27.
42. Witte, *From Sacrament to Contract*, 27-30.
43. Witte, *From Sacrament to Contract*, 42-43.

with a prayer of protection for the marriage. This rite would provide a framework for other Lutheran marriage rites to follow.[44]

Theologically, Lutheran reformers viewed marriage as part of the "earthly kingdom," which involved the natural order of things such as clothing, food, housing, and property. They argued that marriage was not part of the "heavenly kingdom," which involved the sacraments of redemption. With this argument, they did not mean that marriage was unimportant or that the church had no role to play in it. The church should be involved in blessing and praying for marriages. However, it should not be involved in legislating them (outside of the general way church leaders were involved in civil matters) or teaching their salvific efficacy.[45]

Witte summarizes four ways Lutheran reformers believed the church should remain involved in marriage. First, it should preach and instruct on God's will for marriage to inform civil leaders of their duties toward it. Second, all church members should assist couples having marital problems through instruction and prayer. Third, the church would develop a public registry to aid married couples in their instruction. Finally, the pastor would instruct members on the purpose of marriage and discipline those members who acted outside the proper boundaries.[46]

Because the reformers did not consider marriage a sacrament, they did not teach its indissolubility. Therefore, a couple could be divorced if one party was unfaithful. Frequently, the innocent party was permitted to remarry. Some more liberal reformers expanded the grounds for divorce to include abandonment and other reasons. Also, because marriage was to be a public act, so should divorce. Thus, the couple had to go before the judge or civil magistrate to enact the divorce.[47]

John Calvin was a jurist and a theologian, and his marriage rite showed careful consideration. He included the rite in his 1542 book *La Forme des Prières et Chantz Ecclésiastiques* and entitled it "La Forme de confirmer les Mariages devant l'église des fidèles [The Form of Confirming Marriages before the Church of the Faithful]." He taught that the service should occur within the Christian assembly, albeit not on a Sunday with communion. The service contained biblical catechesis, consent, and prayer for the couple. The exchange of rings and joining of hands appeared in later rites.[48]

In his later writings, Calvin described marriage as participating in God's covenant, which was vertical between God and humanity and horizontal between husband and wife. To ratify this covenant, several essential persons had to be involved. The parents acted as God's "lieutenants" by instructing the couple on

---

44. Stevenson, *Nuptial Blessing*, 126-130.
45. Witte, *From Sacrament to Contract*, 51-52.
46. Witte, *From Sacrament to Contract*, 53.
47. Witte, *From Sacrament to Contract*, 66-70.
48. Stevenson, *Nuptial Blessing*, 130-133.

Christian marriage. The witnesses were God's "priests to their peers" by testifying to the couple's promises. The minister acted with "God's spiritual power of the Word" by blessing and instructing the couple, and the magistrate acted with "God's temporal power of the sword" by registering the marriage as a legal union. Calvin echoed Augustine in the three purposes of marriage: mutual love and support, procreation, and protection from sexual sin.[49]

Witte argues that Calvin's covenantal model mediated both the sacramental model of the Roman Catholic Church and the social model of Lutheranism. The covenantal model understood marriage to be a sacred enterprise as participating in God's covenant without making it a sacrament. It was also a social enterprise between the couple and their parents, the church, and the civil community. Thus, this covenantal model proves to be an enduring image for marriage.[50]

"The Forme of Solemnizacion of matrimonie" from the Book of Common Prayer of the Church of England endured with minimal edits from 1549 to 1928. One could consider this rite a synthesis between the medieval rites preceding it and the rites of the Continental reformers. The banns of marriage were required to be pronounced three times preceding the service, a custom coming from Sarum. The service began with a lengthy exhortation that included references to Genesis and Ephesians and the three purposes of marriage: procreation, a remedy against sin, and mutual support. Drawing from Sarum, it asked the congregation if they knew of any impediment to the marriage and then asked the same of the couple. The consent of both parties followed. After the father gave away the bride, the couple joined hands, making their vows to each other. They exchanged rings that were not blessed and tokens of silver and gold. The priest offered a lengthy prayer referencing the marriage of Isaac and Rebecca and the ring as a token of their pledge to each other. The priest joined their hands again, pronounced them married, and blessed them. The couple moved to the choir and the priest to the altar. Several prayers, a kyrie, and blessings followed with the requirement of communion ending the service. In conclusion, Stevenson poignantly asks, "What, then, of Cranmer's marriage rite? It is at root a service which is thoroughly Reformed in theology, but in post-medieval dressing, with a dash of Luther and Hermann here and there."[51]

In his earliest writing on marriage, *Thoughts on Marriage and a Single Life* (1743), John Wesley suggested that celibacy was the preferred state for Christians, but marriage was also permitted for those needing it. He taught that Christians should not marry unbelievers and that parental consent was necessary. His "The Form of Solemnization of Matrimony," found in his 1784 *Sunday Service,* was an adaptation of the marriage rite from the 1662 Book of Common Prayer. He kept the opening rubric requiring marriage banns to be read three times in public. Later editions would allow a marriage license to substitute for reading

---

49. Witte, *From Sacrament to Contract*, 95-96.
50. Witte, *From Sacrament to Contract*, 109.
51. Stevenson, *Nuptial Blessing*, 134-139.

the banns. Then, the public consent of both parties followed. Interestingly, he removed the father's giving of the bride, perhaps because parental consent was already required. He kept the purposes for marriage, which had become traditional in Western rites. However, he removed any mention of the ring, possibly to ameliorate Puritan objections to any sacramental sign and eliminate any remnant of the bridal dowry.

Wesley's writings emphasized the covenantal aspects of marriage, likely gleaned from his Puritan influences. The ministers of the rite were to be ordained elders and deacons. While the 1792 edition would substitute "in the presence of witnesses" for the phrase "in the face of this congregation," journals and diaries from that time still suggest that many weddings occurred in a congregational context.[52]

The history of marriage in the West and the East illustrates the tension between domestic and ecclesial rites. That tension sometimes produced separate rites in the home and the church. Sometimes, that tension unified the rites into a single service in the church. The role the church would play in marriage also changed. Initially, the church only sought to bless the marriage. Eventually, by giving it sacramental status, the church held jurisdiction over marriage, but that view would not persist uniformly as the reformers returned to the role of the church simply blessing the marriage.

Nineteenth and Twentieth-Century Innovations

Thomas Cranmer's marriage rite found in the Book of Common Prayer would have a substantial impact on marriage rites among all Anglican and Protestant English-speaking communities. The Reformation and Counter-Reformation debates would result in two distinct approaches to the rite. Anglicans and Protestants stressed that marriage is an ordinance, not a sacrament. The minister merely presides at the service. The consent of the couple is the pivotal moment, with readings from Scripture and a prayer.[53]

The Counter-Reformation, especially with the Council of Trent, defended marriage's status as one of the seven sacraments. Trent decreed that the nuptial mass was the mandatory form for all churches unless a form older than 200 years existed. In 1614, a new *Rituale* containing a rite for marriage would be promulgated. It would remain in effect until Vatican Two in the 1960s.[54]

As Westerfield Tucker duly notes, the nineteenth and twentieth-centuries involved a significant change in society's understanding of the role of women due in large part to increased urbanization. In some cases, this move toward urbanization produced a view of women that emphasized their domesticity, giving them spiritual attributes of nurturance and altruism. In other quarters, more

---

52. Westerfield Tucker, *American Methodist Worship*, 176-181.
53. Stevenson, *To Join Together*, 113.
54. Stevenson, *To Join Together*, 113-114.

gender-neutral roles emerged, especially as women became more involved in society outside the home.[55]

These changing views of gender mutuality led to reintroducing the wedding ring in Protestant services. Former services influenced by reformed theology banned the wedding ring as a sign of idolatry and out of concern for its possible link with sacramentalism. In 1860, a "Primitive" Methodist rite included the wedding ring. The ring was not placed on a book or blessed, as some Tractarian Anglicans had begun to do, but placed directly on the third finger of the bride's left hand. The groom would say, "I give thee this ring *as a memorial of our union*, and as a pledge of my love and fidelity." To which, the bride replied, "As such I now receive it." This formula would eventually become a primary symbol in marriage rites of the twentieth century.[56]

The attempt to produce a new revision of the Book of Common Prayer in the Church of England included controversy over the marriage rite. The main source of controversy involved the bride's relationship to the groom. Liberals wanted to remove the bride's promise to "obey" from the service, while others desired to keep it. The final draft removed it but also included other significant changes. The bride "gives" her troth, and the groom promises when he gives the ring, "with my body I thee *honour*." Also, quite radically, a nuptial Eucharist is included with its own readings. While this revision did not pass Parliament, these changes were included in revisions of other churches such as the American one. Furthermore, the Scots to the north removed the reference to "obey," included a blessing for the ring, and allowed Eucharist to conclude the service. Thus, Protestants were becoming more comfortable with greater symbolism in the service.[57]

The twentieth century brought further changes regarding the role of women in society. Divorce also became more prevalent. These changes affected the view of marriage in many ecclesial traditions. The Roman Catholic Church responded by emphasizing the importance of marriage with Pius XI's encyclical *Casti Connubii* (On Christian Marriage) in which he stressed the sanctity of marriage and prohibited artificial birth control and abortion. Methodist traditions responded differently with the only significant alteration to the marriage rite in the early twentieth century. They dropped Scriptural references within the rite, though they would eventually return.[58]

The development of modernism brought significant societal changes impacting marriage. The growth of secularism allowed couples to be married outside the church context. Concerns for gender equity grew and found their way into significant shifts in the marital rite. Artificial birth control permitted couples greater choice in procreation, oftentimes extending the average age at marriage. The

---

55. Westerfield Tucker, *American Methodist Worship*, 182-183.
56. Stevenson, *To Join Together*, 116.
57. Stevenson, *Nuptial Blessing*, 150-151.
58. Westerfield Tucker, *American Methodist Worship*, 186-187.

growth of divorce and remarriage would complexify family dynamics as blended families became more normative. Same-sex marriage would present perhaps the greatest challenge of all to the Christian rite. In all these changes, the church needed to respond not only liturgically but also theologically.

Theological Insights[59]

Because marriage predates Christianity by centuries, discussing its theologies involves recognizing the church's role in blessing an existing ritual. In other words, marriage is not uniquely Christian, but that could be said about all pastoral offices. Nonetheless, the church has desired to sanctify marriage in some fashion since its earliest days. Thus, marriage has important theological considerations that are worthy of attention.

One of the most significant shifts in marriage history is the advent of same-sex marriage. Ecclesial traditions strongly differ among and within themselves regarding the church's role in same-sex marriage. Furthermore, not all civil jurisdictions permit it, and, in fact, some jurisdictions actively legislate against it. This book aims not to argue for or against same-sex marriage but to share theological insights on marriage that could inform either position. Space does not allow for an extensive discussion on the theologies of same-sex marriage.[60]

Images of Marriage

Most contemporary marriage liturgies begin with either a rubrical introduction or an exhortation to the congregation describing marriage.[61] These descriptions use scriptural images that are theologically rich and carefully nuanced depending on the ecclesial tradition. They include the imagery of creation (Genesis 1), Christ's presence at the wedding in Cana (John 2), Christ's bond with the church and his sacrificial love on the cross (Ephesians 5), baptism and the empowerment of the Holy Spirit, and the marriage feast of the Lamb (Revelation 19).

The imagery of creation features prominently in marital liturgies. Ecclesial traditions agree about God's involvement in marriage. Some traditions describe marriage as being established or instituted by God or a gift from God.[62] They often include imagery from Genesis 1 that God created humanity and provided marriage as companionship.

---

59. Appendix C contains the marriage rites from the BCP, BCW, BOW, ELW, and OCM in tabular format for easy reference.

60. For additional information on theological arguments for and against same-sex marriage, please see Clare Herbert, *Towards a Theology of Same-Sex Marriage;* and Ludger H. Viefhues-Bailey, *Between a Man and a Woman?: Why Conservatives Oppose Same-Sex Marriage.*

61. See BCP 423-424, ELW 286, BCW 687- 691, BOW 199-200 and *The Order of Celebrating Matrimony,* 11-22, 42, and 57, hereafter OCM.

62. See BCP 423, BOW 200, BCW 687, ELW 286, and OCM 11.

These references to creation imagery recognize that marriage predates the Christian tradition and, more importantly, suggests God's desire for marriage to be a part of the human experience. While not all people may be called to married life, those people who enter it can know that God desires it for them. Scripture and church tradition have sometimes given the impression that marriage is less desirable than celibacy. Marriage is meant for those who cannot keep their passions in check. However, these creation images remind couples and the church that God desires marriage as a blessing for couples.

In one of the nuptial blessings from *The Order of Christian Matrimony*, the priest states, "Father, by your plan man and woman are united, and married life has been established as the one blessing that was not forfeited by original sin or washed away in the flood."[63]

This blessing hearkens back to the Gregorian Sacramentary of the eighth century.[64] This imagery suggests a fortitude to marriage that has resisted the forces of original sin and the flood. Couples receive assurance that God's blessing on their marriage will be equally strong.

In their marital liturgies, many traditions reference Genesis 1:27, which says that God created humanity as male and female. While these references traditionally sought to convey God's blessing on marriage, as mentioned above, today, they can have an additional theological purpose—to convey God's blessing on heterosexual marriage specifically. Same-sex marriage remains a controversial subject both among and within ecclesial traditions.

However, nuance also exists. For example, the Presbyterian *Book of Common Worship* states, "Marriage involves a unique commitment between two people, *traditionally* a man and a woman."[65] This language reflects an amendment to the Constitution of the Presbyterian Church (USA) that now permits same-sex marriage.[66] The Episcopal Church has authorized supplemental liturgical resources for same-sex marriage. These resources avoid this reference in the exhortations, mentioning the imagery from Ephesians 5 regarding Christ's relationship with the church only. The lectionaries list Genesis 1:26-28 as an optional reading in only one of these supplemental services.[67] The ELCA has also authorized "Supplemental Resources for use within the Evangelical Lutheran Worship Service of Marriage" that use gender-neutral language and avoid reference to Genesis 2.[68]

Another scriptural image featured in marital liturgies is Jesus' presence at the Cana wedding, found in John 2. Scholastic theologians used this passage (along with Ephesians 5 and others) to explain Christ's institution of marriage,

---

63. OCM 36.

64. Searle and Stevenson, *Documents of the Marriage Liturgy*, 48.

65. BCW 687, emphasis added.

66. Melody K. Smith, "Presbyterian Church (U.S.A.) approves marriage amendment."

67. *Liturgical Resources 1: "I Will Bless You, and You Will Be a Blessing."*

68. "Supplemental Resources for use within the Evangelical Lutheran Worship Service of Marriage."

an essential component of declaring it a sacrament.[69] Interestingly, though, this imagery occurs infrequently in the euchologies of contemporary marriage liturgies except for being an optional Gospel reading. Even the Roman Catholic marriage liturgy does not reference Christ's presence at the Cana wedding in its euchology, only as an optional lesson.[70]

Two exceptions are the BCP of the Episcopal Church and the BOW of the United Methodist Church, which reference Christ's presence at the Cana wedding. The BCP says, "...our Lord Jesus Christ adorned this manner of life by his presence and first miracle at a wedding in Cana of Galilee."[71] The BOW speaks similarly, "which holy estate Christ adorned and beautified with his presence in Cana of Galilee."[72] This reference to "adornment" indicates a careful theological nuance. While these texts provide no explanations for this word and the other texts do not explain its absence, one presumes that contemporary exegesis has clarified the theological fragility of using this passage to justify Christ's authorization of marriage. Christ was not involved in the marriage rite itself. He did not officiate at it. He did not bless the couple. His involvement occurred only during the post-ceremony celebration when the wine gave out. Thus, it would be theologically challenging to suggest that this passage substantiates Christ's institution, authorization of, a blessing for, or even signification of marriage. At best, one could say that Christ was present at the wedding and, therefore, "adorned" it.

A more explicit theological connection between Christ and marriage occurs with the imagery found in Ephesians 5:22-33. Here, the writer of Ephesians compares the relationship of Christ and the church with the relationship between a husband and wife. According to the culture in which this epistle was written, a wife was subject to her husband, so the church was to be subject to Christ. As disconcerting as that portion of the passage may be to some contemporary readers, it is not its central point.

The main point follows when the writer states that husbands are to love their wives as Christ loved the church and "gave himself up for it." This reference to Christ's self-offering on the cross becomes a pivotal theological theme in contemporary marriage liturgies.[73] The love and self-offering that the couple extends to each other symbolizes the love and self-offering that Christ extends to the church. The connection with Christ's passion signifies that marriage is more than just a romantic gesture or the compatibility of two people. It involves sacrifice, but a sacrifice borne from love for each other.

---

69. Hugh of Saint Victor, *On the Sacraments of the Christian Faith*, 325 and Peter Lombard, *The Sentences*, 159.

70. OCM 112-113.

71. BCP 423.

72. BOW 200.

73. See BCP 423, BOW 200, and OCM 37. It is implied in the opening rubrics in ELW 286 and in the opening exhortation in BCW 691.

Another liturgical and scriptural image in contemporary marriage liturgies is baptism and the empowerment of the Holy Spirit. Explicit references to baptism are infrequent. When they occur, they point to the ongoing sanctification of the Holy Spirit given in baptism. For example, the Presbyterian BCW states, "And the Holy Spirit, given in baptism, renews God's grace within us day by day, enabling us to grow in faith, in hope, and in love."[74] The marriage liturgy of the Roman Catholic Church is more explicit and ties marriage with baptism as part of the overall sacramental system, "Through a special Sacrament, [Christ] enriches and strengthens those he has already consecrated by Holy Baptism."[75]

However, not all contemporary marriage liturgies explicitly reference baptism. This lack of explicit references to baptism may be due to the possibility of interfaith marriages in which one member of the couple is not a baptized Christian. In fact, "The Order for Celebrating Matrimony between a Catholic and a Catechumen or a Non-Christian" of the Roman Catholic Church omits any reference to baptism in its opening exhortation.[76]

Interestingly, most contemporary marriage liturgies feature the Holy Spirit prominently in their nuptial blessings, even if one person is unbaptized.[77] This distinction is understandable since the Holy Spirit works among the baptized and the unbaptized. The Anglican BCP and the Lutheran ELW have almost identical wording for this portion of the nuptial blessing.

> By the power of your Holy Spirit, pour out the abundance of your blessing upon this man and this woman [in ELW, your blessing on _name_ and _name_____]. Defend them from every enemy. Lead them into all peace. Let their love for each other be a seal upon their hearts, a mantle about their shoulders, and a crown upon their foreheads.[78]

The reference to the Holy Spirit empowering them for defense against the enemy hearkens to imagery in confirmation rites.[79] Just as one needs assistance with the challenges of the spiritual life, a couple needs assistance with the challenges of marital life. The final sentence references imagery from the patristic and Eastern churches in which the husband and wife would be veiled with a "mantle about their shoulders" and crowns placed on their foreheads. This

---

74. BCW 691.

75. OCM 28. See also paragraph 7 of the Introduction, OCM 12.

76. OCM 57.

77. The alternative blessing in at BCW 696-697 does not reference the Holy Spirit. The Methodist BOW does not explicitly mention the Holy Spirit but does refer to God as "giver of all spiritual grace," BOW 205. "The Order for Celebrating Matrimony between a Catholic and a Catechumen or a Non-Christian" of the Roman Catholic Church does not reference the Holy Spirit, OCM 52.

78. BCP 430 and ELW 289.

79. See chapter two.

imagery involves protection, support, and joy, attributes that God bestows on the couple.

The second typical edition of *The Order of Celebrating Matrimony* of the Roman Catholic Church added an epiclesis, or invocation of the Holy Spirit, over the couple in the nuptial blessing, "Send down on them the grace of the Holy Spirit.[80] As Paul Turner notes, including an explicit epiclesis in the nuptial blessing is new to the Latin Rite. The Eastern rites have used it in their marriage liturgies, indicating that the priest's blessing affects the sacrament rather than the couple's consent. As Turner aptly states, "The epiclesis enriches the prayers and provides a point of unity among the churches East and West."[81] An epiclesis over the couple mimics its use among some ecclesial traditions over the water in baptism and the bread and wine in the Eucharist.

A final image of marriage involves the end of time and references Revelation 19:1-10. In this passage, the writer summarizes the evocative imagery it describes: "Blessed are those who are invited to the marriage supper of the Lamb [Rev 19:9]." Some contemporary marriage liturgies evoke this image, "Finally, in your mercy, bring them to that table where your saints feast for ever in your heavenly home."[82] The hope is that the couple will enjoy a rich and long life together. One should not read into this blessing any notion that marriage persists into eternity. Christ was clear that it does not (Matt 22:30). Nonetheless, one desires God's blessing, beginning with baptism, continuing with marriage, and culminating with death.

The Purposes of Marriage

As discussed above, Augustine often spoke of three purposes for marriage: *fides* (fidelity), *proles* (offspring), and *sacramentum* (sacred obligation).[83] These three purposes persisted in marriage liturgies throughout the history of the Western church. Contemporary liturgies expand this list to include mutual joy, strength, respect, grace, help, and comfort. Some liturgies also include social good as a purpose for marriage.

Only *The Order of Celebrating Matrimony* of the Roman Catholic Church explicitly refers to marriage as a sacrament.[84] As described above, the reformers contested the sacramental nature of marriage, and their ecclesial traditions do not describe it as a sacrament.[85] However, if one understands *sacramentum* in its

---

80. OCM 37. See also OCM 135 and 139.

81. Paul Turner, *Inseparable Love: A Commentary on The Order of Celebrating Matrimony in the Catholic Church*, section 74.

82. BCP 430. See ELW 289 for identical wording and OCM 37 for a reference to "And grant that, reaching at the last together the fullness of years for which they hope, they may come to the life of the blessed in the Kingdom of Heaven."

83. Stevenson, *Nuptial Blessing*, 29.

84. OCM 11.

85. The Episcopal Church describes marriage as a "sacramental rite" BCP 860.

original Augustinian sense as a "sacred obligation" and not in its later scholastic sense, then additional liturgies reference this obligation.

For example, the BCP exhorts, "Therefore marriage is not to be entered into unadvisedly or lightly, but reverently, deliberately, and in accordance with the purposes for which it was instituted by God."[86] The Methodist BOW uses similar wording.[87] The Lutheran ELW and the Presbyterian BCW refer to the church as surrounding the couple with prayer.[88] Thus, these liturgies emphasize the sacredness of the moment. They all include marriage vows, which create an obligation between the couple. This obligation is sacred and not merely a formal contract between two parties. Thus, Augustine's use of *sacramentum* remains an essential theological theme.

Another theological theme that many contemporary liturgies feature, sometimes prominently and sometimes with nuance, is procreation. Again, the Roman Catholic "Rite for Celebrating Marriage during Mass" discusses procreation most prominently. The introduction describes the procreation and education of children as the "ultimate crown" of marriage.[89] The priest asks the couple, "Will you accept children lovingly from God, and bring them up according to the law of Christ and his Church?" One notes that the rubric gives the option to omit this question "if the couple are advanced in years."[90]

Other contemporary liturgies feature procreation, if not so prominently. The BCP describes procreation as one of the intentions of marriage "when it is God's will."[91] ELW refers to "the care and nurture of children" in its introductory paragraph.[92] However, the Methodist BOW and the Presbyterian BCW do not mention procreation.

A theological challenge exists when linking procreation with marriage in the case of couples who are unable to have children. The couples could be elderly, infertile, or same-sex. Also, some fertile, heterosexual couples of childbearing age choose not to have children for many reasons. Are these marriages inferior to childbearing marriages?

In her book *Un/familiar Theology: Reconceiving Sex, Reproduction and Generativity*, Susannah Cornwall argues for alternative understandings of procreation and marriage. First, she describes the role of "fictive reproduction" in the Christian tradition. "Fictive reproduction" refers to persons who produce children for Christ through spiritual work. These persons could include those who have

---

86. BCP 423.
87. BOW 200.
88. ELW 286 and BCW 691.
89. OCM 11.
90. OCM 29. Interestingly, this question also appears in the "Rite for Celebrating Marriage between a Catholic and a Catechumen or a Non-Christian," OCM 59.
91. BCP 423. The alternative liturgy, "The Witnessing and Blessing of a Marriage," does not refer to procreation, *Liturgical Resources 1*, 91.
92. ELW 286.

vowed celibacy but can also include others. Using Augustine, Chrysostom, and contemporary authors, Cornwall argues, "Generativity in Christ is not limited to those who are generative in the flesh."[93]

Cornwall then refers to psychosocial theorists to discuss generativity as a life-stage process. She critiques Erikson's linear use of life stage progression as too narrow. Generativity can occur at various times in one's life, not necessarily nearing its end. Using the work of John Kotre, a Roman Catholic psychologist, she broadens generativity's definition to include biological, parental (adoptive parents and grandparents), technical (skills or expertise), and cultural generativity.[94]

Thus, she concludes, "Procreation may be generative, but generativity is far more than procreation. Modes of relationship which are not (and never could be) procreative are no less generative on that account."[95] She recognizes that marriage is a gift from God, but a true gift must allow the recipient to use that gift as desired. For some couples, that will entail procreation. For other couples, that might involve other forms of generativity.

Augustine's final purpose for marriage was *proles*, which has been translated as "chastity" or "fidelity." Augustine and later Western marriage liturgies often focused on sexual fidelity. Referencing Paul's discussion of marriage in 1 Corinthians 7:1-16, they believe that sexual lust resulted from the fall, and marriage is the proper container for it. Thus, the couple promises a lifelong commitment to each other. The marriage vows found in contemporary liturgies affirm this principle.[96]

However, contemporary marriage liturgies extend this view of mutual fidelity to include mutual joy, strength, respect, grace, help, and comfort. The BCP speaks of marriage being "for [the couple's] mutual joy; for the help and comfort given one another in prosperity and adversity."[97] In the introduction to marriage, ELW remarks, "Marriage is ... intended for the joy and mutual strength of those who enter it."[98] The BCW states, "Those who marry are called to a way of life marked by grace, fidelity, and mutual respect, as they bear one another's burdens and share one another's joys."[99] Thus, the couple's commitment to each other involves much more than chastity. It involves their "complete fidelity."[100]

The couple not only commits to each other but also to the community. Marriage also involves social good as one of its purposes.[101] This purpose recognizes the social aspect of marriage and, when relevant, its civic responsibility. However,

---

93. Susannah Cornwall, *Un/Familiar Theology: Reconceiving Sex, Reproduction and Generativity*, Rethinking Theologies, 20.

94. Cornwall, *Un/Familiar Theology*, 26.

95. Cornwall, *Un/Familiar Theology*, 38.

96. See OCM 31-32; BCP 424; ELW 288; BOW 208-209; and BCW 694-695.

97. BCP 423.

98. ELW 286.

99. BCW 691.

100. OCM 11.

101. See BCP 423, ELW 286, BCW 686-687, and BOW 208.

theologically, this purpose intends for marriage to be missional. If a Christian marriage is a symbol of the relationship between Christ and the church, then it engages in the same mission of the church: proclaiming the Good News of Jesus Christ through word and deed.

Marriage as Covenant

Marriage as covenant is a primary metaphor in describing God's relationship with Israel and Christ's relationship with the church.[102] This use of marriage as a metaphor for these relationships is understandable, given the ubiquity of marriage throughout human history. Biblical authors have used marriage to try to explain these divine relationships.

However, this method involves a danger because marriage is complex. While many marriage liturgies describe it as created or instituted by God, it is also a human enterprise. A cursory glance at scriptural examples of marriage confirms this truth. The innocence of Adam and Eve's relationship does not endure as the Fall corrupts it (Gen 3). Laban uses trickery to get Jacob to marry his older daughter, Leah, before Jacob's preferred bride, Rachel (Gen 29). David murders Uriah to marry Bathsheba (2 Sam 11). Solomon collects seven hundred wives and three hundred concubines like property (1 Kings 11). The list continues. Even with these mixed scriptural images of marriage, covenantal language still features prominently in contemporary liturgies.[103]

The images of marriage discussed above flow into this covenantal view of marriage. In the creation imagery of Genesis 2, God covenants with Adam to provide him "a helper as his partner." In John 2, Jesus "adorns" the covenant of marriage with his presence. Ephesians 5 speaks explicitly about the covenant between Christ and the church and husband and wife. The church understands baptism as the ritual by which one enters the church's covenant, and Revelation speaks of the fulfillment of the covenant when all the faithful will dine with Christ.

The purposes of marriage also involve covenant. Marriage as a "sacred obligation" is the couple's consent to enter this covenant freely. Fidelity is their promise to remain in covenant with each other, and procreation or generativity is the fruit of that covenant.

As Witte argues, Calvin offered a covenantal model that mediated between the Roman Catholic Church's sacramental model and Lutheranism's social model.[104] Christian marriage is not merely a social contract into which two parties enter. While civil authorities and general society may view it as such, the Christian tradition contradicts this narrow image of marriage. However, the sacramental view of marriage involves a theology to which not all ecclesial traditions can

---

102. For more information on the use of covenant in scripture, see George E. Mendenhall and Gary A. Herion, "Covenant," in *The Anchor Bible Dictionary*, 1:1179-1202.

103. BCP 423, ELW 286, BCW 208, BCW 687, and OCM 11.

104. Witte, *From Sacrament to Contract*, 109.

adhere. A covenantal view of marriage takes seriously the sacredness of marriage. Israel was to worship God alone. The church is to recognize Christ as Lord. However, marriage also has a social aspect. Similarly, God has commanded Israel and the church to care for their neighbor.

Is this covenant indissoluble? The Roman Catholic Church explicitly argues that it is.[105] Other ecclesial traditions recognize the effect sin has on all relationships, marriage being no exception. Some of these traditions accept divorce but counsel one or both parties to avoid remarriage. Other ecclesial traditions recognize redemption in remarriage. Nonetheless, all Christian traditions grieve the pain and harm of divorce and lament its brokenness.

In an increasingly globalized world in which relationships have expanded but simultaneously become much more tenuous, the covenantal nature of Christian marriage stands in contrast. While the divorce rate within Western societies continues to grow, covenantal marriage continues to be an ideal, if not always a reality, to which couples aspire. Whether or not an ecclesial tradition believes marriage to be sacramental, they all agree that God's grace must abound for marriage to endure and prosper.

Cultural Connections

As discussed above, marriage has existed long before the Christian tradition. All cultures across centuries of history have engaged in marriage. It is truly transcultural. As such, marriage involves many cultural connections that the wise pastor considers carefully. The Vatican II document *Constitution on the Sacred Liturgy* provides sage counsel for all Christian traditions when considering how to contextualize cultural practices with liturgical principles:

> Even in the liturgy, the Church has no wish to impose a rigid uniformity in matters which do not implicate the faith or the good of the whole community; rather does she respect and foster the genius and talents of the various races and peoples. Anything in these peoples' way of life which is not indissolubly bound up with superstition and error she studies with sympathy and, if possible, preserves intact. Sometimes in fact she admits such things into the liturgy itself, so long as they harmonize with its true and authentic spirit.[106]

Incorporating cultural practices into liturgy requires a vital balance between "the genius and talents of the various races and peoples" and the "authentic spirit" of the liturgy. This balance is essential for marriage liturgies. Because cultural practices may run deep in the lives of the couple seeking marriage, pastors should take the time to learn more about them and consider creative ways

---

105. RITES 720.
106. *Constitution on the Sacred Liturgy*.

to incorporate them if they "harmonize with [the liturgy's] true and authentic spirit."

This section includes examples from cultures across the globe. Wise pastors will recognize that cultures carry great diversity among and within them. Therefore, this section seeks to encourage pastors to ask culturally-related questions as part of the marriage preparation process.

Community

Increasingly, Eurocentric cultures, especially in Britain and North America, view marriage as an individual, contractual affair based on Enlightenment principles. Marriage is understood not as a sacrament, covenant, or social good but as a contract between two individuals.[107] However, many non-Eurocentric cultural groups recognize marriage as a communal affair. It involves more than just the couple or even the couple's families. It involves the entire community. These two perspectives of marriage create tension, especially for Christians of the Western tradition. Liturgical scholar F. Kabasele Lumbala describes this tension among Africans, "In Africa today, Christians who marry continue to sit astride two worlds: the traditional and the occidental Christian. This coexistence is not always peaceful. The fundamentally communal nature of marriage according to African culture sometimes conflicts with the contractual and individual perspective of the other."[108] This tension exists among other cultural groups as well.

One example of this tension is the difference in understanding marriage as a dynamic process or a punctiliar moment. For example, Lumbala discusses how African cultures understand marriage as a dynamic process that begins with the betrothal and does not end until the firstborn. The scholastic notion that marriage occurs at the moment of the couple's consent is punctiliar and at odds with this more dynamic view of marriage.[109] Post-Vatican II Catholicism and other Western ecclesial traditions no longer view marriage with this sacramental scholasticism. However, the collapse of separate betrothal and post-marital rites into the marriage liturgy still supports this punctiliar view.

Betrothal practices offer a vivid example of the tension between individualistic and communal views of marriage. A popular Eurocentric view of betrothal is a request by one party (often but not always the man) to marry the other (often but not always the woman). It may involve romantic contexts ranging from an intimate dinner to skywriting the proposal in the air, but it primarily remains a practice between two individuals. Even asking permission from the woman's father is often considered quaint but unnecessary. This perspective stems from the cultural view that marriage is a contract between two parties with equal social status and romantic affection.

---

107. See Witte, *From Sacrament to Contract*, 194-215.
108. F. Kabasele Lumbala, *Celebrating Jesus Christ in Africa: Liturgy and Inculturation*, 71.
109. Lumbala, *Celebrating Jesus Christ in Africa*, 71-72.

Other cultures, however, have quite different betrothal practices. An extreme example would be arranged marriages in which two families determine whom their children will marry, and the couple has no say. In some cases, these arrangements even occur in childhood. Individual consent is absent from these marriages.

However, many other forms of communal engagement with betrothal exist that do not involve such extremes. For example, a Liberian groom and his family will come to the bride's family requesting marriage.[110] In the Ethiopian Orthodox tradition, the groom's father will ask the community elders to go to the bride's family requesting marriage. Protestant families in Ethiopia also engage in this practice.[111] These practices reinforce the understanding that marriage is a dynamic process beginning with betrothal and a communal process involving the entire family and often the community.

American Methodism recognized the communal nature of marriage with its insistence on parental consent. Many Methodist traditions expected Methodist women to have their parents' consent before the wedding. The Free Methodists even forbade ministers from performing a marriage without it. Having the bride's father "give her away" continues in this tradition (and others).[112] *The United Methodist Book of Worship*'s marriage liturgy includes a "Presentation" after the consent. The current form has evolved from more traditional forms. First, it is optional, not prescriptive. The genders of the individuals are not mentioned, and both people can be involved. Also, the relationship of the presenters to the couple is not indicated. Thus, they need not be parents. Nonetheless, the presentation includes a communal aspect to the rite.[113]

Instead of seeing the individual view of marriage as opposed to the communal view of it, a more productive perspective could be to see it as a spectrum on which multiple views exist. By engaging the church, no marriage is entirely a private affair. Furthermore, all Western marriage liturgies require the consent of the couple, so arranged or forced marriages are not permitted. Nonetheless, the degree to which the couple wishes to engage with their families and communities in their marriage can also vary greatly. The wise pastor recognizes these cultural and personal complexities when preparing a couple for marriage.

Symbols in Marriage

By their nature, symbols are multivalent, having varied layers of meaning. Symbols are also evocative. They do not merely communicate information like a stop sign informing a driver when to stop. Instead, they conjure feelings, sometimes strong ones, that might include loyalty, sentimentality, disdain, joy, identity, and many others.

---

110. Personal conversation with John Harmon.
111. Personal conversation with Rode Molla.
112. Westerfield Tucker, *American Methodist Worship*, 191-192.
113. BCW 201-202.

Symbols in marriage are no less potent. One cultural group may experience a symbol positively, while another group experiences it negatively. The same is true for individuals within these cultural groups. Wise pastors will approach symbols in marriage liturgies with discernment, listening carefully to the cultural connections involved.

The dowry is a potent symbol of marriage. The practice of the groom or groom's family giving a dowry to the bride or her family has ancient roots and is transcultural.[114] Typically, the groom or his family gives the dowry to the bride or her family at the time of the betrothal.[115] The dowry symbolizes many things. Primarily, it recognizes the communal nature of marriage. Two families, not just two individuals, are entering this new relationship. It also symbolizes the groom's commitment to the bride to marry and support her after marriage.

In some cases, the value of the dowry has socioeconomic implications for the couple. A groom who can give a significant and valuable dowry indicates his socioeconomic status. Familial tension can arise if the groom cannot give a dowry equal to the bridal family's expectations. However, a dowry can also be simple "love tokens" without the weight of socioeconomic expectations. For example, the *nduma* of the Shona people of Zimbabwe might include clothes and contemporary items like computers, watches, cellphones, and sometimes even engagement rings. If divorce occurs, the bride returns the *nduma* to the groom.[116]

Some cultural groups that no longer practice dowry-giving may be inclined to disdain it as a patriarchal practice that monetizes the bride as property to be exchanged. However, such an unnuanced perspective fails to recognize the many additional cultural practices that stem from this original practice. For example, giving *arras*, gifts of coins or other valuables, during the marriage ceremony is popular among some Latine communities.[117] *The Order of Celebrating Matrimony* of the Roman Catholic includes a blessing of the *arras* in its ceremony.[118] The engagement ring is another example of a symbol that comes from dowry-giving. In many North American and European cultures, the groom gives the bride the engagement ring as an individual act. While the groom's family may be involved in its purchase, that fact is not often revealed, making the symbol less about joining two families and more about joining two individuals.

Another communal symbol stemming from the dowry is the financial assistance families offer to the couple. For example, in some Latine communities, family members, including godparents, are involved in the financial arrangements of the wedding. The *padrinos de iglesia* will pay the "stole fee" for the clergy, while others will pay for additional gifts during the service such as the *arras, cojinas, libro*

---

114. To the author's knowledge, the practice of giving a dowry has only occurred among heterosexual marriages where each party identifies as male and female. Therefore, the gendered terms "bride" and "groom" will be used.

115. Other marriage symbols, such as arras and rings, which stem from the dowry, are given during the marriage ceremony and will be discussed below.

116. Chitakure, *African Traditional Religion Encounters Christianity*, 47–48.

117. Mark R. Francis and Arturo Pérez-Rodríguez, *Primero Dios: Hispanic Liturgical Resource*, 104.

118. OCM 64.

y rosario, and *ramo de la Virgen*. Other *padrinos* will pay for the reception after the wedding.[119] In Ethiopian culture, the couple's families will prepare special drinks, known as *bekele sebera*, between the engagement and the wedding that take several months to ferment. After the wedding, the bride takes the groom to her parents' house for the *melse*, a large celebration often involving the entire community.[120]

Other cherished symbols from dowry-giving include the groom asking the bride's family, often the father, for permission to marry his daughter. In some Latine cultures, this practice is called *pedir la mano* "asking for the hand."[121] However, many cultures involve some form of request by the groom or his family for permission from the bride's family to marry their daughter.

A similar symbol during the wedding ceremony is the father giving away the bride. This action symbolizes the joining of two families. The involvement of family members in the wedding ceremony involves many important symbols. These actions often occur immediately before or after the giving of consent. In some cases, the parents might also offer their words of consent. As discussed above, *The United Methodist Book of Worship* includes a "Presentation," which the parents gave historically.[122] Siblings and special friends comprise the "wedding court" of maid/matron-of-honor with bridesmaids and best man with groomsmen. They often stand or sit in a particular place of honor, acting as witnesses to the marriage.

Additional symbols are part of the wedding ceremony itself. One of the most prevalent symbols is the wedding ring. At times, only the bride received the ring. It is becoming more common for both parties to receive a ring. It symbolizes the couple's fidelity and love for each other. In some Latine cultures, the groom gives the bride the libro (often a hand missal in Roman Catholic ceremonies) and rosario (rosary), historically symbolizing the bride's responsibility to pray for the family. The couple would also give a *ramo de la Virgen* (gift to the Virgin Mary), usually flowers presented at the shrine of Mary.[123] Some African cultural groups use kaolin, a white mineral powder that the parents use to anoint the couple in the marriage ceremony. Other times, they will sprinkle it on the dowry to symbolize the conjoining of the families.[124]

Other actions symbolize the joining of the couple. In some Latine communities, the parents, godparents, or priest may wrap a *lazo*, which is a ribbon, cord, or combined rosaries, around the couple. Also, a veil may be placed over the head of the wife and the shoulders of the husband, as Figure 3.4 depicts.[125] In North Cameroon, the couple cuts a cord, symbolizing that the new relationship has forever changed the couple,

---

119. Francis and Pérez-Rodríguez, *Primero Dios*, 102-103.
120. Personal conversation with Rode Molla.
121. Francis and Pérez-Rodríguez, *Primero Dios*, 95.
122. BOW 202.
123. Francis and Pérez-Rodríguez, *Primero Dios*, 104-105.
124. Lumbala, *Celebrating Jesus Christ in Africa*, 71-72.
125. Francis and Pérez-Rodríguez, *Primero Dios*, 105. Also see OCM 35.

from which there is no return.¹²⁶ Some couples may also wish to light a "unity candle," which involves lighting one middle candle from two side candles. The practice has often involved extinguishing the other two candles. Some people have criticized this symbol as representing a more individualistic approach to marriage.¹²⁷ The Eastern Christian traditions involve blessing and placing crowns on the heads of the couple, which symbolizes the joy of marriage and looks forward missionally and eschatologically to their participation in the kingdom of God here and at the end of time.¹²⁸

Figure 3.4: New Liturgical Movement (https://www.newliturgicalmovement.org/2019/02/the-velatio-nuptialis-ancient-and.html) and Schola Sainte-Cécile (https://schola-sainte-cecile.com/2014/07/11/un-antique-usage-la-velatio-nuptialis-ou-le-mariage-au-poele/)

A symbol used among some African Americans is "jumping the broom." Figure 3.5 illustrates that it involves placing a broom on the floor and the couple jumping over it. Recent scholarship has uncovered a deep history behind this practice among enslaved and disenfranchised groups who did not have access to state-sanctioned marriage. This new research has caused a resurgence in the practice today, sometimes with a counter-cultural message.¹²⁹

Marriage rites are rich with symbols. These symbols can have long histories stretching back many centuries. They also have complex meanings. Pastors should avoid two temptations. On the one hand, pastors may be tempted to discard a symbol because it does not align with their cultural norms. Such a practice could have disastrous consequences for the couple, their families, and their communities, as it would likely be interpreted as rejecting their culture.

---

126. Lumbala, *Celebrating Jesus Christ in Africa*, 75.

127. Francis and Pérez-Rodríguez, *Primero Dios*, 106.

128. Alexopoulos and Johnson, *Introduction to Eastern Christian Liturgies*, 249.

129. Tyler D. Parry, *Jumping the Broom: The Surprising Multicultural Origins of a Black Wedding Ritual*.

Figure 3.5: A couple jumping the broom at their wedding (Hipstamatic shots from lisa & lorna, CC BY-SA 2.0 DEED)

On the other hand, pastors may be tempted to use symbols unquestioningly. This practice could allow the symbols to convey a meaning counter to the Gospel. Wise pastors will seek to understand the history and meaning of symbols used in marriage rites, ensuring they align with the Gospel and educating the couple, their families, and the ecclesial community on their richness.

Challenging Marriage(s)

The title of this section intends to convey both how certain practices have challenged marriage customs and how certain marriage customs have been challenging within a Christian framework. Different cultural groups attach different levels of importance to these issues. Also, ecclesial traditions disagree about many of them. Thus, this terrain is complex and should be navigated carefully and with discernment. Unfortunately, this section cannot cover any of these topics with the depth they deserve.

Because marriage holds such an essential place in every culture, some cultures have considered and still consider singlehood a challenge to marriage. Outside of religious celibacy and widowhood, persons choosing to remain single instead of married often receive disdain and even outright ostracization. For example, the Shona people of Zimbabwe consider the refusal to marry outside of physical impairment an insult to the family and the community, as it is one's responsibility to marry and bear children for the future.[130]

For many cultural groups, unmarried children over eighteen years old continue to live with their parents until they are married. With the demands of college education and underemployment, the age for marriage is increasing. Young adults spend more time living with their parents than in previous generations.[131] These changes in contemporary practices can create tension with traditional cultural norms regarding whether one should get married and by what age.

One of the most significant cultural shifts regarding marriage has been the advent of same-sex marriage. The first country to authorize same-sex marriage was the Netherlands in 2001. Since then, more than thirty other countries have authorized it.[132] The list of ecclesial traditions who will perform same-sex weddings or bless same-sex unions is growing.[133]

Nonetheless, same-sex marriage remains a contentious issue. For some countries, same-sex activity of any kind can result in imprisonment or death.[134] Some ecclesial traditions that do not condone same-sex marriage reject violence of any kind perpetrated against members of the LGBTQ+ community and advocate for a loving, pastoral response instead. To further complicate matters, some countries, like the United States of America, have used LGBTQ+ issues to increase political partisanship. Thus, pastors must navigate this issue with great care.

Virginity before marriage poses a considerable challenge among some cultural groups. Many ecclesial traditions and cultural groups forbid premarital sex. While these groups may expect men to refrain from premarital sex, women have carried the burden of shame for it in much greater proportions. Cultural expectations of female virginity have ranged from a woman wearing a white dress as a symbol of her "purity" with no such expectation of the man to physically examining a woman's anatomy as evidence of her virginity. Some cultures will permit a man to divorce his wife if evidence of her lack of virginity is discovered, while the woman has no such option.[135] The Protestant tradition in Ethiopia stresses holiness before marriage, requiring the couple to pray and fast for thirty to forty days before the marriage. If premarital sex occurs before marriage, especially if it results in pregnancy, the couple may not be married in the church. The pastor will perform the marriage in the couple's home instead.[136] At the other extreme,

---

130. Chitakure, *African Traditional Religion Encounters Christianity*, 44.

131. Richard Fry, Jeffrey S. Passel, and D'Vera Cohn, "A majority of young adults in the U.S. live with their parents for the first time since the Great Depression."

132. "Same-Sex Marriage Around the World."

133. "Faith Positions on Marriage Equality."

134. Aditi Bhandari, "Uganda's anti-gay bill is the latest and worst to target LGBTQ Africans."

135. Chitakure, *African Traditional Religion Encounters Christianity*, 47-48.

136. Personal conversation with Rode Molla.

some cultural groups encourage sexual activity before marriage as proof of fertility. Thus, this issue carries great complexity.

Many cultural groups place great emphasis on fertility within marriage. They considered and still consider child-bearing to be a wife's primary responsibility. Thus, infertility can be a challenge to marriage. Before the advent of modern biology, women were blamed for infertility. However, even with the modern understanding of reproduction, infertility still poses a significant challenge, especially for cultural groups that have a more dynamic view of marriage. If this dynamic view understands marriage as beginning with betrothal and not completing until the arrival of the firstborn, infertility leaves a marriage incomplete. The infertile member of the couple may carry great shame for their inability to complete the marriage through procreation.[137]

Divorce and remarriage can also be challenges to marriage. Because of the strong familial and communal ties that many cultural groups attach to marriage, divorce affects the couple and the wider community. Some cultural groups and ecclesial traditions, such as Taiwanese culture, do not permit divorce or have only done so recently.[138] Other cultural groups and ecclesial traditions permit divorce only under specified conditions, such as adultery. The woman's role in divorce remains complex. Some cultural groups do not allow women to initiate a divorce. Only the husband may seek divorce from his wife. Other groups permit the woman to initiate a divorce but only under specific conditions, such as infertility or acts of violence. Remarriage is equally complex as some cultural groups and ecclesial traditions prohibit remarriage, while others permit it only under particular circumstances.[139]

Two practices that pose considerable challenges to the Christian understanding of marriage are polygamy and child marriages. A Pew Research study conducted in 2020 showed that only about 2 percent of the global population lives in polygamous households. Most of those arrangements occur in certain countries within West and Central Africa and, most often, among Muslims. However, the practice of polygamy among most Muslim-majority countries remains rare.[140]

UNICEF defines child marriage as when one or both members are under the age of eighteen. According to data from 2023, four percent of the global population was married by age fifteen, and nineteen percent was married by eighteen. Child marriages disproportionately affect girls and can have devastating consequences for their social well-being.[141]

These challenging marriage practices and challenges to marriage practice pose difficulties for pastors to navigate. Great care and discernment are necessary.

---

137. Chitakure, *African Traditional Religion Encounters Christianity*, 56-57.
138. Personal conversation with John Yieh.
139. Chitakure, *African Traditional Religion Encounters Christianity*, 58-61.
140. Stephanie Kramer, "Polygamy is rare around the world and mostly confined to a few regions."
141. "Child marriage is a violation of human rights, but is all too common."

In some cases, pastors should consult their supervisory bodies before making decisions. The cultural connections with marriage are plentiful and offer richness and beauty but require wisdom.

Pastoral Perspectives

Ideally, marriages are joyous occasions. Two people wish to express their love for each other by committing to support each other. Most Western societies today permit civil weddings without the church's involvement, and the popularity of civil weddings is growing. Thus, it is especially noteworthy when such a couple wishes to commit with the prayers and blessing of the church. Therefore, pastors must be prepared for couples wanting a Christian marriage.

Policies as Pastoral Practice

Marriages may be joyous occasions, but they can also be complicated ones. Especially as church membership and attendance decline, more people are less familiar with how churches operate. Weddings and funerals can often be the only time they attend church. Also, the media has influenced people's perceptions of marriage significantly. To help couples through the marriage process, wise pastors will set up their marriage policies ahead of time in what is often referred to as a customary.

A marriage customary sets out all of a church's policies and procedures for a couple to understand when they inquire about having their wedding in that place. Pastors should check with their judicatory authorities about any policies they have regarding premarital counseling, divorce, and remarriage and reporting the marriage to those bodies. Pastors should also consult their local vestries, board of trustees, deacon board, other congregational bodies, music director, office staff, and volunteers such as altar or flower guilds. A successful customary is a collaborative effort that has everyone's buy-in, as weddings significantly impact the daily operations of a local congregation.

One policy to consider first is who may be married in the church. Some congregations choose to permit only active members to be married. This choice often recognizes the theological implications of marriage in which the congregation is asked to support the couple in their new life together. It is a challenging commitment if the couple does not regularly attend the church. Also, because weddings can significantly impact the church's operations, these congregations only wish to reserve that privilege to their active membership.

Because many people today only visit churches at weddings and funerals, some congregations see weddings as an evangelistic opportunity. Therefore, they welcome non-members to be married to invite them into greater church participation and, perhaps, membership. Also, some congregations, especially if they have a notably beautiful interior or location, will use weddings as a supplemental source of income.

Finally, some ecclesial traditions have certain restrictions on who may be married in that tradition. For example, many traditions require at least one member of the couple to be a baptized Christian. Some traditions do not permit remarriages or have special conditions for the couple in those cases. Customaries should either describe the details of these arrangements or clearly articulate that a preliminary conversation with the pastor is required before approval.

Some ecclesial traditions require premarital counseling. These specifications may include a minimum number of sessions, the involvement of a professional therapist under certain conditions, and the limits of a pastor's involvement in these sessions. Again, a customary should either detail these expectations or require a preliminary conversation with the pastor, who will then discuss them.

The customary should outline liturgical expectations for ecclesial traditions that prescribe resources and lectionaries for marriages. For example, it is popular for couples to write their vows, but not all ecclesial traditions permit this or place parameters on it. Some traditions may permit a couple to write their vows, but they must include specific verbiage from the authorized resource. They may also prescribe specific scripture passages and prohibit (or permit) non-scriptural readings in the ceremony. Even pastors of traditions that do not prescribe specific resources or lectionaries may want to consider these issues beforehand. For example, will the congregational leadership approve of a marriage that includes no Christian scriptures, prayers, or music? Wisdom suggests having these conversations beforehand as the policy can prevent misunderstandings.

If the congregation employs a music director (titles may vary), that person's involvement in the wedding preparations is vital. The selection of music for a wedding can be fraught. The customary can address essential questions about music before they become personal. For example, does the music director need to be involved in the selection of music? Will secular music be allowed in the ceremony? Does the music director have to approve soloists and other instrumentalists? Can the ceremony include recorded music? An experienced music director can assist pastors tremendously in thinking through these questions and more.

The customary should address other logistics. How are the flowers for the ceremony to be arranged? How is the building to be used? Can furniture be rearranged? Under what conditions are photography and videography permitted? What is the relationship of wedding coordinators to the church staff? Can receptions be held onsite, and if so, how are they handled? Weddings involve many logistics.

A final note about marriage licenses is essential. The customary should clarify that the couple is responsible for obtaining their marriage license as determined by the jurisdiction in which the ceremony occurs. If a couple wishes to have the ceremony in a jurisdiction other than where they live, they must ensure they have a license in that jurisdiction, not their home jurisdiction. A couple can have a civil marriage in their home jurisdiction and then have it blessed by a minister in another jurisdiction, but that is not a wedding. It is a blessing of a civil marriage.[142] Also, ministers must ensure they are licensed to perform a wedding in the jurisdiction where it occurs. Some ecclesial traditions also require ministers to be licensed or given permission to perform a wedding outside their home ecclesial jurisdiction. Also, ministers must ensure that any previous marriages have been legally dissolved before performing a new marriage. Asking about previous marriages in front of a couple may feel uncomfortable, but it is crucial. Ministers want to ensure that the wedding they are officiating is legal.

One might think that a customary detailing these expectations is a killjoy. However, such customaries can assist couples with thinking through the logistics and ease the burden of planning. Most importantly, they clearly articulate the congregation's expectations before the couple books the wedding. Then, if a couple feels uncomfortable with the expectations or does not meet them, they can choose to be married elsewhere. Wise pastors will employ creativity and pastoral sensitivity when discussing a customary with a couple to help them plan a beautiful ceremony.

Premarital Counseling

Entering the covenant of marriage requires preparation. Premarital counseling can be an essential way for couples to prepare for their new life together. Even couples that have been cohabitating before marriage can benefit from premarital counseling. As discussed above, some ecclesial traditions require premarital counseling for all couples and may require additional marriage and family therapy for particular circumstances, such as a second or third marriage.

Premarital counseling should not be confused with marriage and family therapy. Pastors should refrain from performing marriage and family therapy unless they are licensed. However, the line between the two can be blurry. One way to clarify the distinction is to limit the number of sessions with the couple. Many ecclesial jurisdictions permit a non-licensed pastor to offer a prescribed number of pre-marital counseling sessions.[143] If issues arise within those sessions that require further consideration, the pastor can refer the couple or the individual to a licensed professional. Some pastors may want all couples to agree to a minimum number of marriage and family sessions, a group premarital counseling program, or some other program before officiating their wedding. That policy can provide couples with robust preparation. However, pastors should still meet with the couple to discuss essential topics outside the wedding logistics. Additional resources at the end of this chapter, such as

---

142. This statement is true for the United States. Other countries may have different laws. Some countries only permit civil marriages that the church then blesses.

143. This restriction is often true of any form of pastoral counseling.

professional development courses and other programs, can equip pastors for this work.

Pastors can use a variety of tools to assist with premarital counseling. Assessments, such as Prepare/Enrich, have couples complete a questionnaire with categories such as money, family, children, social dynamics, and more. The pastor then facilitates a conversation between the couple about the assessment results.[144] Some pastors may have the couple read a premarital counseling book and then discuss it with them. Other pastors develop their topics for discussion. Successful premarital counseling sessions involve in-depth discussions without becoming therapy.

Pastors want to be attentive to red flags that might require a referral to a professional. For example, if one member of the couple mentions past childhood trauma, such as physical, sexual, or verbal abuse, the pastor should make a referral. Indications of active substance abuse, addiction, or untreated mental illnesses, such as depression or chronic anxiety, should flag a referral. If the couple has high levels of unresolved conflict, further therapy may be in order. Even couples cohabitating for some time can experience new challenges as marriage approaches. This turning point toward marriage can be when issues are uncovered, and pastors can help couples navigate them through proper referrals.

A pastor should never feel pressured to officiate a marriage that feels unprepared. If one or both members of the couple refuse to seek therapeutic assistance when the pastor determines its necessity, the pastor can decline to officiate the wedding. If a member of the couple reveals a secret to the pastor, such as an active affair, but will not discuss it with the other person, the pastor can decline to officiate the wedding. The pastor can decline to officiate the wedding if a couple wishes to rush the marriage and not participate in premarital counseling. Pastors want to take these steps carefully and with great discernment, but they will likely encounter scenarios in which they are necessary.

Family Dynamics

The famous saying, "When you marry someone, you marry their entire family," holds great truth. Marriages still involve families, even for couples not formed by cultural groups that prize familial and communal ties in marriage. Families influence a wedding, whether intimate, including only the couple, two witnesses, and the minister, or large with a host of family members. Wise pastors remain attentive to family dynamics.

Pastors will quickly become aware of the couple's family dynamics, whether through conversations in premarital counseling or the preparations for the ceremony. For example, parents can desire control of the wedding preparations whether the couple desires them to or not. Sibling rivalries and animosities can come to the fore as a wedding approaches. Parents' divorces and remarriages

---

144. This assessment requires training to be a facilitator. See https://www.prepare-enrich.com.

can create complexities for the invitation list. Remembering the death of a beloved family member can reintroduce unresolved grief or renew grief more potently.

Furthermore, the couple is forming a new family. Even if they had been cohabitating and whether children would be involved or not, they became a new family with marriage. New traditions will develop. Will they have Thanksgiving at one parent's house and Christmas at another? Where will they live in relationship to their family members? Where will they worship if they attend different churches or faith traditions? Or will they worship separately? If they plan to have children, in which tradition will they be raised? Marriage involves these new questions and many more.

Some marriages involve blended families. One or both members of the couple may have been previously married and have children from those marriages. These children can range in age from dependents to adults. They may be expecting a child at the time of the wedding. The dynamics between step-children and step-parents or among step-siblings can be fraught as the wedding may reignite unresolved grief over the breakup of the previous marriages. The pregnancy may have been unexpected and could have been the impetus for the marriage. Multiple dynamics could be at play in these scenarios.

Pastors can play a pivotal role in this process, but it requires excellent balance. On the one hand, pastors can assist couples in exploring these critical questions and family dynamics together. Premarital counseling can be an opportunity for the couple to discuss these issues in a focused way that previous conversations may not have offered. Pastors can offer needed comfort and support during what can be very challenging conversations and decisions.

On the other hand, pastors must ensure they do not get triangulated into the family dynamics. A classic example can be when a parent calls the pastor to discuss wedding preparations instead of discussing them with their child. Even the couple can triangulate the pastor into resolving difficulties between them. Unless pastors discover a red flag issue about which they will decline to officiate the marriage, they should remain outside them. The best role for pastors is as conversation facilitators when necessary. However, not all conversations can be had, and not all issues can be resolved before a wedding. Pastors must also accept the limited scope of their ability to assist with these complex dynamics.

Marriages Outside the Box

As the previous section implied, not all marriages involve a baptized Christian, heterosexual man and woman of the same race/ethnicity in their first marriage without children. Marriages are complex. More marriages today might be described as "outside the box" than ever before. Pastors must be equipped to handle these complexities.

Interreligious marriages are becoming more and more common. Most ecclesial traditions require at least one of the members of the couple to be a baptized Christian. The other member may be of a different faith or have no faith tradition. Planning an interreligious marriage requires pastoral delicacy and creativity.

Some ecclesial traditions prescribe the use of their liturgical rite, which may or may not account for a non-Christian participant. If the other member is of an Abrahamic faith, they could use scripture readings from the Hebrew Bible. Pastors of eucharistic traditions may want to caution against including the Eucharist in an interreligious wedding. Involving an officiant from the other faith may be permitted but should be carefully considered. For example, a nuptial blessing involving trinitarian language would be inappropriate with a non-trinitarian co-officiant. A couple may choose to get married in one tradition and then have their marriage blessed in the other. These issues and others are important to discuss in premarital counseling.

Same-sex marriage is becoming legal in more jurisdictions and sanctioned by more ecclesial traditions. Pastors in traditions permitting same-sex marriage ought to recognize the unique dynamics of a same-sex wedding. In many ways, joining two people in marriage, regardless of sexuality and gender identity, involves the same dynamics, such as communication strategies, blending finances, social expectations, and many more. Pastors new to same-sex weddings will find many similarities with heterosexual weddings.

However, differences do exist. Most of the differences are not attributed to the different sexualities or gender identities involved but instead to homophobia and transphobia's impact on the couple. If one or both members of the couple come from a cultural group in which same-sex marriage is not permitted or are of an age when same-sex marriage was not legal, they may enter marriage with caution. Internalized homophobia or transphobia may have produced thoughts that they are not worthy of marriage or that marriage is only for cisgender heterosexuals. Homophobic and transphobic messages from society and the church may have created unresolved trauma for one or both members of the couple. This ceremony could be their most public statement about their sexuality or gender identity, which can also produce anxiety. Family members may disapprove of the marriage and refuse to attend. Pastors should be attentive to these issues and identify any red flags that may indicate the need for further therapeutic assistance.

While interracial and interethnic marriages have grown in popularity, they still involve unique dynamics. Because marriage involves many cultural connections, interracial and interethnic marriages require additional attentiveness to those multiple connections. For example, a couple involving one member with strong familial and communal marital ties and another with more individualistic ties will need to navigate those different expectations. Different cultural traditions may be involved in the betrothal period and wedding. Family dynamics will likely be more complicated as they navigate two cultural systems. Past and present racism and ethnic prejudice can traumatize the couple. Interracial and interethnic marriages can be beautiful opportunities for diverse cultural celebrations, but they also need careful planning and care.

Remarriages involve complexities. Whether the previous marriages ended in divorce or death, they still impact the new marriage. Unresolved issues between the previous couple can complicate matters for the new couple, especially when children are involved. Unresolved grief over the death of a previous mate can create unrealistic expectations for the new partner. And, of course, the family dynamics become compounded as not just two but three, four, or more families can be explicitly or implicitly involved in the wedding. Children from previous marriages, especially if they are young, require care. Involving them in the ceremony can be healing, but they should feel free to opt-out if they are uncomfortable with the marriage occurring. It may take time for them to adjust to the new marriage.

Pastors may sometimes be asked to officiate the blessing of a union where the couple cannot marry. Same-sex unions were the typical example of these unions and continue to be in places where they remain illegal. However, other examples exist. Sometimes, elderly couples cannot marry because of the adverse impact of legal marriage on their social benefits such as Medicare, pensions, or Social Security. Divorce and custody arrangements might restrict someone from entering another marriage. Nonetheless, these couples desire the blessing of the church. Pastors should check with their judicatory authorities regarding these unique situations.

Ideally, marriages are joyous, but they are also complex. They involve many cultural and familial dynamics. Sometimes, they can resurface unresolved issues in one or both members of the couple, between the couple, or among family members. They can also be occasions for joyous celebration and even healing. Pastors play a vital role in helping couples navigate the many complexities of marriage. Wise pastors recognize these complexities and assist the couple with discernment and care.

Questions for Discussion

1. If the earliest centuries of the church did not include any distinctive "Christian" marriages nor blessings of marriages, how might this impact how contemporary churches practice marriage today?

2. Are there any practices in the history of Christian marriage rites described in this chapter that practitioners should be careful to avoid? Are there any practices that have fallen into disuse in your tradition that you think should be re-instituted?

3. How have you seen the public ecclesial and private domestic elements of marriage rituals combined? What are some benefits or dangers in emphasizing one side of this tension more than the other?

4. As the chapter details, Augustine and much of the Christian tradition understand the "goods" of marriage to include fidelity, offspring, and sacred obligation. How might practitioners of marriage rites emphasize all these goods with balance and without the complete exclusion of some couples (such as those unable to have biological children)?

5. Have you witnessed different cultural expectations clash in wedding rituals? Have you seen cultural differences handled sensitively or creatively?

6. What are some other "red flags" or problematic dynamics in a possible marriage not mentioned in the chapter that would make you as a practitioner consider making a referral to outside help or even declining to officiate?

Additional Resources

Documents of the Marriage Liturgy. Edited by Mark Searle and Kenneth W. Stevenson. Collegeville, MN: The Liturgical Press, 1992.
For those who desire to view primary sources of marriage liturgies for themselves, this book provides a collection of documents detailing pre-Christian and Christian wedding rituals.

Long, Kimberly Bracken. *From This Day Forward: Rethinking the Christian Wedding.* Louisville: Westminster John Knox, 2016.
From the particular context of the massive North American wedding industry, this book offers an explicitly Christian theology and practice from a PCUSA minister. It also provides a valuable appendix of suggested Scripture readings and wedding hymns.

Prepare-Enrich. www.prepare-enrich.com.
Pastors can use this assessment tool in pre-marital and marital counseling. Each member of the couple takes the survey, and the results show how in agreement they are with each other. It also can raise red flag issues. Pastors will need to receive training to use the assessment. Online options are available.

Skurtu, Angela. *Pre-Marital Counseling: A Guide for Clinicians.* New York: Routledge, 2016.
Though written for clinicians, this book still offers excellent suggestions for pre-marital counseling for pastors. Topics include "Choosing to Love," "Being Empathetic," "Fighting Respectfully," "Asking for Needs and Wants Effectively," and "Keeping the Spark Alive."

Stevenson, Kenneth. *Nuptial Blessing: A Study of Christian Marriage Rites.* Oxford: Oxford University Press, 1983.
Written by an Anglican liturgical scholar, this book comprehensively studies the internal development of marriage liturgies and rituals throughout Christian history.

Thinking Again About Marriage: Key Theological Questions edited by John Bradbury and Susannah Cornwall. London: SCM Press, 2016.
This book provides a variety of perspectives on marriage from British (and predominantly Anglican) theologians amid shifting laws and values in contemporary society.

Turner, Paul. *One Love: A Pastoral Guide to the Order of Celebrating Matrimony.* Collegeville: Liturgical Press, 2017.
While providing plenty of historical and theological discussion, this book gives constructive practical advice for celebrating the current Roman Catholic marriage liturgy with connections to marriage practices generally.

Witte, John Jr. *From Sacrament to Contract: Marriage, Religion, and Law in the Western Tradition.* Louisville: Westminster John Knox Press, 1997.
This book details the social and cultural histories surrounding the transformation of Christian marriage from the late medieval through the reformations to contemporary practice in Western societies.

CHAPTER 4

Rites of Reconciliation and Healing

As 1 Timothy exclaims, "Christ Jesus came into the world to save sinners (1:15)." The Greek word translated here as "to save" is *sōzō*. It can also be translated as "to heal"; thus, the verse could read, "Christ Jesus came into the world to heal sinners." It can also be translated as "to make whole," rendering the verse, "Christ Jesus came into the world to make sinners whole."[1]

Scripture's understanding of salvation is holistic. The ancient world did not differentiate between the spiritual and the physical. Jewish thought at that time understood the person as a whole being, not separated into mind, body, and spirit, as Greco-Roman culture distinguished it. People perceived sin as a cause of illness. Healing included both exorcistic and medicinal properties. Furthermore, grave illness often resulted in death.

Thus, this chapter will discuss ministries of reconciliation and for the sick together. These threads will sometimes intertwine to form a single cord. At other times, they will appear completely separate. At times, these ministries will have an intensely communal quality to them. At other times, they will seem quite individualistic. Cultural groups and pastoral practices will reflect these distinctions as well.

Historical Context

New Testament and Ante-Nicene Period

Arguably, the entirety of Scripture's message is about reconciliation, first with God and then with one's neighbor. In responding to the questioning of the scribes, Christ taught that the first commandment is "Hear, O Israel: the Lord our God, the Lord is one; you shall love the Lord your God with all your heart, and with all your soul, and with all your mind, and with all your strength." And the second commandment is "You shall love your neighbor as yourself (Mark 12:29-31)." Scripture is replete with commandments from God, the

---

1. James Strong, *Interlinear Greek-English New Testament*, term number 4982 on p. 70 in the Greek Dictionary.

prophets, Christ, and the apostles for sinners to repent and be reconciled with God.

However, humanity fails to heed these calls. As the Parable of the Wicked Tenants (Matt 21:33-46 describes, God first sent messengers, i.e., the prophets, but humanity would not listen. Then, God sent the Son, and humanity still did not listen but put that Son to death. The book of Hebrews discusses how Christ's sacrifice on the cross replaces the sacrifices of the Temple, "And it is by God's will that we have been sanctified through the offering of the body of Jesus Christ once for all (Heb 10:10)."

Ephesians connects Christ's sacrifice on the cross with the church's holiness, "Husbands, love your wives, just as Christ loved the church and gave himself up for her, in order to make her holy by cleansing her with the washing of water by the word, so as to present the church to himself in splendor, without a spot or wrinkle or anything of the kind—yes, so that she may be holy and without blemish (Eph 5:25-27)." However, how is the church to remain holy when its members regularly fall prey to the temptations of sin?

The consistent message of the New Testament is first a relational approach to reconciliation and then a punitive one, but only if necessary. Christ taught that a church member is first to go to the one who has offended and seek reconciliation personally. If that fails, then the member is to bring a partner. If that fails, only then should the offending person be excommunicated (Matt 18:15-17). The desire is always for reconciliation.

The church's role in reconciliation begins with the question of apostolic authority in forgiving sins, which has been fraught. In John 20:23, Christ told his disciples, "If you forgive the sins of any, they are forgiven them; if you retain the sins of any, they are retained." For centuries, the church in the East and West interpreted this statement as Christ bestowing on the church the apostolic authority to forgive sins. The nature of this authority, its method of execution, and the sins involved varied over time, but the church's role and authority were not questioned until the sixteenth-century reformations.

References to healing are equally abundant in the New Testament. Jesus' ministry involved healing those who were blind, deaf, mute, having hemorrhages, near death, and even dead (e.g., Mark 10:46-52; Mark 7:31-37; John 5; Luke 8:43-48; Mark 5:21-43; and John 11:38-44). Jesus' ministry also involved exorcising demons (e.g., Matt 8:28-34; Mark 5:1-20; and Luke 8:26-39). Christ gives this power to his disciples (e.g., Matt 10:1; Luke 9:1-2) and extends it to the apostles after his death (e.g., Acts 3:1-10 and Acts 14:8-10). Paul lists healing as one of the gifts of the Holy Spirit available to the church (1 Cor 12:8-10).

However, as with all pastoral offices, the New Testament contains no rite of reconciliation or healing. The closest example and the one most frequently cited by later theologians is James 5:14-16:

Are any among you sick? They should call for the elders of the church and have them pray over them, anointing them with oil in the name of the Lord. The prayer of faith will save the sick, and the Lord will raise them up; and anyone who has committed sins will be forgiven. Therefore confess your sins to one another, and pray for one another, so that you may be healed. The prayer of the righteous is powerful and effective.

This passage is one of only two passages in the New Testament that references leaders anointing the sick with oil. The other is Mark's account of Christ sending the twelve disciples, "They cast out many demons, and anointed with oil many who were sick and cured them (Mark 6:13)."

While not a rite of healing or reconciliation, this passage from James offers notable conditions that the church has considered necessary. First, it refers to "the elders of the church." The Greek word for "elders" is *presbyteroi* and does not mean one of advanced age. While it would be anachronistic to suggest the term refers to the modern-day ordained ministry of a priest or pastor, it signals an officeholder in the church rather than a recipient of the charismatic gift of healing.[2]

These elders are to "pray over [the sick persons]," indicating a grave illness. However, it does not necessitate the nearness of death. Later, Western theologians would posit that the anointing of the sick should be reserved only for the dying and thus called extreme unction. This passage does not indicate that necessity.[3]

The use of oil in this passage corresponds with the ancient understanding of its properties. Oil was used to coronate monarchs, ordain priests, install prophets, consecrate objects, heal the sick, and embalm bodies. People would use it for cooking, bathing, and as a medicinal ointment.[4] Oil is also used in baptism, chrismation/confirmation, marriage, and burial.[5]

James continues, "The prayer of faith will save the sick, and the Lord will raise them up." The Greek word for "save" is *sōzō*, which, as discussed above, can also mean "to heal" or "to make whole." It indicates both spiritual and physical healing. Gusmer suggests the word has this double meaning of spiritual and physical and that the context suggests the latter.[6] However, to make this distinction is a modern anachronism. The word is purposefully holistic and multivalent. The same is true for the Greek verb *egerei* or "to raise up." James could refer to the Lord raising the sick to physical health or the saved one to spiritual reconciliation in the resurrection.

---

2. Charles W. Gusmer, *And You Visited Me: Sacramental Ministry to the Sick and Dying*, 8-9.
3. Gusmer, *And You Visited Me*, 9.
4. Gusmer, *And You Visited Me*, 5-6.
5. For more details, see chapters one, two, three, and five, respectively.
6. Gusmer, *And You Visited Me*, 9-10.

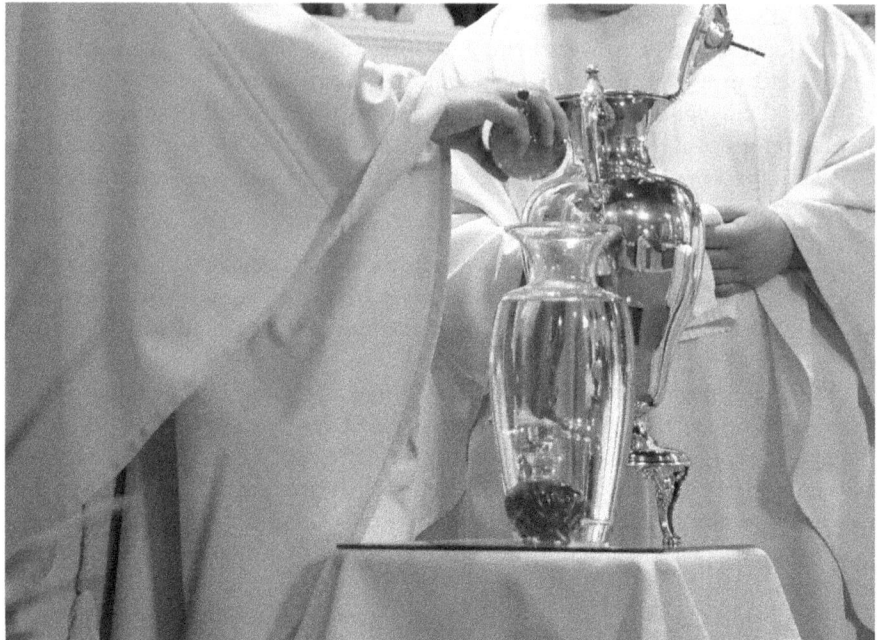

Figure 4.1: Pouring of fragrance into olive oil to create the sacred chism before consecrating it. (Copyright 2019 Arkansas Catholic, www.arkansas-catholic.org. Used with permission.)

Then, James connects healing with forgiveness of sins more closely, "and anyone who has committed sins will be forgiven." Again, Gusmer appears to be speaking anachronistically when he states, "By the forgiveness of sins, serious sins are intended."[7] This distinction between serious and less serious sins will become important in later Western developments. However, nothing in this passage indicates that distinction.

James concludes this passage, "Therefore confess your sins to one another, and pray for one another, so that you may be healed. The prayer of the righteous is powerful and effective." As expected, the Greek verb *iaomai*, or "healed," refers to physical and spiritual healing and salvation. While the passage may imply that one confesses to the elders since they are present, it does not explicitly state that requirement. Confessing "one to another" indeed precludes a solitary confession and involves mutuality but could refer to any fellow believer, whether an elder or not.

The period between the apostles and the Council of Nicea continues the interrelationship of healing and reconciliation without any specific rites for either ministry. Evidence exists of rites for the consecration of oils for healing. The *Apostolic Tradition* contains the earliest reference to this consecration, and it

---

7. Gusmer, *And You Visited Me*, 10.

occurs in the context of the Eucharist, references the anointing of kings, priests, and prophets, and mentions "tasting [it]."[8]

The Prayers of Sarapion of Thmuis, a third-century work, has many similarities to the *Apostolic Tradition* but is much more exorcistic in tone. The fifth and seventeenth prayers in the collection reference ingesting consecrated oil and water.[9] The thirtieth prayer is entitled "Laying on of Hands of the Sick." Its rubrical instruction places it before the prayer of offering in the Eucharist.[10] The fifth and seventeenth prayers also occur in the Eucharist. The seventeenth prayer has significant exorcistic material and references the oil as "an amulet warding off every demon."[11] The eucharistic context is noteworthy as it would imply that the recipients are not always gravely ill. Of course, the consecrated oil and water could be taken to the home of those gravely ill, but the reference to laying on of hands in the Eucharist suggests they were also used for lesser illnesses.

Canons of Hippolytus 21 confirms this practice, "it is a healing for [the sick] to go to the church to receive the water of prayer and the oil of prayer, unless the sick person is seriously ill and close to death: the clergy shall visit him each day, those who know him [sic]."[12] The *Didascalia Apostolorum* 16 describes this ministry of the sick as diaconal and mentions the role of deaconesses in visiting women.[13]

Alexopoulos and Johnson note an essential absence in many of these ancient prayers. They do not include an epiclesis or even mention the Holy Spirit. One important exception is in *Testamentum Domini* 1.24-25., which includes many pneumatic references. Also, this prayer appears to connect this anointing with reconciliation when it mentions "and [that] it may heal the sick and sanctify those who return, as they draw near to your faith." Also, unlike other prayers around this time, this prayer emphasizes the role of the clergy more when it says, "...us your servants whom you in your wisdom have chosen" and "...you who gave the gift of healing to those deemed worthy of this [gift]."[14]

As with healing, no rites of reconciliation exist during this period. Instead, church orders, homilies, treatises, and eventually canons describe the church's changing expectations about reconciliation. As with all documents from this period, one must be careful not to extrapolate a more general pattern of behavior from single sources. Also, these sources tend to address the more extreme cases. They mention very little about the everyday lives of church members at that time.

---

8. Paul Bradshaw, *Apostolic Tradition*, 33.

9. Maxwell Johnson, *The Prayers of Sarapion of Thmuis: A Literary, Liturgical, and Theological Analysis*, 53.

10. Johnson, *The Prayers of Sarapion of Thmuis*, 81.

11. Johnson, *The Prayers of Sarapion of Thmuis*, 53 and 67 respectively.

12. Paul Bradshaw, *The Canons of Hippolytus*, 26.

13. Sebastian Brock and Michael Vasey, *The Liturgical Portions of the Didascalia*, 23.

14. Alexopoulos and Johnson, *Introduction to Eastern Christian Liturgies*, 281-282. See Grant Sperry-White, *The Testamentum Domini: A Text for Students, with Introduction, Translation, and Notes*, 20.

Clement of Rome provides one of the earliest sources on reconciliation. It takes the form of a prayer addressed to God as creator in a *Berakah*-like fashion. The prayer is communal as it pleads with God to forgive the sins of the entire congregation. It likely occurred in a eucharistic context and is an example of *exomologesis*, the ancient form of communal confession. Likewise, Ignatius of Antioch urged the church to avoid certain notorious sinners, and Polycarp implored the church to reconcile sinners.[15]

The church order known as the *Didache*, likely written in the last part of the first century or the beginning of the second century, references confession explicitly concerning church attendance and prayer.[16] The fourteenth chapter references confession as preparation for participation in the Eucharist: "(And) according to [the] divinely instituted [day / rule] of [the] Lord, having been gathered together, break a loaf. And eucharistize, having beforehand confessed your failings, so that your sacrifice may be pure. Everyone, on the other hand, having a conflict with a companion, do not let [him/her] come together with you until they have been reconciled, in order that your sacrifice may not be defiled."[17] The communal nature of this instruction is noteworthy. Not only is one to confess individual sins but also to reconcile with a fellow Christian. Reconciliation involves individual holiness and proper ecclesial relationships. This theme of being adequately prepared for the Eucharist will remain throughout church history.

As church persecutions increased, rigorism did as well. Apostasy became one of the gravest sins, and some church leaders argued that it and other grave sins were irreconcilable. Tertullian is the most well-known exponent of Montanism, a rigorist revival movement that began in the mid-second century and grew in popularity in the third century. He wrote often about the need for repentance. One contrasting example concerns his *De Paenitentia*, written while he was still a Catholic, and *De pudicitia*, written after his Montanist conversion. In the former, he writes that all sinners may receive forgiveness and reconciliation only once for those involved in institutional penitence. In the latter, he denies the church's ability to forgive the most severe sins.[18]

This penitential institution appears to have developed in Carthage around this time. It involved separating those seeking reentry into the church from the faithful. It was similar and often ran parallel to the catechumenate for baptism. Rigorists such as Tertullian taught that one who had committed a grave sin would remain a penitent for one's entire life. God would only offer forgiveness on their deathbed.[19]

Tertullian described this process explicitly as *exomologesis*, often mistranslated as "confession." *Exomologesis* involved the public confession first of faith,

---

15. James Dallen, *The Reconciling Community: The Rite of Penance*, 19-21.
16. Aaron Milavec, *The Didache: Text, Translation, Analysis, and Commentary*, 15 (4:14).
17. Milavec, *The Didache*, 35 (14:1-2).
18. Dallen, *The Reconciling Community*, 30-31.
19. Dallen, *The Reconciling Community*, 34.

then God's praise, and then of sinfulness. Individual sins were not confessed publicly. The point was not inner conversion but rather public acts of repentance. Penitents often knelt in sackcloth and ashes at the entrance to the church, begging the congregation's forgiveness.[20]

Cyprian, who became bishop of Carthage from 249 to 258 CE, sought a compromise. He disagreed with Tertullian and other Montanists that certain sins were irreconcilable. However, he also disagreed with those church leaders who too readily received sinners back into the church. He taught that grave sinners would need to enter the penitential institution and receive a bishop's laying on of hands except under emergency circumstances when a presbyter or deacon could administer it. Those who lapsed (the *lapsi*) and those who had obtained certifications testifying to apostasy through bribery (the *libellatici*) were permitted reconciliation after long penitence. However, those who had sacrificed to idols (the *sacrificati*) would only receive reconciliation on their deathbeds.[21]

Handlaying marked this rite as it often preceded and completed *exomologesis*. For penitents, this action did not involve a conferral of the Holy Spirit. However, for those who had been baptized by heretics outside of the Church, Cyprian and Tertullian insisted that it did confer the Holy Spirit. Augustine would argue to the contrary.[22]

Similar disputes over how to handle the *lapsi* occurred in Rome. Hippolytus and Novation took the rigorist approach. Novation and the later movement of his followers Novationism insisted that the church could not forgive certain notorious sins. This doctrine led to permitting penance only once in a lifetime.[23]

Third-century Eastern Christians took a different approach. Clement of Alexandria taught that all sins were reconcilable. Origen agreed, even with his reputation for asceticism. He was one of the first theologians to offer a systematic approach to reconciliation. Sin has an ecclesial character as it is in discord with the church's holiness. Grave sins do not require a bishop's intervention to exclude from the church because the act of sin has already accomplished that exclusion. Origen's approach to reconciliation involved healing and referenced James 5:14.

Eastern theologians would take this more holistic approach. Spiritual direction and private confessions were regular practices. Public acts of penance with reconciliation by episcopal handlaying occurred but were much less frequent than in the West. Thus, the Eastern church moved more smoothly from exomologesis to private, sacramental penance and retained its ecclesial character.[24]

---

20. Dallen, *The Reconciling Community*, 32-33.
21. Dallen, *The Reconciling Community*, 38-39.
22. See chapter two.
23. Dallen, *The Reconciling Community*, 43.
24. Dallen, *The Reconciling Community*, 44-49.

Nicene Period to Early Middle Ages

Dividing periods of history is always a matter of interpretation and practicality. The history of the anointing of the sick and the rite of reconciliation cannot be easily demarcated. The movement from the Ante-Nicene period to the Nicene period is more gradual for these ministries than others, such as the initiatory rites, and the movement into the Scholastic period of the later Middle Ages is equally nebulous. These rites become more intertwined during this period and affect each other. The rite of reconciliation impacts the ministry of anointing most prominently.

As the church moved into the third and fourth centuries, it needed to address the disparities in the institutional penance system. As described in the last section, rigorists took a very conservative approach to penance, suggesting that the church could not forgive some grave sins. Other ecclesial leaders offered leniency. As could be imagined, these different approaches would cause great confusion. If bishop A excommunicates a member using a rigorist approach, but bishop B welcomes that person back into the church, what is that person's ecclesial status?

Church synods began developing a canonical penance system to address these discrepancies. Furthermore, as persecution lessened and Christianity became legal, more occupations and practices once determined sinful were permitted. Groups within the church criticized this new laxity toward perceived sinful behaviors. Monasticism became one option for more rigor. Another response was canonical penance. In this system, synods attempted to bring uniformity to the penitential system through canons. Penance laws and liturgies became extensive, and penitents became a distinct class of Christians.[25]

One example of a particularly rigorist system came from the Synod of Elvira (between 295 and 314 CE). It provides an example of how penance became juridical. For example, canon 21 instructed temporary excommunication for one who missed Sunday services more than three times. Gambling required excommunication for a year (canon 79). Some canons still required lifetime probation for a consecrated virgin who broke her vows (canon 13). Some offenses resulted in excommunication even on the deathbed, such as adultery (canon 8), abortion (canon 63), or falsely accusing a clergyperson of a crime (canon 75).[26]

These penalties were not uniform across the church, and not all bishops abided by them. The Synod of Elvira also pronounced that the bishop administering the penance must offer reconciliation. However, this practice placed much power in the hands of one bishop. To mitigate this possible abuse of power, the Council of Nicea instructed bishops to gather twice yearly to discuss excommunications. The system became more and more complicated with increasing

---

25. Dallen, *The Reconciling Community*, 56-58.
26. Dallen, *The Reconciling Community*, 58-59.

legislation. Penance became so institutionalized and burdensome that many avoided it unless someone else reported them.[27]

As the church moved into the fourth century with the Peace of Constantine, canonical penance became intertwined with initiation. Given its legal status, the church developed the catechumenal system to handle the influx of new converts to Christianity.[28] Parallel to this development, the canonical penitential system involved similar liturgical forms. Penitents, like catechumens, were separated from communicants and often placed at the back of the church. Sometimes, the bishop would visit them upon entering the church and weep with them. In the final year of their discipline, they underwent particular scrutinies during the period known as Lent in the Western church. Frequently, they would receive episcopal handlaying for reconciliation on Maundy Thursday and be welcomed back into the eucharistic community during the Easter Vigil. As *quam primum* infant baptism replaced the adult catechumenate, Lent became known for penitence rather than initiation.[29]

The practice of deathbed penance increased so dramatically during this period that it became the predominant form of penance. Like baptism, many people would defer penance until they were near death. Originally, Cyprian had authorized deathbed penance as an exception for emergency cases. However, as people feared the consequences of penance and the stricture became rigorous, they avoided penance until their deathbed. Ideally, the bishop would be present to offer handlaying as a sign of reconciliation, but such arrangements could not always be made. The offering of communion (*viaticum*) became the sign of reconciliation.[30]

At about this point, reconciliation became further entwined with the anointing of the sick and dying. Earlier evidence of anointing emphasized the blessing of the oil (and sometimes water) as described above. These descriptions did not discuss how these elements were administered, but other evidence suggests that clergy and laity could administer anointing for healing, including self-administration. However, anointing could not be administered to catechumens or penitents.[31]

Eventually, anointing became associated with three ministries: initiation, healing, and penance. Bishops consecrated chrism for initiation, oil of healing, and oil of reconciliation. These threads became more and more entwined. As questions about the rebaptism of heretics arose, bishops anointed not only catechumens with chrism but also heretics being received into the church. As penitents became a distinct class of Christians and reconciliation became institutionalized, bishops anointed penitents with the oil of reconciliation. As deathbed

---

27. Dallen, *The Reconciling Community*, 62-63.
28. See chapter one.
29. Dallen, *The Reconciling Community*, 61-88;
30. Dallen, *The Reconciling Community*, 78-79.
31. Gusmer, *And You Visited Me*, 15.

penances increased, people deferred clerical visits unless they were gravely ill. Thus, anointing for healing eventually became extreme unction.

The Carolingian Reform and Scholasticism

While canonical penance became the dominant form of the penitential system in the patristic period, its influence would not be long-lasting or widespread. The mass conversion of "barbarians" from the north in the mid-fifth to sixth centuries marked a turning point in the penitential system. Canonical penance presumed a small, tight-knit community seeking to remain pure from the persecution of the outside world. It could not handle a mostly non-catechized host of former pagans. Its elaborate and complicated legalisms were often ignored or, in the case of the British Isles, not implemented.[32]

To meet the needs of these largely superstitious converts, Celtic and Anglo-Saxon monks began to share their method of confession in spiritual direction with the laity around them. Similar to and perhaps influenced by the Eastern Church, these monks had developed a system of individual, private confession in the context of spiritual direction. This system did not have a communal dimension, as did canonical penance. The congregation did not pray for these penitents or rejoice with them when they received reconciliation through episcopal handlaying. Instead, this practice was private and individual between penitents and their spiritual directors.[33]

Another factor that influenced this system differently than canonical penance was the tariff system. In secular law, one had to pay a tariff (a tax or remuneration) to satisfy the requirements of a crime. This secular practice influenced the perception of divine-human interactions. If one committed a spiritual crime, a sin, one had to satisfy that crime with a particular penitential action. The monks developed "penitentials," lists of sins with their corresponding penances. They would offer these satisfactions as part of their guidance to penitents.

This Celtic tariff system differed from canonical penance in essential ways. First, canonical penance involved the community, while Celtic confession was individual and private. Second, the penances involved in the canonical system were meant to be public, involving excommunication and public acts of repentance, such as wearing sackcloth and ashes. The Celtic system of satisfaction could be accomplished without others' knowledge. Finally, the canonical system involved a rite of reconciliation, which included the community and episcopal handlaying. The Celtic system had no liturgical rite of reconciliation. One returned to communion after meeting the satisfaction.[34]

As Celtic missionaries began evangelizing on the continent, they brought this system. It became popular among the people but not among ecclesial leaders,

---

32. Dallen, *The Reconciling Community*, 100-101.
33. Dallen, *The Reconciling Community*, 103-105.
34. Dallen, *The Reconciling Community*, 106-107.

especially bishops, as it circumvented their role as reconcilers. Synods legislated against the practice and attempted to revive canonical penance but to little avail—eventually, a compromise developed. Canonical penance would handle public sins, while private confession handled private sins. Eventually, the time between satisfaction and the completion of penance lessened. By the Romano-Germanic Pontifical (c. 950 CE), penance became immediate. The entire rite would take about twenty to thirty minutes per penitent.[35]

While the prevailing trend was toward private penance, other forms of communal penance existed during this time. The Solemn Penances of Lent remained, even though they were more ceremonial since the ranks of penitents had thinned. Pilgrimages became another form of communal penance, with the Crusades being a notable example. Finally, general absolutions were used in other liturgies, particularly the Eucharist, during the ninth to fourteenth centuries.[36]

At about this time, the anointing of the sick and dying also changed. Previously, any Christian could administer anointing, including for oneself, but the Carolingian reform desired a stronger connection with the clergy in this ministry. However, the sacramentaries at that time only included the consecration of oils, not a complete rite of healing.

H. B. Porter identified a rite he entitled "The Carolingian Unction Order" as the earliest extant rite for anointing for healing. The rite contains Roman, Mozarabic, and Gallican elements. One of the prayers could not be identified with older prayers, and Porter concludes it to have been Carolingian. It contained a lengthy quotation from James 5:14-15, which is atypical for ancient prayers. The sick person is then anointed in all five senses. As these rites developed, the emphasis fell on the spiritual and absolutory benefits of anointing rather than physical ones.[37]

Scholastic theologians attempted to systematize these ministries in the same way as they had others. The modern reader must recognize that these theologians did not have access to the historical information already discussed. They primarily examined their present practices in the light of scripture and limited patristic sources. Had they had access to more historical data, they may have been more nuanced in their pronouncements.

For penance, scholastic theologians were particularly challenged. Their sacramental system required a sacrament to have matter and form. The Eucharist easily fulfilled this requirement as the bread and wine were the matter, and the priestly pronouncements over them were the form. The form for penance was not challenging to determine. It was the indicative formula, *Te absolvo*, "I absolve you."

However, the matter was more challenging. Peter Abelard believed contrition was the critical factor. Confession was not enough. Penitents needed to feel

---

35. Dallen, *The Reconciling Community*, 108-116.
36. Dallen, *The Reconciling Community*, 118-126.
37. H. B. Porter, "The Origin of the Medieval Rite for Anointing the Sick or Dying," 214-220.

deeply grieved about their sin to enact the mercy of God. Other theologians, such as Hugh of St. Victor, believed the power of the keys (John 20:21) was the matter. Thomas Aquinas took a compromise position. He believed that the penitent's acts (contrition, confession, and satisfaction) were all the matter, and absolution was the form.[38]

Another question the scholastic theologians considered was the order of operations. Did confession cause one to feel contrition? Or did contrition cause one to confess? Also, when does forgiveness of sins occur? Does it occur when one feels contrite or when one is absolved? If absolution can cause contrition when one feels God's mercy after hearing forgiveness pronounced, how does that affect this relationship?

Subsequent scholastic theologians taught that the sacrament was the direct cause for grace and two separate ways in which that grace was conferred. When contrition (love of God's mercy) was present, it was the effective cause for grace. However, if contrition was not present but only attrition (the self-interested concern for forgiveness and lack of punishment), then the power of the keys was sufficient cause for grace. Eventually, the acts of the penitent (sincere contrition, full confession, and satisfaction) became less prominent as the effective cause of grace, while absolution became more prominent.

Eventually, this view would become the prevailing one. Private confessions became even more popular, with other forms of communal penance falling into disuse. The Fourth Lateran Council (1215 CE) would enshrine it by requiring every Christian of rational age to offer a private, oral confession to their priest annually before receiving communion. However, despite the threat of damnation, many people only partook of this sacrament as obligated.[39]

The anointing of the sick underwent an equally significant transformation during scholasticism. Some early scholastic theologians like Hugh of St. Victor believed that anointing had both spiritual and physical benefits. It was tied to the forgiveness of sins but also could convey physical health. Later scholastic theologians, however, believed that it was only efficacious to forgive sins. They claimed that sacraments only conveyed grace, a spiritual power, not physical benefits. Therefore, anointing for healing could only convey the forgiveness of sins.[40]

But what kinds of sins could this anointing effect? Penance was necessary to forgive grave sins, now called mortal sins. This question stirred controversy between the Dominican School with Aquinas and the Franciscan School with Bonaventure and Scotus. The Franciscan School taught that anointing would cause the forgiveness of lesser sins, known as venial sins. The Dominican School believed it caused the remission of the "remnants" of sin that might impede one's

---

38. Dallen, *The Reconciling Community*, 144–146.
39. Dallen, *The Reconciling Community*, 147–148.
40. Gusmer, *And You Visited Me*, 28–29.

passage to glory. Both schools agreed that its principal purpose was the forgiveness of sins.[41]

However, when was this to occur? Both schools believed it should occur when death was imminent as a final preparation for heaven. Because penance is the normative sacrament for the forgiveness of sins, anointing should be reserved only when one is *in extremis* so that the recipient cannot sin any further. Thus, it became known as "extreme unction." These theologians transformed anointing from a sacrament for the sick to a sacrament for the dying.[42]

By the late Middle Ages, these two sacraments dominated Western Christian spirituality. Fear of dying in a sinful state became the prevailing mood. Infant baptism was an exorcistic rite for original sin, often done in private homes by midwives out of fear of infant mortality. "First Confession" became a prerequisite for First Communion. Eucharist occurred in an ancient language while the laity prayed private devotions and received communion annually at best. As private penances increased, priests found alternatives for satisfaction through private Masses and indulgences. Eventually, Mass stipends and the sale of indulgences led to increasing clerical abuses. The reformers would respond vociferously.

The Reformations

Indeed, the sale of indulgences sparked the continental and English reformations with Martin Luther's adamant condemnation, "those indulgence preachers are in error who say that a man is absolved from every penalty and saved by papal indulgences."[43] Luther considered it egregious that preachers taught that a Christian's sins could be forgiven by purchasing a papal indulgence.

However, Luther did not despise confession and absolution. He had quite the opposite viewpoint. In his "The Babylonian Captivity of the Church," he lauds not only public confession as described in Matthew 18:15-17 but also private confession, "As to the current practice of private confession, I am heartily in favor of it, even though it cannot be proved from the Scriptures. It is useful, even necessary, and I would not have it abolished."[44]

What Luther considered abominable was forced confession, "Concerning confession we have always taught that it should be voluntary."[45] Private confession could be worthwhile for a person in need of unburdening themselves to another but should not be compulsory. He also felt that enumerating sins was unnecessary. He considered spending too much time listing one's sins as a form

---

41. Gusmer, *And You Visited Me*, 30-31.
42. Gusmer, *And You Visited Me*, 31-32.
43. Martin Luther, *Luther's Works*, 31:27.
44. Luther, "The Babylonian Captivity of the Church," in *Luther's Works*, 36:86.
45. Martin Luther, "A Brief Exhortation to Confession," in *The Book of Concord: The Confessions of the Evangelical Lutheran Church*, 476.

of gaining merit before God and emphasized instead the importance of hearing the absolution. While he affirmed the power of the ordained minister to declare absolution from the "power of the keys," he emphasized God's grace and mercy at work in the absolution.

While Luther taught that one should not be coerced into confession, he also taught it was necessary to identify as a Christian and to receive communion, "However, if you despise it and proudly stay away from confession, then we must come to the conclusion that you are not a Christian and that you also ought not receive the sacrament."[46] Thus, Luther tied the worthy reception of the Eucharist with confession. He also believed that "public, obstinate sinners should not be admitted to the sacrament or other fellowship in the church until they improve their behavior and avoid sin."[47] Thus, he took the confession of sin very seriously.

Luther's views of confession, or more particularly absolution, as a sacrament are less than systematic. At the beginning of his "The Babylonian Captivity of the Church," he states forthrightly, "To begin with, I must deny that there are seven sacraments, and for the present maintain that there are but three: baptism, penance, and the bread."[48] However, by the end of the work, he nuances his response, "*Hence there are, strictly speaking, but two sacraments in the church of God—baptism and the bread.* For only in these two do we find both the divinely instituted visible sign and the promise of forgiveness of sins. The sacrament of penance, which I added to these two, lacks the divinely instituted visible sign, and is, as I have said, nothing but a way and a return to baptism."[49] Thus, technically, Luther concludes that confession does not fulfill all his requirements for a sacrament since it lacks a visible sign, like water or bread and wine. Instead, confession acts sacramentally by returning one to the sacrament of baptism. Luther's collaborator, Philip Melancthon, often described as the first Lutheran systematic theologian, described absolution as "the sacrament of penance."[50]

As for the anointing of the sick, Luther was much more straightforward. As with confirmation, matrimony, and holy orders, anointing, or extreme unction as it had become identified by this time, lacked a divinely instituted sign and, *ipso facto*, could not be a sacrament. With extreme unction, Luther went further. First, interestingly, he took issue with the apostolicity of James from which the scholastics drew their authority for its sacramental status. However, even if one accepts the book's apostolic authority, James lacked the authority to institute a sacrament as an apostle and not Christ himself. Furthermore, Luther claimed the Roman Catholic Church was not following the words of James by restricting anointing

---

46. Luther, "A Brief Exhortation to Confession," 479.
47. Luther, "Smalcald Articles," in *The Book of Concord*, 323.
48. Luther, "The Babylonian Captivity of the Church," in *Luther's Works*, 36:18.
49. Luther, "The Babylonian Captivity of the Church," in *Luther's Works*, 36:124.
50. Philip Melancthon, "Apology of the Augsburg Confession," in *The Book of Concord*, 193.

to one's deathbed. Finally, the sacrament lacked an "effective sign" because it did not produce the healing it purported to do, or, if it did, then it was no longer the sacrament of extreme unction.[51]

Luther continued with an important point that other reformers would make regarding the nature of miracles. The anointing in James was a miracle Luther believed was restricted to the early church and no longer applied after the close of the apostolic age. Nonetheless, Luther recognized the benefit of forgiveness of sins through this action because the one seeking such forgiveness believes it to be present. Thus, it had some merit as a sacred action.[52]

Luther's views on healing changed toward the end of his life. When his good friend Philip Melancthon lay gravely ill, Luther visited and prayed with him. After the visit, Melancthon's health improved, and he fully recovered.[53] In his letter to Severin Schulze on June 1, 1545, Luther referenced an incident in which he and others prayed for a cabinetmaker who was "afflicted with madness and we cured him by prayer in Christ's name."[54] He would later compose a short liturgy for healing that included prayers for exorcism and handlaying.[55]

John Calvin's view of extreme unction was very similar to Luther's. He referred to it as a "fictitious sacrament."[56] Like Luther, he believed that miraculous healing was a sign Christ and his apostles used to spread the gospel during that age. However, those miracles no longer occur in the age following the apostles. He agreed that healing was a ceremony appointed by God with a promise, his two criteria for a sacrament. However, it is not a promise for this present age. Thus, the sacrament is not efficacious. He suggested it might be called a sacrament during the apostolic age but could not be now. Unlike Luther, he does not take issue with the apostolicity of the book of James, nor does he engage with the concern of an apostle instituting a sacrament.

Calvin, Luther, and other reformers believed in cessationism, a doctrine that the miracles of the New Testament ceased after the apostolic age. This doctrine suggests that miracles were signs (*vis-à-vis* the Gospel of John) that Christ and the apostles used to spread the Gospel. However, those signs no longer occur. Instead, the stories of those miracles are intended to inspire one toward faith and works of charity. This doctrine predates the reformers and can be seen in the writings of Ambrose of Milan, Origen, and John Chrysostom. However, not all patristic and medieval theologians were consistent in this view. For example, both Augustine and Gregory the Great taught that miracles had ceased with the close of the apostolic age but also affirmed

---

51. Luther, "The Babylonian Captivity of the Church," in *Luther's Works*, 36:117-120.
52. Luther, "The Babylonian Captivity of the Church," in *Luther's Works*, 36:121-122.
53. Carl J. Scherzer, *The Church and Healing*, 67-69.
54. Martin Luther and Theodore G. Tappert. *Letters of Spiritual Counsel*, 51-52.
55. Richard G. Ballard, "Lutheran Ambivalence toward Healing Ministry," 18-19.
56. John Calvin, *Institutes*, IV:XIX:19 (637).

miracles related to the sacraments and the saints. While Calvin remained quite strict in his adherence to cessationism, other reformers like Luther and Melancthon allowed exceptions such as the efficacy of prayers for healing and exorcism.[57]

Again, Calvin's views on penance aligned with Luther's views. Calvin considered the early practice of public penance salutary. However, it was a "ceremony ordained by men [sic], not by God, which indeed are not to be despised, but occupy an inferior place to those which have been recommended to us by the word of the Lord."[58] Like Luther, he questioned the matter of the sacrament. Was it contrition or satisfaction? He also proposed that it should be the absolution.[59] Instead of being a separate sacrament, penance should be an extension of the sacrament of baptism. He noted Augustine's reference to baptism as "the sacrament of faith and repentance" and that John the Baptist preached "the baptism of repentance for the remission of sins."[60]

Following the continental reformers, English reformers did not consider penance a sacrament. Thomas Cranmer agreed with Luther that private auricular confession had merit but should not be enforced.[61] In the 1549 Book of Common Prayer, one of the exhortations before communion and the visitation of the sick referenced private confession. However, no complete rite existed, only a form of absolution in the visitation of the sick.[62]

While the reformers taught that penance was not a sacrament, they also taught the importance of repentance and worthy reception of communion. The practice of "fencing the table," in which ministers warned and even sometimes actively prevented communicants from receiving unworthily, was common during that time. Reformed liturgies often included an exhortation for worthy reception as a preface to communion. General confessions were part of the liturgy; more remarkably, elders issued communion tokens to worthy communicants.[63]

Liturgically, the 1549 Book of Common Prayer included an exhortation citing 1 Corinthians 11:27-29 and warning the congregation, "yf wee receive the same [Christ's Body and Blood] unworthily, for then wee become gyltie of the body and bloud of Christ our savior, we eate and drinke our owne damnacion, not considering the Lordes bodye."[64] The general confession came after the

---

57. Pavel Hejzlar, "John Calvin and the Cessation of Miraculous Healing," 31-77. Also see Beth Langstaff, "A Case of Apostolic Discontinuity: John Calvin on the Anointing of the Sick for Healing," 217-233.

58. Calvin, *Institutes*, IV:XIX:14 (633).

59. Calvin, *Institutes*, IV:XIX:16 (634).

60. Calvin, *Institutes*, IV:XIX:17 (635).

61. Stuhlman, *Occasions of Grace*, 132.

62. Cummings, *The Book of Common Prayer*, 25 and 75 respectively.

63. Stuhlman, *Occasions of Grace*, 132.

64. Cummings, *The Book of Common Prayer*, 22-23.

eucharistic prayer and immediately before communion to ensure one received communion with a pure heart.⁶⁵ Subsequent editions added another exhortation and moved the general confession after them.⁶⁶

The reformers also considered public repentance and excommunication necessary when dealing with serious crimes. Calvin devoted a chapter in his *Institutes* entitled "Of the Discipline of the Church, and Its Principal Use in Censures and Excommunication."⁶⁷ He never produced a liturgical form, but his student John Knox did.⁶⁸ *The Liturgy of John Knox* includes four orders related to repentance: "The Order of Ecclesiastical Discipline," "The Order of Excommunication and of Public Repentance," "The Form of Excommunication," and "The Ordoure to receave the Excommunicat agane to the Societie of the Church."⁶⁹ These various orders reflected a significant commitment to public discipline.

As for healing ministries, *The Liturgy of John Knox* took the reformed approach of extended prayer, but it included no opportunity for communion for the sick, handlaying, or anointing.⁷⁰ The form that found its way into t*he Book of Common Order* included additional prayers, scripture readings, and a prayer, "When the Holy Communion is administered," but no handlaying or anointing.⁷¹

Cranmer's 1549 edition of the Book of Common Prayer includes a liturgy for the Visitation of the Sick with several prayers and anthems. As mentioned above, it offers the opportunity for confession and absolution. It also includes both the reception of communion and anointing.⁷² However, the more reformed 1552/59 version removed the anointing.⁷³

Following the reformed approach, John Wesley did not regard penance as a sacrament.⁷⁴ Wesley rejected the Catholic distinction between mortal and venial sins.⁷⁵ However, he distinguished between "sin, properly speaking" and "sins of infirmity,"⁷⁶ with the former being "a voluntary transgression of a known law of

---

65. Cummings, *The Book of Common Prayer*, 32.

66. Cummings, *The Book of Common Prayer*, 131-134 for 1559 edition and 397-400 for 1662 edition.

67. Calvin, *Institutes*, IV:XII (452-471).

68. Bryan Spinks, "A Seventeenth-Century Reformed Liturgy of Penance and Reconciliation," 190.

69. *The Liturgy of John Knox: Received by the Church of Scotland in 1564*, 34-37, 38-60, 61-75, and 76-81 respectively.

70. *The Liturgy of John Knox*, 82-90.

71. *Euchologian, A Book of Common Order*, 337-351.

72. Cummings, *The Book of Common Prayer*, 72-81.

73. Cummings, *The Book of Common Prayer*, 164-170.

74. John Wesley, *The Works of the Rev. John Wesley: With the Last Corrections of the Author*, 10:152-153.

75. Wesley, *The Works*, 10:444.

76. Wesley, *The Works*, 12:448.

God"[77] and the latter being unconscious "deviations from the holy and acceptable and perfect will of God."[78] Wesley believed that confession to a "spiritual guide" could be beneficial but rejected it as necessary. He thought prescribing penance to be "teaching for doctrines the commandment of men." He also taught that the priest's absolution is only "declarative and conditional" because only God can pardon sin.

In his *The Sunday Service of the Methodists in North America*, he followed the 1662 Book of Common Prayer closely except for the absolutions. In Morning and Evening Prayer, he replaced the lengthy absolutions from the 1662 BCP with the collect for the twenty-fourth Sunday after Trinity.[79] In the communion service, he changed the pronouns from "you" to "us," indicating a declaration of forgiveness rather than a priestly absolution.[80]

Wesley considered communal repentance and forgiveness of paramount importance. In 1755, he celebrated a service first published by Richard Alleine in 1663 entitled *Vindiciae Pietatis: or, A Vindication of Godliness in the Greater Strictness and Spirituality of It*. Later, this service would be known as the Covenant Service and often celebrated on New Year's Eve or Day. The introduction to the service in the *United Methodist Book of Worship* states, "The heart of the service, focused in the Covenant Prayer, requires persons to commit themselves to God. This covenant is serious and assumes adequate preparation for and continual response to the covenant."[81] It continues to be celebrated in United Methodist churches to this day.

Wesley also did not regard extreme unction as a sacrament. He acknowledged that anointing the sick with oil was a rite in the early church, but the Church of Rome had made it a sacrament. The early church meant the rite to be for healing the body. The Church of Rome intended it for spiritual healing only. The early church used it for sickness with the expectation of healing. The Church of Rome intended it only for those "past recovery." Thus, he concluded that it had no scriptural warrant.[82] Wesley excluded "The Order for the Visitation of the Sick" found in the 1662 Book of Common Prayer from his *The Sunday Service*. He only includes "The Communion of the Sick."[83]

---

77. Wesley, *The Works*, 12:239 and 444.

78. John Wesley, *The Works of John Wesley*, 1:241.

79. *God in Christ Reconciling: On the Way to Full Communion in Faith, Sacraments, and Mission.* Also see Cummings, *The Book of Common Prayer*, 241 for the absolution in Morning Prayer, 251-252 for the absolution in Evening Prayer, 364 for the collect for the twenty-fourth Sunday after Trinity; and John Wesley, *John Wesley's Sunday Service of the Methodists in North America*, 8 for Morning Prayer and 15 for Evening Prayer.

80. Wesley, *The Sunday Service*, 132 and Cummings, *The Book of Common Prayer*, 399.

81. BOW, 365.

82. Wesley, *The Works*, 10:153-154.

83. Wesley, *The Sunday Service*, 155-156 and Cummings, *The Book of Common Prayer*, 442-450.

Theological Insights[84]

The historical context for the ministries of reconciliation and the sick reveals the intertwined nature of these ministries. Much like baptism, confirmation/chrismation, and the Eucharist, these ministries work together and can become problematic when artificially separated. Therefore, these theological insights will take this more holistic approach and speak of the rites separately only when the distinction is significant. Also, these insights rely on contemporary rites, which involve a theological evolution from the time of the reformers.

Reconciliation

All Christian traditions recognize the need for reconciliation with God and one's neighbor. Sin has disrupted those relationships, and the Christian church teaches that Christ's passion, death, and resurrection were the progenitors of that reconciliation. As 1 Corinthians 15:20 states, "But in fact Christ has been raised from the dead, the first fruits of those who have died." Christ has paved the way for the reconciliation of the world. Second Corinthians speaks of this ministry of reconciliation and the responsibility of the church, "All this is from God, who reconciled us to himself through Christ, and has given us the ministry of reconciliation; that is, in Christ God was reconciling the world to himself, not counting their trespasses against them, and entrusting the message of reconciliation to us." The church is responsible for sharing this message of reconciliation with the world.

All Christian traditions also agree that baptism is the first sign of reconciliation. While God's forgiveness is not confined to baptism and may certainly precede it, baptism is the central rite, a sacrament for many traditions, that publicly declares reconciliation. Some ecclesial traditions also believe that baptism cleanses one from original sin.[85]

Several traditions make this connection to baptism explicit when discussing reconciliation. The Introduction to *The Order of Penance* of the Roman Catholic Church paraphrases Romans 6:4-10, "The victory over sin first shows itself in Baptism, in which the old self is crucified with Christ, that the body of sin may be destroyed and that we should no longer be slaves to sin but, rising again with Christ, we should henceforth live for God."[86] *Evangelical Lutheran Worship* uses vivid language for this connection between baptism and reconciliation in its introduction to the rite of "Corporate Confession and Forgiveness," "Confessing our sin involves a continuing return to our baptism where our sinful self is drowned and dies; in the gift of forgiveness God raises us up again and again to

---

84. Appendix D contains the rites of reconciliation from the BCP, BCW, BOW, ELW, and OPN in tabular format for easy reference. Appendix E contains the rites of public healing from the BCP, BCW, BOW, ELW, and RITES in tabular format for easy reference.

85. See chapter one for further details.

86. *Order of Penance: Revised Rite*, 12.

new life in Jesus Christ."[87] This statement elucidates the truth that while baptism is a one-time, unrepeatable event, the need for reconciliation is necessary "again and again."

Celebrating the Eucharist or Lord's Supper is a reconciling event that occurs repeatedly. However, understanding the connection between reconciliation and the Eucharist differs dramatically among ecclesial traditions. For example, the Roman Catholic Church understands this connection to be an active, present reality, "In the Sacrifice of the Mass the Passion of Christ is made present, and the body handed over for us and the blood poured out for the forgiveness of sins are again offered to God by the Church for the salvation of the whole world."[88] Anglicans also understand the Eucharist to be an event in which "the sacrifice of Christ is made present."[89] Eucharistic Prayer C from the Book of Common Prayer directly connects the table and reconciliation: "Deliver us from the presumption of coming to this Table for solace only, and not for strength; *for pardon only*, and not for renewal."[90] Luther's Large Catechism connects the Sacrament of the Altar with the proclamation of the Word and, thus, recognizes it as a sacrament of reconciliation, "Therefore it is absurd for them to say that Christ's body and blood are not given and poured out for us in the Lord's Supper and hence that we cannot have forgiveness of sins in the sacrament."[91] However, the reformed tradition understands the connection to be one of celebration rather than active presence, "The Lord's Supper is a celebration of the reconciliation of men [sic] with God and with one another, in which they joyfully eat and drink together at the table of their Savior."[92]

Each of these ecclesial traditions understands the Eucharist to involve reconciliation. All traditions recognize the Eucharist as a celebration of Christ's redemption on the cross and its reconciling effect on the world. Some traditions go further by seeing the connection as an active one in which the sacrifice of Christ is made present in the event of the Eucharist. Thus, the Eucharist is a reconciling act.

Christian traditions also recognize the need to prepare oneself for the Eucharist. Many ecclesial traditions offer a general confession as part of the eucharistic liturgy, occurring either at the beginning of the service or in the transition between the Service of the Word and Holy Communion (or the Service of the Table).[93]

However, the Roman Catholic Church instructs that "individual and integral confession and absolution constitute the only ordinary means by which a member

---

87. ELW, 238.
88. *Order of Penance*, 12.
89. BCP, 859.
90. BCP 372, emphasis added.
91. *The Book of Concord*, 469.
92. "The Confession of 1967" in *The Book of Confessions*, 378.
93. See BCP 330-331 and 359-360; ELW 94-95; BOW 51; and BCW 19-21.

of the faithful conscious of grave sin is reconciled with God and the Church."[94] This statement requires some unpacking, which will also elucidate how other ecclesial traditions differ from it. "Individual and integral confession and absolution" refers to what is commonly known as private confession and absolution, in which a penitent confesses sin privately to a priest and receives absolution individually. Other ecclesial traditions recognize the value of individual confession or spiritual guidance and even provide rites for them.[95]

"The only ordinary means" indicates that exceptions may occur but should be rare. Such exceptions include the imminence of death without the time for individual confession or a large number of penitents and insufficient confessors such that penitents "are forced to be deprived for a long while of sacramental grace or Holy Communion through no fault of their own."[96] This requirement is the most significant distinction between the Roman Catholic Church and other ecclesial traditions. Most other ecclesial traditions do not require private, individual confession before receiving communion or as "the only ordinary means" of reconciliation with God and the church.[97]

"Conscious of grave sin" is another distinction between the Roman Catholic Church and other ecclesial traditions. The Roman Catholic tradition recognizes a difference between "venial sins" and "mortal (or grave) sins." Examples of mortal sins include murder, adultery, pre-marital sexual relations, etc.[98] Private confession and absolution are required if one has committed such a grave sin. Other ecclesial traditions do not make this distinction among sins. The distinction is necessary in the Roman Catholic Church due to the requirement for private confession. For other ecclesial traditions, the distinction is moot since they do not require private confession.

Some ecclesial traditions exclusively practice absolution, which only a bishop or priest may pronounce.[99] Some ecclesial traditions exclusively practice declarations of forgiveness, which may ordinarily be pronounced by the pastor but also can be pronounced by lay people (and deacons, if they have them).[100] Other ecclesial traditions practice a mixture of both absolution and declarations of forgiveness.[101]

This distinction indicates different understandings of the role of the "power of the keys" (Matt 16:19)." Traditions who practice absolution believe the power of the keys authorizes bishops and priests to declare absolution in the name of the

---

94. *Order of Penance*, 23.

95. BCP 447-452 and ELW 243-244.

96. *Order of Penance*, 24.

97. The practice among Eastern churches differs, see Alexopoulos and Johnson, *Introduction to Eastern Christian Liturgies*, 39-56.

98. This author lacks the expertise in Roman Catholic canon law to explicate this distinction fully.

99. For example, the Roman Catholic Church and many Eastern churches. See *The Order of Penance*, 17 and Alexopoulos and Johnson, *Introduction to Eastern Christian Liturgies*, 39-56.

100. For example, the Methodist and Presbyterian churches. See BOW 52 and BCW 21-22.

101. For example, Anglican and Lutheran churches. See BCP 448 and ELW 244.

church. They understand that forgiveness comes from God alone, but the church directly declares forgiveness and reconciles the penitent to the church through the order of the bishop or priest. A strong ecclesial connection exists between reconciliation and the church for them.

Traditions who do not practice absolution believe that only God declares forgiveness. The church's role is to proclaim God's forgiveness to all people. The pastor plays a vital role in this ministry and often declares forgiveness in public liturgies, but the authority is not through the pastor's office.

All ecclesial traditions recognize the ever-present reality of sin and the need for reconciliation. They also understand the church's primary mission is to proclaim God's desire for reconciliation with the world through Jesus Christ. This proclamation begins in baptism, continues in the Eucharist, and may occur through other services, both individual and corporate. Reconciliation always starts as a gift from God. Humanity may receive that gift through confession and be assured of God's forgiveness. Where ecclesial traditions differ is how that assurance of forgiveness is offered. For some traditions, it is offered directly through the church's orders of bishops and priests. For other traditions, the church plays the role of declaring forgiveness only.

Holistic Healing

The church's understanding of healing has evolved. One of the most significant evolutions has been a return to a holistic understanding of healing.[102] Healing is no longer reserved for the end of life but may be requested at any time and received multiple times for the same illness.[103] Furthermore, modern rites reflect an understanding of physical, emotional, and spiritual healing.

Most ecclesial traditions offer both private and public rites for healing.[104] These rites have a similar structure. They begin with a greeting, proceed into a ministry of the Word, offer a confession (either an individual rite of reconciliation or a general confession), provide a blessing of oil and anointing (although this can sometimes follow communion), and communion. Each of these sections of the rite involves theology that supports a holistic view of healing.

Many greetings at the beginning of healing services recognize Christ's healing ministry. For example, *Evangelical Lutheran Worship* begins with "Our Lord Jesus Christ healed many as a sign of the reign of God come near."[105] The Roman Catholic rite of "Anointing within Mass" begins by recalling Christ's presence among the assembled congregation.[106] These greetings also remind the com-

---

102. See the Historical Context section above for detail of this evolution.

103. This theological change is most notable in the Roman Catholic Church. See RITES, 814-816.

104. More will be said about the interplay of communal and individual rites below.

105. ELW 276.

106. RITES 832.

munity that Christ's healing ministry continues in his disciples, "...and sent the disciples to continue this work of healing—with prayer, the laying on of hands, and anointing."[107] Some greetings begin with recalling God's power to "banish all affliction both of soul and of body"[108] and Christ's promise, "Ask and it will be given you; seek, and you will find; knock, and it will be opened to you."[109]

The ministry of the Word often follows this greeting, depending on the context. Sometimes, public healing services occur within the context of the weekly or daily Eucharist, and the readings for the day are used. When these services are intended to focus primarily on healing, selected passages may be used. For example, the Book of Common Prayer offers 2 Corinthians 1:3-5 that God comforts the afflicted, Psalm 91 that God has charge over the angels, and Luke 17:11-19 with Christ's declaration to the tenth leper that his faith made him well. It offers additional scripture readings for penitence, anointing, and communion.[110] Of course, James 5:13-16 features among the suggested passages in all rites.

These passages reflect the wide range of healing ministry. The *Book of Common Worship* lists 1 Kings 19:4-8 in which Elijah despairs in the wilderness, along with Job 7:11-21 when Job complains to God. Illness and other forms of suffering can lead to the need for lament. These passages affirm that lament is scripturally warranted. *The United Methodist Book of Worship* offers several psalms that refer to God as a source of strength, assurance, and refuge, comforting those who hear these words. Some resources also offer scriptural passages for specific incidents such as a sick child, surgery, extended treatment, incurable, chronic, or terminal illness, addiction recovery, and organ or tissue donation.[111] While every possible illness or injury cannot be listed, offering specific examples can help the afflicted know that God is present in all forms of suffering.

The inclusion of confession in the rite of healing varies among different ecclesial traditions and between private and public rites. For example, the Book of Common Prayer offers the Rite of Reconciliation or a general confession, both optional. The Roman Catholic rite of "Anointing outside Mass" offers the penitential rite, while the "Anointing within Mass" presumes that one has utilized the sacrament of penance beforehand.[112] The Presbyterian *Book of Common Worship* and the Methodist *Book of Worship* include the general confession as an expected part of the service.[113] *Evangelical Lutheran Worship* does not have the option for confession.[114]

---

107. ELW 276.
108. BOW, 573.
109. BCW 734.
110. BCP 453-454.
111. ELWPC169-197.
112. RITES 820-822 and 831, respectively. The sacrament of penance may be used instead of the penitential rite in the rite of "Anointing outside Mass" if the sick person wishes; see RITES 815-816.
113. BCW 734-736 and BOW 575, respectively.
114. ELW 276-278.

These varied liturgical practices reflect different understandings of the interplay between healing and confession. Since *Evangelical Lutheran Worship* offers no opportunity for confession in its rite, this absence suggests a theological understanding that illness is not the result of sin, so confession is unnecessary. The general confession in other rites coincides with its use as preparation for communion rather than being a response to the illness. Even among traditions that offer the Rite of Reconciliation or the sacrament of penance, care is taken not to associate it with the onset of illness. In the Book of Common Prayer, the rubrical instructions state, *"The Priest may suggest the making of a special confession, if the sick person's conscience is troubled, and use the form for the Reconciliation of a Penitent."*[115] Thus, the motivation for using that rite is the sick person's troubled spirit, not a connection between the illness and sin. Similarly, the Roman Catholic rite of "Anointing outside Mass" states, "If the sick person wishes to celebrate the sacrament of penance, it is preferable that the priest make himself available for this during a previous visit."[116] Having two visits, one for penance and the other for anointing, suggests the desire to separate the two sacraments in the sick person's mind.

These changes illustrate a radical theological shift in the connection between sin and healing. Previous rites made this connection much more explicit. As discussed above, the sacrament of extreme unction was primarily about forgiveness of the "remnants" of sin to prepare one for death.

Other traditions also made this connection explicit. For example, in the 1662 Book of Common Prayer, "The Order for the Visitation of the Sick" begins with "Remember not, Lord, our iniquities, nor the iniquities of our fore-fathers: Spare us, good Lord, spare thy people whom thou hast redeemed with thy most precious bloud, and be not angry with us for ever."[117] A sick person would inevitably believe that the illness resulted from God's punishment for sin, generally or particularly.

Modern rites of healing wish to sever that connection with God's punishment. Some rites take a more extreme view by not even offering a confession. Other rites recognize that illness can stir up spiritual concerns and wish to relieve the sick person spiritually. Nonetheless, special care is taken not to draw a connection between illness and punishment.

Another significant theological shift is the inclusion of anointing with oil, especially among traditions from the reformations. Of course, the Roman Catholic Church includes anointing with oil as it is the "matter" of the sacrament and, therefore, necessary. Anglican, Methodist, Lutheran, and Presbyterian traditions also include anointing with oil, but optionally in all cases.[118] These traditions do

---

115. BCP 454.
116. RITES 815.
117. Cummings, *The Book of Common Prayer*, 443.
118. See BCP 456, BOW 580, ELW 277, and BCW 738.

not recognize anointing as a sacrament; therefore, anointing with oil is not a sacramental action.[119]

Evangelical Lutheran Worship offers a poignant explanation for using "physical gestures of healing" such as handlaying and anointing, "These signs, first given in baptism, tell us again that we are sealed by the Holy Spirit and marked forever with the cross of Christ, who is health and salvation for the whole world."[120] Thus, handlaying and anointing in the healing rite reminds one of their baptism. They make a direct connection to Christ through baptism.

Likewise, offering communion in the healing services makes a connection with Christ. Baptism symbolizes the beginning of life in Christ, and the Eucharist sustains that relationship. Thus, it is fitting for healing to occur within a eucharistic context. In nearly all liturgical rites, the handlaying and anointing occur before communion.[121] This placement within the service recognizes that communion is the theological "climax" of the service.

Communion involves the entire Body of Christ, even at a hospital bedside. Not only is Christ present in communion, but so is the Body of Christ, the church. This theological truth reminds the sick person that they are not alone. The church's prayers accompany them on this journey of illness and hope for healing. It is vital for one to feel a part of the communion of saints during illness.

Sickness, especially grave illness, can evoke fear of death. The Eucharist is eschatological, pointing toward the hope of Christ's return. Communion reminds the sick person that Christ has destroyed the power of death through his resurrection. They can be assured of eternal life, whether physical healing will occur or not, and communion sustains that hope.

Individual and Corporate Participation

All pastoral offices involve a tension between corporate and individual or familial participation. For example, baptism and marriage often involve this tension between the family and the church. However, ministries of reconciliation and the sick can feel this tension most keenly due to the contexts in which they often occur. When a pastor visits a sick person at home, in the hospital, or when a congregant seeks reconciliation in a pastoral conversation, the ministry feels individualistic. Nevertheless, public ministries of healing and reconciliation are regular parts of the life of most churches.

Theologically, this tension is essential to consider. Beginning with reconciliation, the historical practice of canonical penance clearly illustrated a corporate practice. In this practice, the church excommunicated one who committed

---

119. The Anglican tradition recognizes anointing as a "sacramental rite," which is a "means of grace, [but] not necessary for all persons in the same way that Baptism and the Eucharist are." See BCP 860.

120. ELW 276.

121. The *United Methodist Book of Worship* includes it after communion but with the option to move it before communion; see BCW 579.

a grave sin and offered reconciliation to penitents through a very public process. This somewhat rigid discipline gave way to a much more individual practice that began with personal spiritual guidance and eventually became the modern-day practice of penance. One consults privately with a priest. This practice retains an ecclesial dimension in seeking reconciliation with God and the church. Nonetheless, the practice feels personal and individual.

Many ecclesial traditions practice a general confession and absolution as part of their liturgical services. This practice differs from canonical and individual penance in that the community recites the confession together. No persons are singled out as the designated penitents. The assumption is that the entire assembly confesses their sin. This distinction is evidenced by using the first-person plural rather than singular in these rites.[122]

At times, confusion can occur regarding the nature of general confession. Is it a moment in the liturgy when each person contemplates their sins and then aggregately confesses them and receives an aggregated absolution? Or is it a corporate confession of sin as the church? Some forms of general confession leave this distinction obscure. For example, the general confessions in the Book of Common Prayer and the *Book of Common Worship* use the first person plural but do not reference the church or any other corporate entity.[123] Thus, one could believe that one is confessing sins aggregately or corporately. On the other hand, *The United Methodist Book of Worship* explicitly refers to the church: "We have failed to be an obedient church."[124] *Evangelical Lutheran Worship* gives a similarly corporate confession with "God of all mercy and consolation, come to the help of your people."[125]

The lack of an explicitly corporate referent in the general confession could be an example of liturgical multivalence. The editors may have deliberately sought multiple meanings in the formulation to allow participants to experience both an aggregated confession and a corporate one. The corporate nature of sin remains a controversial idea, especially in predominantly Western cultures. Many people formed by Western cultures are comfortable confessing their personal sins but are much less comfortable with confessing a sin "done on our behalf."[126] While awareness of systemic evils, such as racism, misogyny, and homophobia, rises, some people remain unconvinced and resist the idea of corporate sin.

Scripture offers a blended approach. The prophets preached against the corporate sin of the people of Israel and called them to corporate repentance.[127]

---

122. For example, "Most merciful God, we confess that we have sinned against you..." from BCP 360. See also ELW 95, BCW 20, and BOW 51.

123. BCP 360 and BCW 20-21.

124. BOW, 51.

125. ELW 239.

126. *Enriching Our Worship 1: Morning and Evening Prayer, The Great Litany, and The Holy Eucharist*, 56.

127. See Isaiah 1; Ezekiel 14:6; Hosea 6 as examples.

However, individuals like Cain, Jacob, and David committed personal sins. In the New Testament, Paul speaks of corporate sin in Romans 1:18-32, and James speaks of "confessing your sins to one another (5:16)." A fulsome view of sin recognizes its personal and corporate natures.

Similarly, reconciliation is both individual and corporate. However, this view involves theological complexities with which not all ecclesial traditions will agree. Three permutations exist. One is individual to individual (God). Another is individual to corporate (the church). A third is corporate (the church) to individual (God).

All ecclesial traditions agree that God offers reconciliation to all people. Where ecclesial traditions disagree is the church's role in that form of reconciliation. The Roman Catholic Church teaches that sin is simultaneously against God and one's neighbor. Therefore, reconciliation must also involve both. The sacrament of penance is necessary for grave sins and is recommended for venial sins. The sacrament of penance requires a priest and, thus, is corporate because the priest represents the church.[128]

Other traditions do not distinguish between types of sins and, therefore, do not require the sacrament of penance. In the case of the Anglican tradition, bishops and priests offer absolution, but deacons and laypeople may declare forgiveness. In other ecclesial traditions, pastors and lay people only declare forgiveness. So, the priest or pastor does not act as a necessary intermediary for grave sins, as in the Roman Catholic Church. Nonetheless, the pastor symbolizes the church and acts as an agent of the church in its mission to proclaim repentance and reconciliation. Thus, reconciliation can occur between individual and individual, but the church is involved when proclaimed in liturgical rites, whether publicly or privately.

All sin affects the Body of Christ, the church, but notorious sins are particularly harmful by their scandalous publicity. From its inception to today, the church has recognized that certain scandalous sins require a public response. Historically, that public response was canonical penance. Today, that response occurs more rarely and often in a more muted fashion. Nonetheless, ecclesial traditions excommunicate members when necessary.

However, the Roman Catholic Church's understanding of the corporate effect of sin holds even if the sin is not publicly scandalous. All sin weakens the Body of Christ and interferes with the church's mission to offer reconciliation to the world. Therefore, general confessions in other traditions acknowledge this effect with the Scriptural quotation, "We have not loved our neighbors as ourselves."[129] Thus, reconciliation is always individual to corporate as well.

What about corporate (the church) to individual (God)? Does the church confess and seek reconciliation with God as a corporate body? Some ecclesial traditions affirm that belief by explicitly including the church in their general

---

128. *The Order of Penance*, 13-17.
129. BCW 20, BCP 360, BOW 51, and ELW 95.

confession formularies: "We have failed to be an obedient church."[130] However, the theological challenge with this view is the belief held by most ecclesial traditions from the Nicene-Constantinopolitan Creed that the church is "one holy catholic and apostolic." What does it mean for the church to be "holy"? When referring to God's holiness, it means without sin. Does that apply to the church? If so, how can the church confess sin if it is sinless? If individual church members are not sinless, how can the church be holy?

Ecclesial traditions answer this question differently. The Vatican Two document, "Dogmatic Constitution on the Church" states, "While Christ, holy, innocent and undefiled knew nothing of sin, but came to expiate only the sins of the people, the Church, embracing in its bosom sinners, *at the same time holy and always in need of being purified*, always follows the way of penance and renewal."[131] Thus, the Roman Catholic Church acknowledges that the church is holy but needs confession and reconciliation. The distinction is that this tradition does not distinguish among its members. This view also corresponds to the church being "one."

The Anglican tradition states, "The Church is holy, because the Holy Spirit dwells in it, consecrates its members, and guides them to do God's work."[132] This simple statement does not preclude acknowledging that members of the church sin. Instead, it recognizes the agent of holiness as the Holy Spirit. Similarly, the Lutheran tradition recognizes the church as " the assembly of saints who truly believe the gospel of Christ and have the Holy Spirit. Nevertheless, we admit that in this life many hypocrites and wicked people, who are mixed in with these, participate in the outward signs."[133] The church is holy because the Holy Spirit works in it even when its members sin.

The reformed tradition takes a different view. This tradition understands the church as comprising an invisible and visible component. The invisible component is "the whole number of the elect, that have been, are, or shall be gathered into one, under Christ the head thereof, and is the spouse, the body, the fullness of Him that filleth all in all."[134] The visible church "consists of all those throughout the world that profess the true religion."[135] Thus, the invisible church comprises the elect who genuinely align with Christ. The visible church comprises those who "profess" that they are but may not indeed be so. Therefore, "This catholic Church hath been sometimes more, sometimes less, visible. And particular churches, which are members thereof, are more or less pure, according as the doctrine of the gospel is taught and embraced, ordinances administered,

---

130. BOW 51.
131. Second Vatican Council, "Dogmatic Constitution on the Church, sec. 18, emphasis added.
132. BCP 854.
133. *The Book of Concord*, 178.
134. *The Book of Confessions*, 27.1 (243).
135. *The Book of Confessions*, 27.2 (243).

and public worship performed more or less purely in them."[136] Furthermore, "the purest churches under heaven are subject both to mixture and error: and some have so degenerated as to become apparently no churches of Christ."[137] Thus, the reformed tradition also recognizes that the church contains error but claims that some may contain so much error as to no longer be considered a church.

Thus, if an ecclesial tradition recognizes the church to already be "holy" because of its intrinsic relationship with Christ, it could not participate in confession and repentance corporately. Individual members could and are urged to do so, but not the church corporately. However, if a tradition understands the church to be "holy" through the agency of the Holy Spirit as a process, it could be possible to corporately confess and seek reconciliation as part of that ongoing process of sanctification.

The ministry of healing also involves both individual and corporate aspects. Sickness besets individuals but has a corporate effect, especially with serious illnesses. Families and caregivers feel the impact of serious illness. Congregation members may also feel the burden as they pray and care for the ill among them. Thus, when congregants seek the ministry of healing, whether in a public service or a private space such as their home or the hospital, the church is involved through their prayers and the ministry of the pastor or other designated person sent from the church.

Theologically, all pastoral ministries are individual and corporate, especially those of reconciliation and the sick. Whether publicly in a worship service or privately in one's home or the hospital, how the ministry occurs does not alter the theological truth that the entire Body of Christ is involved. Nonetheless, pastors need to share this theological truth with those to whom they minister, especially if they are isolated from the corporate body.

Cultural Connections

The understanding of sin, guilt, shame, and reconciliation are deeply contextual. This section offers cultural examples from across the globe. These are not monolithic examples of any one culture. Instead, the wise pastor will recognize them as opportunities for further exploration.

Cultural Understandings of Sin

Theology is deeply contextual.[138] Cultural factors strongly influence theological understandings of sin, guilt, and shame, which will also affect one's theology of reconciliation. It is essential to understand that a Eurocentric view of sin, guilt, and shame has influenced the history of reconciliation and its current liturgical

---

136. *The Book of Confessions*, 27.4 (244).
137. *The Book of Confessions*, 27.5 (244).
138. Stephen B. Bevans, *Models of Contextual Theology*, 3-7.

rites in many ecclesial traditions. Diverse theological traditions further influence this Eurocentric view.

For example, a Eurocentric Protestant view understands sin as a personal breach of God's commandments. Even when violating these commandments involves others, this view primarily recognizes the issue as being between God and the sinner. One might be encouraged to seek reconciliation with the offended person, but this reconciliation would be between two individuals, not a communal affair. Even when ecclesial traditions use general confessions and absolutions/declarations of forgiveness, the experience of sin and reconciliation is individualized.

A Eurocentric Roman Catholic view of sin and reconciliation involves the church but in a more abstract manner. The church plays an intermediary role but still on an individual-to-individual basis. One confesses to an individual priest, who symbolizes the church. Thus, the experience of confession and reconciliation remains individualized even when the theology explains it as communal.

Many non-Eurocentric cultures understand sin, shame, and guilt differently, even when strongly influenced by Western theology. For example, Empereur and Fernández recognize an interesting dichotomy among Latine communities, especially more traditional ones. Latine cultures are intensely communal. Familial and communal ties run deeply in these communities. Thus, many Latines recognize sin in a communal way. It is not unusual for a Latine Roman Catholic to mention in confession not only their offenses but also the offenses committed by a family member. Even though they may not have committed the offense themselves, they feel responsible for it because of their deep familial connections.[139]

Individual, auricular confession is juxtaposed against this communal view of sin, especially among traditional communities. Thus, these communities have not yet fully received the reforms of Vatican Two, which have attempted to restore reconciliation as an ecclesial affair rather than an individual spiritual practice.[140] Many Latines, especially traditional ones, only wish to confess their sins individually to a priest, but those sins may not necessarily be just their own. Thus, the practice is individualized, but the concept of sin is communal.

In addition to this communal view of sin, many Latines carry a deep shame that extends beyond personal or familial sins. Empereur and Fernández explain that "the *mestizo* culture was born of conflict and violence, whether that of the conquistadors of long ago or that between immigrants and the dominant culture in the U.S. today."[141] These historical and present experiences produce trauma, which can be internalized as cultural shame. Of course, not all Latines will feel this shame, nor will it always be felt. This shame should not be confused with the guilt of sin but is a cultural reality for many Latines to which pastors must attend.

Other cultures differ in their understanding of sin and its relationship with God and others. For example, Lumbala describes "sin" in the Bantu context of

---

139. Empereur and Fernández, *La Vida Sacra*, 231.
140. Empereur and Fernández, *La Vida Sacra*, 231.
141. Empereur and Fernández, *La Vida Sacra*, 218.

Africa as "anthropocentric" in that offenses are committed among people rather than against God. They believe God cannot be offended, so a person's sin is not an offense against God but rather an offense only against one's community. Like Latines, they understand sin communally. The wrong affects the individual, that person's family, and the entire community. Therefore, "A wrong, once committed, even in private, is a disorder that is introduced into the universe and the social tissue."[142] This disorder has cosmic and social consequences. It has created an imbalance, which the parties directly involved and everyone in the community feel. Because the sin is not an offense directly against God, it can be reconciled more readily among those offended. This distinction produces a sense of optimism in that sin is not a pernicious characteristic of all humans for which only a divine remedy is available but, instead, is something that can be conquered and resolved.

East Asian cultures, highly influenced by Confucianism and Buddhism, have a similarly optimistic view of human nature. The Augustinian notion of original sin has a more pessimistic view of human nature with its understanding of human depravity. This view, introduced into East Asian cultures by Jesuit missionaries, has clashed with the more optimistic outlook of Confucianism and Buddhism.[143]

Chow identifies two further cultural elements that challenge the reception of the Western understanding of sin. The first is linguistic. The Jesuit missionaries appropriated the use of the Chinese character *zui*, and its Japanese cognate *tsumi* and Korean cognate *choe* from Chinese folk religion and Japanese Shintoism. These cognates carry the sense of a societal wrong one has committed and been caught doing. Thus, they have both a communal understanding and a juridical one. A "sinner" could be understood as a "convicted criminal," which has a very different connotation than the Western view of private, individualized sin.[144]

The third East Asian cultural element that challenges the Western notion of sin is the national movements of the twentieth century. Traditional Protestant Christian communities preserved the more Augustinian view of sin. However, more liberal East Asian Christians understood this view as challenging their country's desire to pursue modernity.[145]

Since the Second World War, East Asian Christian theology has rediscovered the doctrine of sin. In the late 1980s in China, a growing area of academic research known as Sino-Christian Theology developed. Scholars in this field may identify as atheists rather than Christians but find Christian teaching helpful in explaining philosophical ideals. In this case, they believe the Christian view of sin explains the trouble in the world with greater accuracy than the optimism of Confucianism or Buddhism.[146]

---

142. Lumbala, *Celebrating Jesus Christ in Africa*, 61.
143. Alexander Chow, "The East Asian Rediscovery of 'Sin,'" 127-128.
144. Chow, "The East Asian Rediscovery of 'Sin,'" 127.
145. Chow, "The East Asian Rediscovery of 'Sin,'" 129.
146. Chow, "The East Asian Rediscovery of 'Sin,'" 129-130.

Other East Asian cultures have developed a theology of sin stemming from the South Korean Minjung theologians of the early 1970s when they were under dictatorial rule. The "minjung" are the poor and the oppressed. Like Liberation Theology, they argue that Jesus identified himself with the "minjung" rather than the ruling class. Therefore, the term "sinner" could not be applied to the "minjung" as the oppressed but only to the oppressors. Thus, they deemphasize the Augustinian notion of original sin in favor of a more socially constructed understanding of sin.[147]

Finally, Kazoh Kitamori's *The Theology of the Pain of God* understands sin as *tsurasa* or "pain." He draws from Japanese folk drama that recognizes one may suffer and die to provide life for others. Thus, Christ's suffering and death on the cross enacted this human pain. God the Father experienced pain, not on the cross but through the Son. As Chow explains, "…the pain and suffering of humanity points to the pain and suffering of God. That is, the suffering of humanity points to the extent of God's wrath against sin and God's love to unforgivable sinners."[148]

Cultural groups understand the doctrine of sin differently. Sometimes, these different understandings result from deep cultural roots, often connected to indigenous cultures and religions that predate Christianity's arrival. Sometimes, they stem from recent or even contemporary experiences of oppression. Liberation, feminist, womanist, and other contextual theologies have challenged the Augustinian doctrine of original sin and the Western view of individualized sin among Eurocentric cultures. All these contexts could influence one's view of sin and, therefore, of reconciliation.

Communal Reconciliation and Lament

Since many cultural groups recognize sin differently, they also recognize reconciliation differently. The prevalent view of reconciliation in the West has become individualized and private. In the Roman Catholic tradition, that view is most explicit with private, auricular confession. An individual sinner goes to an individual priest to confess their sins privately and receives individual absolution.

As noted above, Anglicans made private confession optional, and Lutherans offered it optionally in their most recent liturgical resources. Most Protestant groups rejected private, auricular confession in favor of a general confession. However, it often remains unclear if the general confession is a combination of individual confessions of sin or a communal confession of sin, especially given the Eurocentric view of sin as individualized and private.

Other cultures share some similarities with Western reconciliation but also involve significant differences. For example, the reconciliation process of the Bantus begins with the "unmasking," in which guilt is determined.[149] This process involves confession and contrition. Offenders confess their wrongdoing or sin

---

147. Chow, "The East Asian Rediscovery of 'Sin,'" 131.
148. Chow, "The East Asian Rediscovery of 'Sin,'" 132.
149. Lumbala, *Celebrating Jesus Christ in Africa*, 62.

and express remorse, or contrition, for it. However, rather than occurring in the presence of a priest alone or privately with God, it occurs in a communal setting with the community elders present.

How the offense will be remedied is then discussed. The remedies could range from saying a good word to replace a bad word previously uttered to acts of public humiliation. Thus, satisfaction is necessary but toward the person offended and the community rather than toward God. Lambala provides an example of a daughter-in-law who had badmouthed her father-in-law. When the father-in-law died, and the funeral proceeded near his son's home, the daughter-in-law approached the coffin on her knees, asked for forgiveness of the corpse, and paid a sum to the man's brothers. Then, the coffin could proceed to the son's home.[150]

Lumbala shares another example of reconciliation within a Christian context. Two individuals in conflict came before the community elders to identify culpability and remedy. Later, they convened at the church for a rite of reconciliation. It began with readings from Scripture. The parties in conflict came forward, and the elder allowed each to speak, recognizing their error publicly. They spat on the ground to renounce vengeance. The guilty party paid the fine and shared tea and milk as a symbol of reconciliation. The rite concluded with a song of thanksgiving and a prayer.

Interestingly, Lumbala states, "This is not a sacramental reconciliation, but the Christians hold it in high esteem, especially when a priest is present for the ritual."[151] Within his Roman Catholic context, this rite lacks sacramental efficacy. One wonders if a Eurocentric view of individual confession to a priest constricts this theological interpretation. Later, Lumbala recognizes that "God does not limit forgiveness to sacraments alone. The effectiveness of a rite of reconciliation outside of the sacrament of penance does not in any way diminish the privileged place of the sacraments in the economy of salvation."[152]

As described above, many Latine communities, especially traditional ones, juxtapose a communal understanding of sin with an individualized approach to reconciliation. They come to private, auricular confession and will confess family members' sins and their own. Another example of this juxtaposition is the tendency to participate in the rite of reconciliation on major feast days such as Our Lady of Guadalupe for Mexicans, Lent and Holy Week retreats, or *El Dia de los Muertos*. These festivals unite the community for celebration in a very communal way. And they often include private, auricular confessions beforehand. As Francis and Pérez-Rodríguez explain, "[Confession] is a private moment to 'come clean' before God through naming one's personal sins and receiving absolution from the priest. The phrase *me acuso, padre* (I accuse myself, Father) introduces the penitent's listing of sins and serves as a key phrase which sums up the meaning of 'confession' for many Hispanics."[153]

---

150. Lumbala, *Celebrating Jesus Christ in Africa*, 62.
151. Lumbala, *Celebrating Jesus Christ in Africa*, 64.
152. Lumbala, *Celebrating Jesus Christ in Africa*, 67.
153. Francis and Pérez-Rodríguez, *Primero Dios*, 86.

Empereur and Fernández describe three types of communal reconciliation that can assist pastors in understanding these cultural complexities. Beginning with one's estrangement from God, they describe this experience as having less to do with violating a commandment as being out-of-synch with God and the church. Thus, reconciliation becomes more holistic in deemphasizing a recital of cataloged sins and emphasizing restoration of wholeness with God and neighbor.[154]

The next type of communal reconciliation involves "the overcoming of self-estrangement" and "the movement to greater self-integration.[155] Initially, this type may appear individualized. However, to be self-integrated, one must be open to the community and the resources it can provide. Empereur and Fernández recognize the strength of the communal aspect of Latine cultures in this regard.

The final form of reconciliation involves "the overcoming of the alienation from society."[156] This form of reconciliation can be incredibly challenging because of the historical and contemporary oppressions that many Latines have experienced. Justo González speaks of this alienation as a form of bondage. It is more than just an inner or psychological alienation. It "is an usurpation of rights, leading to an improper subjection of one part of creation to another."[157] Early Christian theology saw this as a bondage to the Devil, who has usurped authority from God over humanity. González recognizes another form of usurpation, political oppression. People have usurped control over others through slavery, war, and economic and racial injustice.

Andrew Sung Park, a Korean liberation theologian, describes the results of this oppression as *han*. When one is the victim of sin or oppression, be that individual, such as domestic abuse or societal racism, they experience suffering, marginalization, and powerlessness. "Han is the suffering of the innocent who are caught in the wicked situation of helplessness. [It] is a physical, mental, and spiritual repercussion to a terrible injustice done to a person, eliciting a deep ache, a wrenching of all the organs, an intense internalized or externalized rage, a vengeful obsession, and the sense of helplessness and hopelessness."[158]

This usurpation by oppression can produce varied responses in the victims. One response is to internalize the oppression. Some members of oppressed communities may feel that they deserve the oppression. They may begin to believe themselves inferior, just as their oppressors do. Reconciliation becomes about more than just the guilt of individual sins. It may include overcoming the shame of oppression.

Another response can be externalized. It might be experienced as anger and rage. Destructively, one may seek revenge on the oppressors. Constructively, one

---

154. Empereur and Fernández, *La Vida Sacra*, 216.
155. Empereur and Fernández, *La Vida Sacra*, 216.
156. Empereur and Fernández, *La Vida Sacra*, 217.
157. Justo L. González, "The Alienation of Alienation," in *The Other Side of Sin: Woundedness from the Perspective of the Sinned-Against*, 67.
158. Andrew Sung Park, "The Bible and Han," in *The Other Side of Sin*, 47–48.

may seek to eradicate the causes of oppression through social justice advocacy. If the situation does not change for the victim, their *han* deepens.[159]

Rites of reconciliation may assist but may not be fully effective, especially if they involve only private, auricular confession. Rites of public lament may be more effective. "If confession is the cry of the sinner, then lament is the cry of the victim."[160] The Psalms are filled with lament. In his *Liturgies of Lament*, Frank Henderson provides helpful guidelines for creating these rites.[161]

Finally, the church must go beyond rites of reconciliation or lament in addressing oppression. The church must actively engage in social justice work to dismantle systems of racism and oppression more broadly. The church will also need to investigate its complicity in these systems of oppression and seek reconciliation with the victims on which it has perpetrated them.

Cultural Understandings of Healing

Like sin and reconciliation, many cultures understand sickness and healing socially and cosmically rather than just individually and physically. Western medicine has emphasized physical symptoms and treatments, although more attention has recently been paid to social, emotional, and spiritual factors. Non-Western cultures accept the physical dimensions of sickness and healing but often include social, emotional, and spiritual elements.

For example, Lumbala discusses how the Bantu people of Africa recognize illness as "a disorder introduced into the social and cosmic fabric."[162] Sometimes, illness is understood as the result of human neglect, such as a failure of proper hygiene, poor nutrition, etc. In this regard, illness is understood physically. It might also be understood socially. An enemy might inflict one with an illness. Cosmically, illness can be the result of divine punishment.

Latine communities also understand sickness in social and cosmic terms. When one is ill, the family gathers to provide support. Francis and Pérez-Rodríguez describe two views on illness that Latines may hold. The first view understands sickness as divine punishment. God may be upset with the individual and the whole family. Thus, when family members gather, they will use rituals that involve *promesas* (promises), *mandas* (pilgrimages), candles, novenas, Masses, and other activities to appease God's anger on the family.[163]

Another view stems from this view of God's punishment but involves a more passive approach. Some Latines may describe illness as *es su destino* (it is his/her destiny) or *estabas escrito* (it was written). These expressions can accompany a

---

159. Park, "The Bible and Han," 48.
160. Ruth C. Duck, "Hospitality to Victims: A Challenge for Christian Worship," in *The Other Side of Sin*, 168.
161. J. Frank Henderson, *Liturgies of Lament*.
162. Lumbala, *Celebrating Jesus Christ in Africa*, 79.
163. Francis and Pérez-Rodríguez, *Primero Dios*, 124.

feeling of despair or helplessness in the face of God's divine wrath. However, it can also indicate a surrender to God's will. The expression *resignarse a la voluntad de Dios* is literally translated as "to resign oneself to the will of God." However, *resignarse* has more of the connotation of a faithful surrender to God's plan than a hopeless despair.[164]

Additional cultural factors play an important role in healing ministries in non-Western cultures. For example, the role of indigenous faith healers is typical in many non-Western cultures. For example as Figure 4.2 depicts, Mexican and Mexican-American communities have *curanderos(as)*, healers who trace their lineage back to the Mayans and Aztecs. Caribbean cultures have *santeros* and *espiritistas*, which include elements of African cultures.[165] The Bantu in Africa might call "a strong one," or divine healer, when an illness persists and appears grave.[166] These indigenous faith healers can be male or female and often are part of a long lineage of such healers passed down from generation to generation.

Figure 4.2: Traditional healers (Larry Lamsa, CC BY 2.0 DEED, https://www.flickr.com/photos/larry1732/19906598281)

The Charismatic Movement also plays a vital role in cultural understandings of healing. While this movement is global and interfaces with many Christian traditions, its growth has been robust in African and Latine communities. This

---

164. Francis and Pérez-Rodríguez, *Primero Dios*, 124-125.

165. Empereur and Fernández, *La Vida Sacra*, 237.

166. Lumbala, *Celebrating Jesus Christ in Africa*, 79.

tradition recognizes the healing ministry among any congregation member, lay or ordained, male or female. Frequently, persons who have had a grave illness and experienced healing from it become faith healers in their communities.[167]

In her study of women faith healers, Oliva Espín recognizes a dichotomy between Western medicine and psychotherapy and these practices. Western medicine and psychotherapy understand the causes of illness to be internal in terms of physical symptoms or intrapsychic in terms of psychological issues. However, the remedies are external in terms of doctors and psychologists. Indigenous and faith healers recognize the cause of illness to be external, often divine, but the remedy is personal through faith and personalized rituals. Espín notes, "The traditional healing system thus places responsibility outside clients and helps them recover an internal locus of control. The prevailing psychodynamic psychotherapeutic approaches, in contrast, make clients responsible for their difficulties but externalize their control."[168] These indigenous faith-healing practices empower people amid the disempowerment of serious illness.

Healing as Prophetic Ministry

When sickness and healing are understood holistically, they inevitably include ailments beyond the individual or family. Social ills, such as racism, misogyny, and classism, among others, become not just socio-political issues but contribute to health issues that impact the well-being of those affected.[169] Not only can they produce or exacerbate physical ailments such as diabetes, cancer, and heart disease, but they also create psychological problems, such as depression and anxiety, and spiritual conditions, such as hopelessness and despair.

Healing ministries return the church's focus to the sick, elderly, and dying. These church members can easily be seen as castaways, especially in the Western medical infrastructure, which favors institutionalization over family care. The emphasis on caring for one's family members, which constitutes many non-Western cultures, provides a prophetic voice for the church, calling its members to recognize the sick, elderly, and dying as full members. James Empereur poignantly draws this connection between the anointing of the sick and prophetic ministry.

> Anointing is a major form of proclamation of the Christian community. And while it surely proclaims to the sick and elderly that they can transcend the debilitating confines of the present because it promises a future as something which is human, it voices even more loudly to the believers once anointed in baptism, that there is freedom from the

---

167. Empereur and Fernández, *La Vida Sacra*, 247-248.
168. As quoted in Empereur and Fernández, *La Vida Sacra*, 249.
169. For an instructional article on the impact of institutionalized racism on health, see Belinda L. Needham, Talha Ali, et al., "Institutional Racism and Health: A Framework for Conceptualization, Measurement, and Analysis," 1997-2019.

suffocating attitude which capitulates to the present with its brokenness and loss of integrity.[170]

Ministries of healing bring this prophetic call to the forefront of the church's ministry, especially when all members, regardless of order or gender, are involved.

Ministries of healing can also be ministries for social justice. In raising awareness of the challenges many people living with chronic illness, disabilities, and old age experience, the church can respond prophetically by calling for societal changes. Empereur and Kiesling proclaim, "A prophetic community will raise issues about national health policies, everyone's right to health care, a wholistic approach to health and healing, hospices, and medical care that promotes human dignity."[171] Embracing people with conditions that may be regarded as socially stigmatizing, such as HIV/AIDS, obesity, lung cancer from smoking, and others, proclaims the Gospel message of Christ's healing ministry to the dispossessed of his time.

Ruth Duck also suggests that healing liturgies could be a fruitful way for victims of oppression to experience relief. She cautions that the tendency to include confession and forgiveness of sin with these healing rites could suggest to victims that they are somehow culpable for the oppression they have experienced. Therefore, they should be excluded from rites involving them.[172]

Many cultural groups understand healing and reconciliation as intertwined. Their holistic view of illness and sin contributes to this understanding, as does the oppression many have endured. Pastors should be cautious in attempting to draw lines of causality between sin and illness, but they should also be attentive to how healing and reconciliation operate synergistically.

Pastoral Perspectives

Public Services of Healing as Pastoral Care

Most ecclesial traditions offer a public service of healing. These services can be essential moments of pastoral care for congregants. Sometimes, people are reluctant to seek pastoral care from the clergy. They may feel that their illness is not severe enough to warrant a personal visit or that the clergy only visit when one is nearing death. Also, if someone is relatively new to a congregation, they may not feel comfortable or understand the process of calling on the clergy for pastoral care. Public services of healing can be a way to offer pastoral care in these circumstances.

Public healing services are also helpful for congregants who may not be ill. It reminds the entire church of their vocation to be "communities of care."[173] If

---

170. James Empereur, *Prophetic Anointing: God's Call to the Sick, the Elderly, and the Dying*, 200.
171. James Empereur and Christopher Kiesling, *The Liturgy That Does Justice*, 227.
172. Duck, "Hospitality to Victims," 173-174.
173. Richard Wall, personal communication, May 23, 2023.

healing ministry is perceived as the responsibility of only the clergy, lay people miss out on the opportunity to be involved. Even in ecclesial traditions that recognize anointing as a sacrament or sacramental rite, the laity can be involved through their prayers. Public healing services embody the need for intercessory prayer poignantly.

Also, as noted above, public healing services can offer opportunities for lament and healing from less tangible ills than physical sickness, such as abuse, systemic injustice, mental illness, addictions, etc. These services can be tailored to address a particular set of pastoral concerns. They can be especially fruitful for spiritual retreats, quiet days, and other special gatherings. If they occur at a regularly scheduled public service, it would be wise to offer clear and plentiful communication so that congregants are not surprised by the particular emphasis on the service.

For communities that celebrate the Eucharist frequently, public healing services may be incorporated into a eucharistic service and require some special attention. First, a public healing service involving anointing and/or handlaying will require congregants to come forward to receive prayers and those healing gestures. This additional procession will require time and should be factored into planning the entire service. Congregants will likely understand the extra time involved if the service is dedicated to healing.

Second, the expected attendance should be factored into the number of healing ministers present. If a significant number of people are expected, it would be wise to have additional healing ministers than just the presider of the service. Some ecclesial traditions require only ordained clergy to offer healing ministry. For ecclesial traditions that permit lay people to be healing ministers, pastors should select those volunteers with discernment. Lay healing ministers can speak powerfully to the comprehensiveness of the church's vocation toward healing.

Catechesis around healing ministries is another crucial factor when offering public healing services. Some traditions that recognize anointing as a sacrament or sacramental rite may have specific teachings on who may receive this ministry. For example, one might wish to come forward in a public healing service out of concern for a family member or friend's illness rather than one's own. Sacramental traditions do not typically offer sacraments by proxy. However, this person has presented a pastoral need by coming forward. One could offer this person prayer without anointing. Or one could offer anointing, recognizing that sickness affects more than just the ill person but also family members and friends.

Finally, when public healing is within the context of the Eucharist, it typically occurs before communion. This order recognizes that communion is itself an act of public healing. In fact, one might argue the supreme act of healing. Thus, each Eucharist is also a public healing service. Pastors can emphasize this truth through preaching and catechesis.

Visiting the Sick

Arguably, one of the most important ministries for any pastor is visiting the sick and elderly in a community. As discussed above, ministry to the sick is an integral part of the vocation of any Christian community. Christ's ministry centered on the sick, not only due to his compassion for them but also as a recognition of how easily they can become outcasts in society and the church. Pastoral care for the sick is as much an issue of social justice as it is pastoral ministry.

Due to differing congregational sizes and clerical resources, the senior pastor may not always be able to visit all the sick and elderly in the community. Some traditions have deacons who can assist in this ministry. Some traditions also have lay ministers, sometimes called lay eucharistic ministers or visitors, who can assist in this ministry. Including all orders of ministry in visiting the sick reinforces that this ministry is one for the entire church. Nonetheless, a senior pastor should not delegate all pastoral visits to assisting clergy, deacons, or lay ministers. It is just as crucial for the senior pastor to be involved in the intimacy of this ministry as others are.

Most formational programs for clergy include training in pastoral care. Nonetheless, senior pastors would be wise to confirm that new clergy have received training and recognize that further mentoring will likely be necessary. Similarly, a wise pastor will carefully discern the lay people asked to participate in this ministry. Pastors may want to distinguish between lay eucharistic ministers, whose ministry is primarily to bring the sacrament to the sick and elderly, and pastoral care, which may entail more involved conversations. Of course, some lay people may be well trained, even better trained, than clergy as professional pastoral counselors or through other formation programs. They are a gift to any church.

When discerning lay eucharistic ministers, certain qualities are essential. First, the person should have appropriate emotional boundaries. The sick and elderly are often in a vulnerable state. They may not want extensive conversation. Troubling them with one's challenges and even joys may be burdensome for them. Second, the person should understand the limits of the ministry. Sometimes, the sick and elderly may face additional challenges beyond their illness. Maybe they are having trouble with their insurance, receiving proper health care, maintaining their expenses, family issues, or facing other challenges. Lay eucharistic visitors are not equipped to be social workers. Recognizing the boundaries of the ministry is a critical quality in a lay eucharistic minister and an essential item to emphasize in training. Finally, lay eucharistic ministers should have a mature faith. Again, they may not be equipped to answer all spiritual questions that the sick and elderly often carry, but they should be people of prayer and mature Christian faith. All these qualities are equally crucial for clergy as they are for lay ministers.

Preparing for a pastoral visit with the sick and elderly requires a few considerations. First, one should honor the agency of the person. Sometimes, well-meaning congregants will inform the pastor that someone in the community is in the hospital or sick at home and that they "should go and see them right away." However, not everyone desires a visit from their pastor or other church members when sick. A wise pastor will call the person first to see if they want a visit. Calling the spouse, partner, or close family member is appropriate if the person cannot receive calls. Also, it is best to ask if the person would like to receive communion during the visit. Sometimes, people do not desire communion for varied reasons.

Responding to a pastoral visit request requires discernment. If death is imminent and the person or their close family and friends desire a visit, that visit should be a "drop everything" priority. However, discerning the imminence of death can be challenging. Also, most pastoral visits are not near the point of death. For example, praying with someone before they enter surgery is a beautiful gift but may not always be possible given the many demands on a pastor's time. A post-surgical visit may be all one can do. Every pastoral visit is not nor should be considered an emergency.

Care should also be taken about the time spent on the visit and the frequency of visits. Elders confined to living at home or in an assisted care facility often experience loneliness and would gladly welcome a weekly visit for an extended time. Wise pastors do not promise what they cannot keep. A consistent monthly thirty-minute visit is much better than weekly visits of two hours that cannot be maintained. Some people have difficulty tracking time and may need a gentle reminder that the time for the visit is approaching its end. Pastors need healthy boundaries around their family and personal time.

An introduction is appropriate when visiting someone in a hospital or assisted care facility, even with a previous acquaintance. People recovering from an illness and some elders can experience confusion when they are in unfamiliar surroundings. Also, confirming that it is still a good time for a visit allows the person to readjust if they are not feeling well enough for a visitor. Being confined to a bed, especially in a hospital or in greater levels of care in assisted living, can be very challenging for many people. Wise pastors will not sit on the bed and will request permission to move personal items if space is needed for setting up communion to honor the person's confinement.

Beginning the visit with a personal conversation helps establish a connection with the person. If they are seriously ill, they may not wish much conversation or be unable to converse. In those circumstances, limited conversation is warranted. Lulling conversation can be the cue to turn to the liturgical rite. However, as mentioned above, some people may not track their time well, and gently moving in that direction could be appropriate. Concluding the visit with a short personal conversation can also be helpful, but an extended conversation at this point could be especially burdensome. If regular visits are warranted, and the person is cognitively alert, an approximate notice of the next visit can be comforting. However, giving a specific date is to be avoided unless one is confident it can be kept.

General Confessions, Penitential Rites, and Liturgies of Lament

The common perception of the rite of reconciliation recognizes it as occurring privately between the penitent and the priest, which will be discussed in the next section. However, the most common form of reconciliation in many ecclesial traditions occurs publicly within the liturgical rite. General confessions, penitential rites, and liturgies of lament are examples of reconciliation within public liturgical rites and require pastoral provisions.

In many ecclesial traditions, a general confession is a regular part of the Eucharist.[174] Without care, this part of the service can become rote and lose its potency. Pastors can mitigate against that tendency with the judicious use of silence. For example, if one rushes from the bidding to the general confession, one encourages the congregation to give little thought to what they are about to confess. Pausing after the bidding allows the congregation to collect their thoughts, ponder their corporate or personal complicity in sin, and offer a more heartfelt confession. Similarly, the absolution or declaration of forgiveness should be said from a prominent location and with authority. People need and want to hear the words of forgiveness proclaimed boldly.

Some ecclesial traditions have a penitential rite or rite of corporate confession and forgiveness that can be incorporated into the Eucharist or act as a stand-alone service.[175] Offering these services during penitential seasons, especially Lent, allows the congregation to participate in reconciliation more thoroughly than just a general confession. Also, moving the general confession or the penitential rite to a different place in the liturgy draws attention to it. So, for example, if the general confession occurs typically after the congregational intercessions or right before communion, moving it to the beginning of the service will make it more prominent. If this movement occurs with the change in the liturgical season, such as from the season after Epiphany to Lent, that also draws attention to the new season.

For particular circumstances, a pastor may offer the penitential rite or rite of corporate confession and forgiveness outside of penitential seasons. For example, it could be a meaningful offering during specific retreats or quiet days. If the congregation has experienced a period of contention, this public rite could be healing for the parties involved. However, care should be taken to prepare for the rite through instruction and conversations among the hurt parties. Using the rite without preparation could worsen the divisions rather than heal them.

Liturgies of lament can be poignant services in which people, especially people who have experienced a great deal of oppression or other forms of calamity, can corporately express their myriad feelings to God. Because of the powerfully personal aspects of these services, they do not lend themselves to regular use in

---

174. For example, see BCP 330-331 or 360; ELW 94; BOW 51; BCW 19-21.
175. BCP 319-320 or 351-353; ELW 238-242.

the primary Sunday worship service. Incorporating them in a particular service around the focus of the lament prepares the participants for the poignancy of the service. These liturgies could be a powerful part of a retreat or a particular service after a community calamity. Gathering ecumenically for these services can emphasize the importance of the lament more strongly. In all cases, wise pastors will plan these services with great care.

Hearing Confessions[176]

Some ecclesial traditions provide rites for individual reconciliation.[177] For Roman Catholics, the sacrament of penance is required to receive communion faithfully. For other ecclesial traditions, it is not required but may be beneficial. Sometimes, congregants want to share their sins and hear the words of forgiveness through a more personal encounter than general confessions or penitential rites permit. The rite of reconciliation can also help someone mark a significant passage of time that private prayer may not do as well. Some congregants may need help confessing particular sins or hearing moral guidance from the pastor. For some people, a particularly destructive secret must be brought to light. The rite of reconciliation can provide spiritual relief in these cases where a general confession may not.

Anyone can hear a confession and offer a declaration of forgiveness. However, some ecclesial traditions permit only bishops and priests to declare absolution because of their ecclesial role. Nonetheless, any pastor should be prepared to hear a confession. Confessions differ from pastoral counseling but can often arise within pastoral conversations. Pastors need to discern when a pastoral conversation becomes a confession, especially in traditions that see it as a sacrament or sacramental rite.

Pastors should also be mindful of gender and power dynamics. While any pastor can hear a confession, should a pastor hear one in particular situations? For example, it might not be wise for the senior pastor to hear a confession from another staff member. Will all women feel comfortable confessing to a man or vice versa? When hearing the confession of minors, pastors must assure privacy and safety. Offering referrals to other confessors could solve some of these potential puzzles. Pastors can also ensure that the space is private but still visible and that other people are in the building during the visit.

All pastors ought to avail themselves of the rite of reconciliation. Before one can hear a confession, one should understand the vulnerability of offering a confession. Sharing the deep burdens of one's heart requires trust. Receiving such burdens requires a significant level of pastoral sensitivity. By participating as a penitent, a pastor can see that sensitivity modeled toward them.

---

176. This section is heavily indebted to Julia Gatta and Martin L. Smith, *Go in Peace: The Art of Hearing Confessions*.

177. See *Order of Penance*, 31-33; BCP 446-452; and ELW 243-244.

Furthermore, regular confession can be a great benefit to all pastors. Congregants often project their aspirations of perfection on pastors. The rite of reconciliation affords pastors a place to be fully human and able to share all their sins and failures. Also, pastors need to hear the good news of forgiveness proclaimed to them as they often proclaim it to others. Many pastors are prone to perfectionism, and regular participation in the rite of reconciliation reminds them of their regular imperfections. Also, regular participation in the rite of reconciliation may bring the temptation toward scrupulosity to light.

If someone has never offered a confession, they may wish to offer what is known as a "first confession" or "life confession." It usually involves examining one's entire life. Martin Smith's book *Reconciliation* provides exceptional guidance for anyone preparing their first confession.[178] The preparation process can take between three to six weeks. Dividing one's life into significant sections balances the reflection between too much detail and too little consideration. Scriptural passages such as 1 Corinthians 13 on the qualities of love, Exodus 20 on the Ten Commandments, Mark 12:28-31 the Summary of the Law, Matthew 5 and 6 on the Sermon on the Mount, and Galatians 5:22-26 on the fruits of the spirit can be valuable guides for self-reflection.

Preparing a life's confession has several benefits. By reviewing one's life entirely, one can see specific patterns emerge. Perhaps many sins are rooted in pride, greed, envy, or other of the "seven deadly sins." These patterns can be spiritually illuminating. If one struggles with the sinfulness of a particular thought or behavior, the rite of reconciliation can help make that distinction more transparent. When no new material comes up during self-reflection, the preparation time ends.

Pastors should prepare a special place for hearing confessions. The traditional "confessional booth" may or may not be appropriate or available. Nonetheless, the vulnerability of this rite requires consideration. The church's worship space is often the best place to hear confessions as it reminds the penitent of the corporate nature of reconciliation. However, it needs to be a private area within that space. If other people in the building frequent the worship space, using it would not be advisable. Confidentiality is paramount. Also, if the penitent offers a life confession, its length might necessitate another area. Some churches may have a particular office for spiritual direction or pastoral counseling. A simple space with two chairs, a bible, the text of the rite, and an icon or cross can suffice. The pastor's office might be appropriate if it can provide confidentiality and avoid distractions.

When the penitent arrives in the space, the pastor should greet them neither too cheerfully nor too somberly. This greeting is not the time to catch up on personal business. The penitent may choose to sit or kneel, depending on the space.

---

178. Martin L. Smith, *Reconciliation: Preparing for Confession in the Episcopal Church*, 65-100. For a Lutheran discussion of the importance of private confession, see Dietrich Bonhoeffer, *Life Together*, 87-99.

The penitent will choose the desired form if the rite offers more than one form. The pastor can offer an extemporaneous prayer, giving thanks for God's forgiveness, and then begin the rite after a moment of silence.

As the penitent confesses their sins, the pastor listens deeply, asking the Holy Spirit for guidance. Especially during a life confession but also at other times, the pastor is listening for underlying patterns that may indicate a deeper issue. Also, pastors are listening to issues confessed that may not be examples of sin. If the penitent expresses emotion, the pastor should be present but not offer comfort. The upcoming declaration of forgiveness or absolution is the most superb comfort that can be offered.

After the penitent has confessed their sins, the pastor will offer counsel. For the novice pastor, this portion of the rite can be nerve-wracking. Therefore, one should remember that the most critical counsel is the proclamation of forgiveness. Nonetheless, the penitent will expect some form of response. Pastors need to remember that counsel is neither therapy nor advice.

First, the pastor can remind the penitent of God's grace and forgiveness and the bravery it took to be this vulnerable. The penitent may be expecting some form of judgment or punishment, so these first words of comfort are essential. The pastor can ask open-ended questions if portions of the penitent's confession are vague. Then, the counsel can focus on the underlying patterns observed and questions of sinfulness. Pastors must be equipped enough in moral theology to guide a penitent through a moral problem.

The temptation to minimize the sins confessed should be avoided. The fact that the person confessed the act indicates the seriousness with which they regard it. Also, a seemingly superficial act may point to a deeper spiritual issue that was left unconfessed. Discerning pastors will recognize those signs.

However, some penitents can become scrupulous in their confessions. This scrupulosity could be a desire to prove their ultimate righteousness and, therefore, a source of pride. It may also be the product of deep shame or even past spiritual abuse. Pastors may want to inquire gently, especially if the person seeks confession regularly and the pattern of scrupulosity persists.

If the penitent confessed actions involving another person, such as sexual impropriety outside of marriage, the pastor wants to be judicious in suggesting restitution. Sometimes, asking the penitent to speak to the other party can cause more harm than good. Pastors need wisdom in these circumstances.

Offering penances requires discernment. Superficial penances unrelated to the acts confessed have dubious benefits, but penances that lead the penitent to deeper spiritual engagement can be beneficial. For example, asking someone who has confessed lustful thoughts to say ten "Our Fathers" may feel like a technical solution without any connection to the act confessed. However, asking that person to read and reflect on a specific Scriptural passage about lustful thoughts might be more helpful to their spiritual growth.

Many ecclesial traditions consider the seal of confession as absolute. Before hearing a confession, pastors should clarify the expectations of their ecclesial and civil jurisdictions concerning this seal. Suppose someone confesses a sin that a civil authority would consider subject to mandated reporting, such as abusive behavior toward a minor or elder, threats of violence toward someone or themselves, or a crime. In that case, the pastor needs to be clear about their civil and moral responsibility.

Using discretion and understanding can assist in these circumstances. For example, suppose someone unknown to the pastor requests the rite of reconciliation. In that case, the pastor should have a preliminary conversation to get a general sense of the person and what they may confess. Also, because pastoral conversations do not fall under the seal of the confession, it is crucial to have clear boundaries of when the rite begins and ends. Most ecclesial traditions expect contrition; some will withhold absolution until contrition is expressed. Requiring someone who has committed a crime to report it can express contrition. However, unless one works in prison ministry or a similar setting, most confessions do not involve criminal or violent behavior.

After the confession and counsel, the pastor offers the absolution or declaration of forgiveness. Laying hands on the penitent's head or shoulders during this time can express the weight of this proclamation and allow the penitent to hear the words and feel the forgiveness bodily. Most rites will conclude with a final prayer, which could be extemporaneous.

As the rite concludes, the pastor should ask the penitent to discard any notes they brought, especially for a life confession, to symbolize God's forgiveness of those sins. The end of the rite is not the time for frivolous conversation. The penitent can leave in silence or after a short farewell. The pastor should not reference anything discussed during the rite with the penitent unless they bring it up.

Reconciliation and healing are deeply intertwined. Pastors may find congregants desire the rite of reconciliation when visiting them during an illness or other health procedure. Also, ministration at the time of death might involve reconciliation. Depending on the setting, pastors may need to attend to confidentiality issues more closely, especially if the congregant is in a shared hospital room or other family members are present.

The church's central message is salvation, which is reconciliation and healing. A holistic view understands these practices as spiritual, physical, personal, and communal. They are deeply intertwined and incorporate cultural elements that precede the history of Christianity. Wise pastors recognize that they require deep discernment and wisdom to offer them faithfully. They also acknowledge their need for these practices to continue their pastoral ministry fruitfully.

Questions for Discussion

1. Did any elements of the historical material in this chapter discuss practices that you think should be reinstituted in contemporary Christian practice? Should any be avoided?

2. Are there any practices or common beliefs in your place of ministry that might be working against understanding healing holistically, including physical, emotional, and spiritual well-being? How might you encourage a more holistic conception with pastoral sensitivity?

3. In your cultural context, is sin and reconciliation understood as more individualistic or communal? As a minister, how might you work to support your congregation while guiding them towards a more balanced understanding?

4. How might a practitioner in ministries of reconciliation attempt to avoid linking illness with punishment for sin while maintaining a connection between reconciliation and healing?

5. What practices in ministries of reconciliation and for the sick and dying that you learned about in this chapter or that you know from elsewhere might you use to maintain a connection between public and private rites?

6. This chapter discussed the importance of taking questions of oppression seriously when engaging in ministries of reconciliation. What new liturgies or new emphases in current practices might you introduce in your context in addressing oppressive systems and actions in these ministries?

Additional Resources

Evans, Abigail Rian. *Healing Liturgies for the Seasons of Life.* Louisville: Westminster John Knox Press, 2004.
This book assembles a wide collection of modern healing liturgies from many churches. The liturgies are helpfully sorted by applicability to a particular season of life or a particular crisis for ministers' reference.

Gatta, Julia and Martin L. Smith, *Go in Peace: The Art of Hearing Confessions.* New York: Morehouse Publishing, 2012.
Two experienced Episcopal priests provide a practical guidebook to hearing confessions. It provides both historical and theological overviews and a section that includes texts of sample confessions with the authors' practical and pastoral commentary.

Gusmer, Charles. *And You Visited Me: Sacramental Ministry to the Sick and Dying*, rev. ed., Studies in the Reformed Rites of the Catholic Church, Vol. 6. Collegeville: The Liturgical Press, 1990.
This book comprehensively introduces the post-Vatican II Roman Catholic rites of anointing the sick and dying. While certainly focused on contemporary Roman Catholic practices and liturgies, it also provides a detailed history of Christian anointing, theological perspectives on sickness and healing, and pastoral considerations relevant for any practitioner of Christian liturgies of healing.

Kidder, Annemarie. *Making Confession, Hearing Confession: A History of the Cure of Souls.* Collegeville, MN: The Liturgical Press, 2010.
Written by an ordained Presbyterian, this book introduces practices of confession. It is beneficial for clergy and ministers interested in these practices, who come from traditions that do not practice sacramental confession.

Morrill, Bruce. *Divine Worship and Human Healing: Liturgical Theology at the Margins of Life and Death.* Collegeville: Liturgical Press, 2009.
A well-known Catholic liturgical theologian gives a recent theological treatment of Christian liturgy and healing. While richly philosophical and predominantly academic, it also includes stories from the author's experience as a priest and pastor.

The Other Side of Sin: Woundedness from the Perspective of the Sinned-Against. Edited by Andrew Sung Park and Susan L. Nelson. Albany, NY: State University of New York Press, 2001.
This edited volume by various theologians provides different themes on reconciliation and healing from the point of view of those who have been sinned against. This perspective is critical to consider when engaging in reconciliation and healing ministries.

Smith, Martin. *Reconciliation: Preparing for Confession in the Episcopal Church.* Cambridge, MA: Cowley Publications, 1985.
While this book is written in the context of the Episcopal Church, it is useful for anyone exploring the rite of reconciliation. It offers practical advice on how to prepare for the rite, as well as spiritual and theological considerations.

CHAPTER 5

Ministration at the Time of Death and Burial

Death is ubiquitous in the human experience. Rituals surrounding death are equally ubiquitous. The eminent cultural anthropologist Margaret Mead remarked, "I know of no people for whom the fact of death is not critical, and who have no ritual by which to deal with it."[1] Like many other pastoral offices, the rites of ministration at the time of death and burial are not uniquely Christian. Such rites predated Christianity by centuries and are found among all human communities today. Nonetheless, Christianity has influenced these rites with its theology, particularly regarding the resurrection.

Historical Context

The New Testament to Pre-Nicene Periods

The Hebrew Scriptures attest to the importance of burial in the Judaic roots of first-century Christians. Being buried in one's land with one's ancestors was treasured (Genesis 23, 49, 50, and Joshua 24:32-33). After the exile, rabbis taught the importance of burying Jews and non-Jews out of charity. No Jewish funeral rites from the first century exist. Still, it is believed that the ninth-century *Tzidduk Ha-din* ("Justification of Judgment"), with its realistic simplicity, likely was the experience of first-century Jews.[2]

Greco-Roman rites influenced rituals around death in first-century Palestine. Fear was the most significant emotion involved in their burial rites. Loss and grief were also present, but fear of the dead was most prominent. Many believed the dead sought revenge on the living and needed to be appeased. They believed a burial with all the proper rituals would comfort the dead and prevent them from exacting revenge on the living. Even strangers who died were to be given a proper burial to prevent their spirits from wandering among the living.[3]

---

1. Margaret Mead, "Ritual and Social Crisis," in *The Roots of Ritual*, 89-90.
2. Rutherford, *The Death of a Christian*, 4-5. See also Tobit 1:16-20.
3. Richard Rutherford, *The Death of a Christian: The Order of Christian Funerals*, 3-4.

The New Testament speaks of death significantly. Of course, the most essential message of the New Testament is the death and resurrection of Jesus Christ. This message transformed the early church's approach to death. Different sects of Judaism contested the reality of the resurrection (Acts 23). However, as the church expanded to include Gentiles, the emotional tenor of burial rites would radically change. The theology of resurrection and the eschatological hope of the paschal message would feature prominently in Christian theologies of death and burial.

Another prominent feature of the New Testament and subsequent centuries was the theology of martyrdom. The church recognizes Stephen, the deacon, as the first martyr (Acts 6:1 – 8:3). All the apostles, except for John, are believed also to have been martyred. Due to the persecution of the church, martyrdom became a poignant experience in the lives of Christians. Martyrdom was considered so important that if a catechumen who had not been baptized was killed for the faith, the church understood that person to be "baptized by blood." In 256 CE, Cyprian responds to Bishop Jubaian that if a catechumen is "seized and killed for the confession of the Name," they should not lose hope of salvation because "they are baptized with the most glorious and greatest baptism of blood."[4]

Around the beginning of the third century, some Christian communities built public cemeteries around the tomb of a martyred saint. After the Peace of Constantine, this practice became more widespread.[5] However, even before the third century, contrary to popular belief, Christians were not buried in secret but in public cemeteries, often next to pagans. Christian markings would have distinguished their graves from pagan graves. Such decorations and inscriptions included Christ as the Good Shepherd, meals of loaves, fishes, eucharistic wine, and baptismal water, indicating rebirth in Christ. These images of resurrection theology emphasized the distinction between Christian and pagan views of death. While personal grief was real, Christians believed death was not to be feared but celebrated as the passage to new life.[6]

Vigils became an important Christianization of an older pagan practice. Initially, a vigil-like service was held in anticipation of Christ's return. Christians became known as "nightwatch people." Initially, the disciples gathered after sundown on the sabbath to await Christ's return. This custom continued for decades and included pouring baptismal waters, celebrating the Eucharist, and laying on of hands for the power of the Holy Spirit. They were not quiet, contemplative services as the modern person might expect but vigorous services involving the entire assembly. These services eventually would lead to celebrating the Eucharist on Sundays, especially after Christians were expelled from the synagogues.[7]

---

4. Cyprian, "Epistle 73," in *Saint Cyprian Letters (1-81)*, 282-283.

5. Frederick S. Paxton, *Christianizing Death: The Creation of a Ritual Process in Early Medieval Europe*, 25.

6. Rutherford, *The Death of a Christian*, 6-7.

7. Rutherford, *The Death of a Christian*, 8-9.

These vigil services extended to commemorating the death of martyrs. Rather than commemorating a martyr's birthdate, early Christians commemorated their death date by gathering at their tomb annually for a vigil. These Christians viewed their death date as their "new birthdate," signifying when the person entered a new life in Christ through the resurrection. Eventually, these commemorations included prominent people who may not have been martyred, leading to the theology of sainthood. As the commemorations grew, a liturgical calendar formed that not only commemorated the essential points in Christ's life, death, resurrection, and ascension but also these saints.[8]

One practice that developed from earlier Roman practice was the *refrigerium*. At the anniversary of the death of a loved one, third-century Christians would visit the gravesite. Near the gravesites would be a *triclinium*, a little kitchen providing a meal, which the family would eat near their loved one's gravesite.[9]

These Christians, who met for a *refrigerium*, wrote prayers on the walls, like graffiti. Many of these prayers have survived. They illustrate a prevalent theology of the dead during this time. For example, they often involve the living asking the dead to remember them rather than the living offering remembrances of their dead loved ones. These prayers indicate a resurrection theology in which the dead are witnesses of the living (Heb 12:1).

They also describe scenes of peaceful waiting. The diary of the African martyr Perpetua described her vision of her deceased brother. He was in peace as he awaited his final rest in heaven. These early Christians did not see this intermediary state as one of torment but instead of peace.[10] However, this intermediary state was more likely to have been a Christianization of Greco-Roman myths than an early form of purgatory, as that doctrine would develop later.

Another example of the inculturation of Greco-Roman myths connected death, particularly martyrdom, with the Eucharist. This ritual became known as *viaticum*, giving the Eucharist to a Christian right before death, and it comes from a pagan practice. Ancient Greeks and Latins prepared a meal for those dying, known as *viaticus*, "of or pertaining to a journey," in Latin, and *ephodion*, "provisions for a journey," in Greek. This meal was meant to sustain the dead in their journey to the afterlife. Eventually, this practice evolved into placing a coin, *obolus*, on the mouth of the deceased as payment to Charon, the ferryman over the river Styx into the afterlife. Thus, *viaticum* became the payment for the journey after death.[11]

Early Christians adopted and Christianized this practice. However, it took on a very different theology. Instead of a coin or even a basic meal, the Eucharist became the *viaticum*. Because Christians believed that the Eucharist joined them

---

8. Rutherford, *The Death of a Christian*, 8-9.
9. Peter Brown, *The Ransom of the Soul: Afterlife and Wealth in Early Western Christianity*, 36-37.
10. Brown, *The Ransom of the Soul*, 37-38.
11. Gusmer, *And You Visited Me*, 107.

with Christ's death and resurrection, they also believed that receiving the Eucharist before death fortified that connection with Christ.

For example, during his imprisonment, Paul spoke of his desire to connect with Christ through death, "For to me, living is Christ and dying is gain. If I am to live in the flesh, that means fruitful labour for me; and I do not know which I prefer. I am hard pressed between the two: my desire is to depart and be with Christ, for that is far better; but to remain in the flesh is more necessary for you (Phil 1:21-24)." Thus, Paul laid the theological foundation for the *viaticum* by connecting death with Christ. Death was not just a journey to a better place but being in the presence of Christ.

Ignatius of Antioch (died c. 110) went further in his yearning to be with Christ through death by connecting it with the Eucharist, "I desire the bread of God which is the flesh of Jesus Christ . . . and for drink I desire his blood which is incorruptible love."[12] The Eucharist joins the Christian with Christ both during one's lifetime and at its end. However, the journey continues beyond death. Ignatius also described the Eucharist as "the medicine of immortality, that antidote that results not in dying, but in living forever in Jesus Christ."

Another early Christian martyr, Polycarp of Smyrna (died c. 157), connected his desire to be with Christ with eucharistic language in his final prayer, "I bless thee for granting me this day and hour, that I may be numbered amongst the martyrs, to share the cup of thine Anointed and to rise again unto life everlasting both in body and souls, in the immortality of the Holy Spirit."[13] Thus, the *viaticum* was not simply an inculturation of an existing Greco-Roman practice. It was not just food for a journey, albeit Christianized food. It had evolved. The Eucharist was more than food. It was identification with Christ, who would accompany one through death to everlasting life. This desire to connect with Christ through the Eucharist near death has continued in the church in many ecclesial traditions.

When death occurred, it involved the preparation and burial of the body. Again, Christians adopted and adapted surrounding practices. Jewish and pagan practices involved some form of preparation for the body, usually at home, with accompanying prayers and rituals. For pagans, this process involved exuberant expressions of grief. When a pagan died, the family was expected to enter mourning immediately. The quality of the mourning was almost violent. The family would often hire professional mourners, who would beat their breasts, pluck out their hair, roll around in the dirt, and chant dirges. These exuberant displays of grief would continue as the family processed the body from the home to the gravesite for the burial and its accompanying rituals.[14]

Similarly, Christian burial practices began at home with a wake or vigil. Christians prepared the body by washing it and laying it out. They would pray, light candles, and burn incense. They would then proceed to the gravesite in

---

12. Ignatius, *To the Romans*, in *The Apostolic Fathers*, 1:279.

13. Ignatius, *To the Ephesians*, in *The Apostolic Fathers*, 1:241.

14. Rush, *Death and Burial*, 163-171.

a funeral procession for the burial. A vigil might also be held at the gravesite. However, the quality of the Christian funeral was significantly different. It did not involve the violent, dramatic expressions of lament as with pagan funerals. Instead, Christians sang psalms and hymns.[15]

The significant distinction between Christian and pagan funerals was the spirit. Christians had a spirit of joy based on the hope of the resurrection. They believed death to be more than just the passage from this world to the next but also an identification with Christ, the Resurrected One. This contrast with the pagan view of funerals was significant for Christians to maintain. They wanted to distinguish themselves by the way they celebrated the death of their loved ones. Cyprian, a bishop during this time, encouraged his people in a pastoral letter not to fall back into the pagan mourning rituals.[16]

This processional nature of Christian burial, moving from the home to the gravesite with accompanying rituals, would continue. Later in church history, the procession would include a stop at the church for rites in that location, developing an almost stational character. As time progressed, different stations—home, church, or gravesite—would receive different emphases. For example, the rites in the home might be truncated or disappear, with the rites at the church taking prominence. The same might be true of the rites at the gravesite. Variations regarding the stations and their accompanying rites would occur, but the basic threefold structure persisted in some fashion.

The Nicene and Early Medieval Periods

As the church moved into the Peace of Constantine after the Edict of Milan, much changed in how it operated concerning the world around it. Moving from a persecuted church to a public church permitted an openness in worship that was less prominent before. The funeral procession now added the church as a station. Rites in the home continued, but they were now followed by rites in the church and then at the gravesite. While liturgies from this period remain nonexistent, other sources, such as sermons, treatises, and other literature, provide evidence of practices. Of course, such evidence should always be considered specific to a region and time.

Like baptism, increased Christian membership during this time impacted the theology of the dying. The earlier emphasis on resurrection theology remained strong during this period. Patristic sermons attested to the hope of resurrection. While Christian funeral practices remained similar to pagan practices, their spirit continued to emphasize the resurrection. Personal grief was acknowledged, but the despair that often accompanied pagan funeral practices was strongly discouraged. Christians were a people of hope.[17]

---

15. Rush, *Death and Burial*, 163-171.
16. Rutherford, *The Death of a Christian*, 11.
17. Rutherford, *The Death of a Christian*, 14-17.

Praying for the dead originates early in the Christian church and is referenced in Christian literature from the second century.[18] However, Augustine was the theologian whose teachings would later influence the importance of this practice in medieval spirituality. In his short treatise "On the Care to be Taken for the Dead," Augustine commended the practice of praying for the dead.[19]

However, in his *Enchiridion*, he went beyond simply commending prayer to adding two elements, "There is no denying that the souls of the dead are benefited by the piety of their living friends, when the sacrifice of the Mediator is offered for the dead, or alms are given in the church."[20] Not only was prayer beneficial for the dead, but so was almsgiving and especially the Eucharist. It is important to note that he defined almsgiving as "given in the church." The implication undoubtedly was that they would be given to the poor. However, this practice of offering the Eucharist and alms for the church would lead to abuses centuries later.

Augustine also significantly impacted church doctrine by teaching an intermediary state between heaven and hell. "For there is a mode of life that is neither so good as not to need such helps after death nor so bad as not to gain benefit from them after death."[21] He explains that some people have lived a life so good that the prayers, almsgiving, and Masses on their behalf would have little effect. The same is true for some people who have done such evil. However, these "sacrifices, whether of the altar or of alms, are offered for the baptized dead, they are thank offerings for the very good, propitiations for the not-so-very-bad, and, as for the very bad—even if they are of no help to the dead—they are at least a sort of consolation to the living."[22]

Augustine's teaching would have a profound impact on medieval spirituality. The afterlife became a tripartite state: heaven, hell, and what would become known as purgatory. Only the "very good," a category usually reserved for martyrs, were believed to go immediately to heaven. All others were left with two options. Hell awaited them if they had committed mortal sins without confession and absolution. Otherwise, they would enter purgatory to be "purged" of their venial sins with the hope of entering heaven. Augustine argues that appealing to God's mercy would have little effect. The practice of offering Masses and alms for the dead instead would be productive.

Augustine's teaching connecting the efficacy of the Eucharist for the souls of the dead would lead to abuses in the medieval church. Some examples include offering communion to the dead. The frontals and other linens

---

18. John F. Baldovin, "Mass Intentions: The Historical Development of a Practice," 873.

19. Augustine, "*De cura pro mortuis gerenda,*" in *Corpus Scriptorum Ecclesiasticorum Latinorum*, 41:629-630.

20. Augustine, "Enchiridion," in *The Library of Christian Classics*, 7:405.

21. Augustine, "Enchiridion," 405.

22. Augustine, "Enchiridion," 405-406.

associated with the Eucharist would be used as shrouds and talismans. People requested internment near the altar, which led to multiple bodies being buried in a single grave.[23]

As might be expected, great concern developed over the souls of departed loved ones. Since the opportunities for martyrdom were slim in the Christendom that developed, how might one enter heaven? One option became indulgences.

Today, the Roman Catholic Church defines an indulgence as

> the remission before God of the temporal punishments for sins whose guilt is already forgiven, which a properly disposed member of the Christian faithful gains under certain and defined conditions by the assistance of the Church which as minister of redemption dispenses and applies authoritatively the treasury of the satisfactions of Christ and the saints.[24]

This definition emphasizes that indulgences only remit "temporal punishments," not eternal punishments. This distinction involves the penances one might be given as satisfaction for a sin. The guilt is already forgiven through the absolution of confession. Therefore, indulgences understood today do not affect one's eternal destination.

However, this distinction was the product of centuries of theological discussion. The theology of indulgences in the early Middle Ages was less distinct. Furthermore, the church used indulgences to promote participation in the Crusades, among other examples.[25] Thus, the ordinary person might understand their participation in a crusade or other examples in which indulgences were given to ensure their eternal destiny in heaven.

However, the proliferation of private or solitary Masses for the dead significantly impacted medieval spirituality, which would become a rallying cry for sixteenth-century reformers. Faithful Christians believed that offering Mass for a deceased loved one would benefit that person, allowing them easier passage from purgatory to heaven. A "private Mass" had few or no communicants and sometimes only the server. A "solitary Mass" had only the priest. However, the benefit of the Mass had nothing to do with the number of people present. A solitary Mass with only the priest present was as efficacious as any other Mass. Eventually, the "low Mass," with no singing, developed from the proliferation of solitary Masses.[26]

From the New Testament, the church has commended almsgiving for not only the poor but also the upkeep of the church, including provisions for the priest. However, during the Middle Ages, Mass stipends with intentions increased

---

23. Rutherford, *The Death of a Christian*, 23.

24. *Code of Canon Law, Latin-English Edition*, 318 (can. 992).

25. For a thorough treatment of this topic, see Ane L. Bysted, *The Crusade Indulgence: Spiritual Rewards and the Theology of the Crusades, c. 1095-1216*.

26. Baldovin, "Mass Intentions," 880.

due to this desire to ease the deceased's passage from purgatory to heaven. Eventually, multiple solitary Masses were said in a single day, each receiving a stipend. The wealthy even donated money to erect special side altars, known as chantries, in which priests could say solitary Masses for them and their families perpetually.[27] Thus, Augustine's "sacrifices" of almsgiving and offering Masses became intertwined into stipendiary Masses. These stipendiary Masses became a point of rebuke for the reformers.

As with all pastoral offices, full liturgical rites were unavailable until the Middle Ages. Beforehand, information about funeral liturgies can be gleaned from other sources. In the sixth century in Syria, an author, formerly believed to be Dionysius the Areopagite but now believed to be someone writing in his name, Pseudo-Dionysius, wrote a commentary on the funeral liturgy.

The *ordo* of this funeral liturgy differs in the details from other funeral liturgies, but the faith expressed in it remains familiar. The bishop gathered people in the church. Thus, the addition of the church in the tripartite procession had occurred by then. The bishop offered a thanksgiving prayer. The deacons read passages from Scripture and chanted Psalms about the resurrection. One of the deacons would then dismiss the catechumens and call out the names of the previously deceased. The deacon would bid the congregation to pray for "a blessed end in Christ."[28] The bishop would then offer a prayer for the deceased. These practices appear similar to modern-day liturgies.

However, two practices less familiar to modern-day services followed. First, the bishop would offer a kiss of peace to the deceased, and others would come forward to do the same. Commentary later in the text explains that the kiss of peace is given "because one who has finished a divine life is dear and honorable to all the god-like."[29] Then, the bishop anointed the deceased with oil. The commentary connects this anointing with the anointing received at baptism. However, it makes a distinction, "Then, the anointing with oil called the one being initiated to the holy contests, but now, the pouring of the oil signifies that the deceased has fought to the finish in those same holy struggles."[30] This connection with baptismal imagery will find its way into some modern rites. The internment of the body occurred next. Interestingly, there is no mention of Mass in this commentary.

In the seventh century in the West, Pope Gregory the Great discussed funerary practices and the theology associated with them in his *Dialogues*. These Dialogues make it clear that the Western church had evolved its funerary theology into a pessimistic view of the afterlife. Rather than the previously optimistic view of the hope of resurrection, the teaching of purgatory had taken hold. As mentioned in chapter four, this period was also when the

---

27. Baldovin, "Mass Intentions," 881-882.
28. Dionysius, *Dionysius the Pseudo-Areopagite: The Ecclesiastical Hierarchy*, 82.
29. *Dionysius*, 88.
30. *Dionysius*, 88.

anointing for healing became extreme unction, reserved only for those near death.[31]

For example, in his *Dialogues*, Gregory details an account of how efficacious Masses for the dead could be for the state of one's soul. One of Gregory's monks, Justus, fell ill. The other monks discovered that Justus had hidden three gold pieces in his room, which was against the rule of life for the monastery. As punishment, Gregory ordered that no Masses be said for him in his last moments before death and after it, even though Justus died repentant. Gregory permitted no Masses to be said for Justus for thirty days. Finally, out of compassion, he agreed that the monks could say Masses on Justus' behalf for thirty additional days. After that period, Justus appeared to Gregory and told him that he had been released from purgatory and received into heaven on that thirtieth day. Gregory explained that this was proof of the efficaciousness of private Masses for the dead.[32]

Like all liturgical rites, funerary rites began more as a collection of prayers than a complete rite. Sometimes, these prayers would be included in sacramentaries, which priests would use for celebrating the Mass. Other times, they may be a series of rubrical instructions in *ordines*, which were collections of rubrical material. Much of these materials began to appear in the eighth century with Gregory the Great's influence.[33]

Funeral liturgies varied greatly depending on whether they occurred in an urban setting for a cleric or monk, which would be more elaborate, or in the country for a peasant, which would be more straightforward. During this period, local churches had their practices. Nonetheless, a basic pattern emerged that continued from ancient pagan practice. The funeral liturgy would begin in the home with certain practices near death and for the preparation of the body occurring there. Then, the body would be processed into the church compound. The church compound included the church and the churchyard, cemetery, and cloisters. Because burial typically happened within the church compound, the cemetery, or the church building, the liturgy made no distinction between the church and the burial site.

However, these church compounds were typically found outside the city walls. Basilicas were built inside the city walls but without cemeteries. If a funeral occurred in a basilica, an additional procession had to occur from the church outside the gates to the cemetery. Eventually, this procession from church to cemetery would overshadow the procession from home to church.

Another example of the emphasis on the funeral procession from the church to the burial site occurs in the Sacramentary of Rheinau, which dates around 800 CE. This document includes an extended vigil service for the deceased. After the vigil, the procession from the church to the burial site within the church

---

31. Rutherford, *The Death of a Christian*, 25.
32. Rutherford, *The Death of a Christian*, 25-26.
33. Rutherford, *The Death of a Christian*, 38-39.

compound was considered the main funeral procession. Nonetheless, the tripartite structure of liturgies in the home, church, and gravesite remained.[34]

Liturgical sources from this period indicate that the service in the home had two main sections. The first section was meant for the dying person and included *viaticum* and a final commendation at the time of death. This attention to the dying person before death rather than the corpse after death distinguished Christian liturgies from other pagan practices. After death, the second section included the preparation of the body. Psalms, antiphons, and prayers might have accompanied this preparation process. These preparations would have been more elaborate in monastic houses or for clergy than in the homes of lay people. These services in the home concluded with a short prayer.[35]

The body would then have been carried to the church. Although, this action would not have been considered the principal funeral procession. The main service in the church was the vigil, which involved psalms and responsories. However, complex ritual elaborations evolved. These elaborations eventually drew the funeral liturgy's focus to the church service. Earlier sources describe only wake services without the celebration of Mass.[36]

The funeral procession proper came next. Sometimes, the body was moved from one part of the church to another if it was to be interred in the church building. Other times, the procession would go to the cemetery. These processions included candles and incense, a Christian contextualization of earlier pagan practices. Psalms and antiphons were sung. Psalms 25 and 118 were popular.[37]

The burial itself was a liturgical service. The body would be placed in the grave or sarcophagus accompanied by singing psalms and antiphons. Rubrics were minimal, indicating a lack of complex ritual gestures. Two prayers are noted. The first is an invitation to prayer. The second is the final commendation prayer, which concluded the service.[38]

The development of the funeral Mass was gradual. As described above, the rites in the church initially centered on the vigil. Psalms, antiphons, and prayers were said, but not Mass. Eventually, as the desire to offer Mass as expiation for the deceased grew, the body would remain in the church for an extended time. Then, the regular schedule of Masses would occur, at which time prayer for the deceased would be offered.[39]

Eventually, references in liturgical sources to celebrating Mass at "an opportune time" indicate that special Masses were said at the funeral rather than the regularly scheduled Masses. By the thirteenth century, the *Requiem* Mass, which

---

34. Rutherford, *The Death of a Christian*, 40-42.
35. Rutherford, *The Death of a Christian*, 43-47.
36. Rutherford, *The Death of a Christian*, 47-48.
37. Rutherford, *The Death of a Christian*, 49-51.
38. Rutherford, *The Death of a Christian*, 51-53.
39. Rutherford, *The Death of a Christian*, 58-59.

had been part of the liturgies of the papal court, became normative. Eventually, it was included in the *Missale Romanum* (1570) as the funeral Mass until the revised Missal of Pope Paul VI (1970). The inclusion of the sequence *Dies irae*, and other chants further drove the funeral liturgy toward the pessimistic and dark views characteristic of medieval life.[40]

A radically new element, later known as the *absolutio* or Absolution Service, entered the funeral service in the Carolingian period of the ninth and tenth centuries. Initially, this new element involved the suffrages said at the time of death. However, by the twelfth century, they included the responsory "Deliver me, O Lord, from eternal death." These suffrages occurred after the Mass at the bier before the funeral procession to the gravesite. Interestingly, if a Mass were not celebrated as part of the funeral, the *absolutio* would be said the next day at the next Mass rather than as part of the burial service. Thus, it created another connection between the offering of Mass as an expiation for the deceased.[41]

As the Middle Ages ended with the Black Death and the Dance of Death, funeral liturgies varied greatly. The church service began to wane during this period, and additional rites at the gravesite increased. Unfortunately, many of these elaborations were not documented in liturgical sources due to the cost of replacing manuscripts. They became evident in the sixteenth century after the invention of the printing press, which allowed dioceses and local churches to produce their manuals more readily.[42]

Funerals for children during this time further developed the medieval theology surrounding death. Initially, the same funeral rites for adults were used for baptized children. However, eventually, different prayers developed. These prayers were atypically optimistic. Because these children had original sin washed away by baptism but had not yet committed sins of their own, an expiatory Mass was unnecessary. Mass would be celebrated, but it was for the families, not for the deceased.

However, if an infant died unbaptized, they received no rites from the church. Priests were forbidden to say Mass or any prayers for them. They would be buried at night outside of the cemetery. Some sources recorded that priests and lay people might bury them near the eaves of the church in the hope that the water dripping on their graves would provide some semblance of baptismal grace. Catechumens who died unbaptized were treated similarly. The Braga Council referred to the death of unbaptized infants and catechumens in the same terms as people who died by suicide. This custom continued in the Roman Catholic Church into the twentieth century until the revised Roman Rite.[43]

---

40. Rutherford, *The Death of a Christian*, 59-60.
41. Rutherford, *The Death of a Christian*, 61-65.
42. Rutherford, *The Death of a Christian*, 75-76.
43. Rutherford, *The Death of a Christian*, 90-93.

The Reformations

As discussed above, the medieval church had utterly changed the theology surrounding death and how the Mass related to death. Before the Middle Ages, Christians celebrated the Eucharist as a joyous occasion, believing that Christ's resurrection had defeated death. While personal grief was expected, funerals and the theology surrounding them emphasized the hope of the resurrection. However, as the doctrine of purgatory developed and became popular, the emotions surrounding death changed from joy and expectation to anxiety and fear. Judgment became a dominant theme.

To mitigate this dread of death, the church emphasized Mass as an expiation for sins for both the living and the dead. While the Eucharist had long been understood as "medicine for immortality," its principal feature was propitiatory. The church offered Masses to assuage God's wrath against sinners and alleviate judgment. Eventually, the belief took hold that the more Masses offered for someone would produce more significant benefit. This belief led to stipendiary Masses in which patrons would pay priests to say Masses on their behalf.

From the Scholastic period, the church taught that Mass was an *opus operatum*, literally translated as "the work wrought." This doctrine taught that the grace of Mass was efficacious regardless of the recipient's spiritual state. As long as one had not committed a mortal sin, the grace of Mass would be of benefit whether or not the person received it or was even present. As a result, the average Christian received communion infrequently, usually only at Easter, because canon law required communion at least annually.

The priest would offer Mass on behalf of the people and typically be the only one to receive communion. Private, stipendiary Masses were the result of this practice. If communicants were unnecessary, priests could offer Mass much more frequently. If a priest were paid a stipend for each Mass, the more Masses offered would increase the income.

In *The Babylonian Captivity of the Church*, Martin Luther harshly criticizes this practice.

> This has been the fate of the mass; it has been converted by the teaching of godless men into a good work. They themselves call it an *opus operatum*, and by it they presume themselves to be all-powerful with God. Next they proceed to the very height of madness, and after inventing the lie that the mass is effective simply by virtue of the act having been performed, they add another one to the effect that the mass is none the less profitable to others even if it is harmful to some wicked priest who may be celebrating it. On such a foundation of sand they base their applications, participations, brotherhoods, anniversaries, and numberless other lucrative and profitable schemes of that kind.[44]

---

44. Luther, 'The Babylonian Captivity of the Church," in *Luther's Works*, 36:47.

Here, Luther connects the stipendiary Mass with the underlying theology of *opus operatum*. The almsgiving that Augustine taught was efficacious became primarily for the church's upkeep rather than for the poor.

Luther also attacked Mass as a work rather than an act of grace, "You have seen that the mass is nothing else than the divine promise or testament of Christ, sealed with the sacrament of his body and blood. If that is true, you will understand that it cannot possibly be in any way a work; nobody can possibly do any thing in it, neither can it be dealt with in any other way than by faith alone."[45] Luther's main theological critique was how the church had abandoned grace in favor of works. Such a critique is understandable in the environment created by stipendiary Masses.

Interestingly, Luther did not criticize the act of private Masses nor that of priests receiving money for their needs. He clarified, "The private mass does not differ in the least from the ordinary communion which any layman [sic] receives at the hand of the priest, and has no greater effect."[46] He emphasized that it was not the offering of Mass that was efficacious but rather the offering of prayers. Priests must distinguish between the two.

Concerning "votive Masses," which were offered with a special intention, usually for the dead, Luther criticized them as well, "If a priest is requested by others to celebrate so-called 'votive masses,' let him [sic] beware of accepting a fee for the mass, or of presuming to offer any votive sacrifice." However, Luther distinguished between offering Mass and praying for the living and the dead, "Rather, [the priest] should take pains to refer all this to the prayers which he offers for the dead or the living, saying to himself: 'Lo, I will go and receive the sacrament for myself alone, and while doing so I will pray for this one and that one.'"[47] Luther considered it permissible for priests to be paid to offer prayers as their livelihood. However, he wanted to distinguish between such prayers and offering Mass as a propitiatory sacrifice.

However, in his later work, "The Abomination of the Secret Mass," Luther critiqued the practice of praying for the dead in his commentary on the section known as the "Commemoration of the Dead." That section of the Mass stated, "Remember also, O Lord, Thy servants, men and women, *N.*, who have gone before us with the sign of faith and repose in the sleep of peace. For these and all who rest in Christ we pray, O Lord, that Thou wilt grant a place of refreshment, light, and peace. Through the same Christ our Lord. Amen."[48] In his commentary following that section, Luther responded sarcastically, "Now the priest comes again to the dead. This part is worth money, so that they do not say mass in vain."[49] He continued that it was foolish for priests to pray for those who have

---

45. Luther, "The Babylonian Captivity of the Church," in *Luther's Works*, 36:47.
46. Luther, "The Babylonian Captivity of the Church," in *Luther's Works*, 36:54.
47. Luther, "The Babylonian Captivity of the Church," in *Luther's Works*, 36:55.
48. As quoted in Luther, "The Abomination of the Secret Mass," in *Luther's Works*, 36:321.
49. Luther, "The Abomination of the Secret Mass," in *Luther's Works*, 36:322.

"the sign of faith and repose in the sleep of peace." Thus, Luther's opposition to Masses for the dead was clear, but his position on praying for the dead became less clear as time evolved.

The Brandenburg Church Order (1549) provides significant information about Lutheran liturgical practices during this time. Regarding communion for the sick and dying, it commended the practice. If possible, the sick person should come to the regular public service to receive communion. However, if they were too weak, the pastor could offer communion from reserve or celebrate the Lord's Supper at a private service in the church or the sick person's home. If an emergency occurred and the dying person needed *viaticum*, the pastor was to go to the church to consecrate the elements and then bring them to the dying person. This practice would indicate that reservation of the sacrament for *viaticum* was not regularly practiced but was not expressly forbidden.[50]

Luther did not produce a funeral liturgy. Nonetheless, funeral practices in Lutheran regions would retain and eschew older traditions depending on the underlying theology. One retained tradition was the continuation of *viaticum* at the time of death. If communion was not received, the expectation of repentance and absolution remained. If one died without repentance, absolution, or communion, then no burial rites were offered, and the corpse would be laid in unconsecrated ground. This attachment to burial in consecrated ground remained essential to many people.[51]

The location of burials also changed. Because Luther and other reformers rejected the doctrine of purgatory, the need for bodies to be buried in or near the church disappeared. It was no longer necessary to intercede on behalf of a lost loved one. Thus, proximity to the church was irrelevant. Furthermore, Luther recommended that they be moved outside the city due to the possibility of graveyard diseases.[52]

One would expect the funeral sermon to be popular in the Lutheran regions of Europe, but they were not. Funeral sermons were typically reserved for the wealthy. When funeral sermons occurred, they were modeled after Luther's death, considered the perfect Christian death. One exception to this trend was the Free Imperial City of Nördlingen in Bavaria. Funeral sermons there were used as teaching tools for the laity.[53]

While Luther permitted private Masses, at least in his early work "The Babylonian Captivity of the Church," John Calvin forbad them entirely. "I hold that private masses are diametrically opposed to the institution of Christ, and are, therefore, an impious profanation of the sacred Supper." He continued by explaining that Christ instituted the "sacred Supper" as a meal to be shared

---

50. Philip H. Pfatteicher, Some Early and Later Fathers on the Visitation of the Sick," 217-219.

51. Gordon D. Raeburn, "The Reformation of Burial in the Protestant Churches," in *A Companion to Death, Burial, and Remembrance in Late Medieval and Early Modern Europe, c. 1300-1700*, 159.

52. Raeburn, "The Reformation of Burial in the Protestant Churches," 162.

53. Raeburn, "The Reformation of Burial in the Protestant Churches," 166-167.

among all the members of the church. He referenced 1 Corinthians 10:16 "that the breaking of bread is the communion of [Christ's] body and blood." In fact, Calvin believed that without the "breaking of bread for the communion of the faithful, there is no Supper of the Lord, but a false and preposterous imitation of the Supper."[54]

Like Luther, Calvin completely rejected Mass as a propitiatory sacrifice because that would repeat the sacrifice of Christ on the cross, which was once for all. Instead, the "eucharistic sacrifice" commemorates Christ's sacrifice, "And yet we deny not that in the Supper the sacrifice of Christ is so vividly exhibited as almost to set the spectacle of the cross before our eyes."[55] Thus, the response is praise and thanksgiving, a eucharistic response.

Calvin also distinguished between the sacrificial nature of Mass and the meal-like nature of the Lord's Supper.

> But now that the sacrifice has been performed, the Lord has prescribed a different method to us—viz. to transmit the benefit of the sacrifice offered to him by his Son to his believing people. The Lord, therefore, has given us a table at which we may feast, not an altar on which a victim may be offered; he has not consecrated priests to sacrifice, but ministers to distribute a sacred feast.[56]

Thus, the meal is not a sacrifice being offered to God to appease God's wrath for the sins one has committed. Instead, it is a meal at which one celebrates the grace received through the once-for-all sacrifice of Christ.

Calvin concluded that it was "an abominable insult and intolerable blasphemy" that one might attempt to repeat the sacrifice of Christ and, especially, to purchase forgiveness of sins through it. Since the Lord's Supper was meant to be received by all the faithful as a thank offering and commemoration of Christ's sacrifice, it could not be applied to specific people or for specific purposes, "or rather, to any one who is willing to purchase their merchandise from them for a price paid." Thus, Calvin struck at the heart of the abuse of stipendiary Masses.

Calvin also did not produce a funeral liturgy. In fact, burial rites were eschewed completely in Reformed regions. For example, the Walloon synods and Strasbourg, in the Rhineland instituted very simple burials without any prayers or sermons until about 1533. At about that time, the first Strasbourg Synod attempted to permit some graveside prayers. Simplicity remained the norm. John Knox in Scotland followed Calvin's instructions for Geneva and permitted no graveside ceremony. The minister was allowed to exhort the people in the church after the burial. One exception was in Frankfurt in 1554, where Pollanus

---

54. Calvin, *Institutes of the Christian Religion*, IV:18:8, 612-613.
55. Calvin, *Institutes of the Christian Religion*, IV:18:11, 614.
56. Calvin, *Institutes of the Christian Religion*, IV:18:12, 615.

published a liturgy in which the pastor was instructed to give an exhortation and prayer at the graveside.[57]

Reformed regions attempted to follow the Lutheran practice regarding burial sites outside the church and even outside the city. Calvin's burial was in the churchyard with no ritual or gravestone as was Knox's burial in Scotland. However, public outcry for burials in the church continued. Wealthy members of the community especially desired burial in prominent places in or near the church. Compromises were made.[58]

Thomas Cranmer and the other English reformers followed their continental counterparts in renouncing the doctrine of purgatory and the practice of stipendiary Masses. Mass as a propitiatory sacrifice was also condemned. The 1549 Book of Common Prayer contained exhortations in which the priest would address the congregation that they must duly prepare their hearts to receive communion worthily. In one of these exhortations, the priests urges the congregation to seek forgiveness from God and restitution with their neighbors before receiving communion because "Neither the absolucion of the priest, can any thing avayle them, nor the receiving of this holy sacrament doth any thing but increase their damnacion."[59]

Nonetheless, the 1549 Book of Common Prayer retained a rite for the Visitation of the Sick in which communion would be offered to them. The opening rubric for this section recognized the ever-presence of death,

> *Forasmuche as all mortal men be subject to many sodaine perils, diseases, and sicknesses, and ever uncertain what time they shall departe out of this lyfe: Therefore to the entente they may be always in a readinesse to dye, whensoever it shall please almighty God to call them: The curates shall diligently from tyme to tyme, but specially in the plague tyme, exhorte theyr paryshoners to the ofte receyvyng (in the churche) of the holy communion of the body and bloud of oure saviour Christe: whiche (yf they doe) they shall have no cause in theyr sodaine visitacion, to be unqueted for lacke of the same. But if the sick person be not hable to come to the churche, and yet is desirous to receive the communion in his house, then he must geve knowledge over night, or els early in the morning to the curate, signifying also howe many be appointed to communicate with hym.*[60]

Thus, while receiving communion offered no propitiation, it was encouraged in times of illness when death could be approaching. If the priest happened to be in the home right before death, these prayers and communion would be a means of preparing for death.

---

57. Raeburn, "The Reformation of Burial in the Protestant Churches," 159-160.
58. Raeburn, "The Reformation of Burial in the Protestant Churches," 163-166.
59. Cummings, *The Book of Common Prayer*, 25.
60. Cummings, *The Book of Common Prayer*, 79.

The 1662 Book of Common Prayer added a commendatory prayer at the time of death.[61] The prayer recognizes that one might die with sin still on one's soul and asks, "Wash it [the deceased's soul], we pray thee, in the bloud of that immaculate Lamb that was slain to take away the sins of the world; that whatsoever defilements it may have contracted in the midst of this miserable and naughty world, through the lusts of the flesh, or the wiles of Satan, being purged and done away, it may be presented pure and without spot before thee."[62] Thus, it makes a clear connection to Christ's sacrifice as the expiation for sin.

Unlike the continental reformers, the English reformers retained a full liturgy for burial. "The Order for the Burial of the dead" in the 1549 Book of Common Prayer could be said either in the church or in procession to the gravesite.[63] The service opened with a quotation from John 11, "I am the resurrection and the life (saith the Lord) he that believeth in me: yea, thoughe he were dead, yet shall he live. And whosoever liveth, and believeth in me, shall not dye for ever." Thus, the tone of the service was the hope of the resurrection.

The 1549 version included a commendation said by the priest as the body was lowered into the grave.[64] The 1552 and 1559 versions changed the wording of the commendation from the first person singular referencing the priest to the first person plural referencing everyone gathered. The 1549 version had the priest alone casting earth on the corpse, while the 1552/1559 versions permitted anyone to do it. The 1552/1559 versions significantly shortened the office, eliminating portions from the Sarum rite.[65]

One prayer in the 1549 version that was eliminated in the 1552/1559 versions included this plea, "Graunte we beseche thee, that at the daye of judgement his soule and all the soules of thy electe, departed out of this lyfe, may with us and we with them, fully receive thy promises, and be made perfite altogether thorow the glorious resurrection of thy sonne Jesus Christ our Lorde."[66] As Raeburn notes, "It could be suggested that this was a form of intercessory prayer and as such would not have sat comfortably with other Reformed denominations, leading, perhaps, to its subsequent removal."[67] Indeed, the 1552/1559 versions took a much more Reformed theological approach. Thus, any prayer appearing to intercede on behalf of the dead would likely have been considered suspect and removed.

While these liturgies referenced the hope of the resurrection, they retained a somber tone. Judgment after death remained a primary focus for them. God's

---

61. Cummings, *The Book of Common Prayer*, 448.
62. Cummings, *The Book of Common Prayer*, 448.
63. Cummings, *The Book of Common Prayer*, 82.
64. Cummings, *The Book of Common Prayer*, 82.
65. Marion J. Hatchett, *Commentary on the American Prayer Book*, 479-480.
66. Cummings, *The Book of Common Prayer*, 83.
67. Raeburn, "The Reformation of Burial in the Protestant Churches," 161.

mercy was available but must be appealed on behalf of the deceased. The pessimistic tone of the medieval rites was beginning to break, but not entirely.

John Wesley followed suit with the other reformers in utterly rejecting the doctrine of purgatory and the grace of the Mass working *ex opere operato*.[68] He taught that souls went to an intermediary state after death but not to be purged. This state was like a foretaste of the eternal state to which they would go. For the faithful, he called it "the ante-chamber of heaven," "Abraham's bosom," and "paradise." For the wicked, it was a prelude to eternal damnation.[69]

Because Wesley believed Christians were assured a place in heaven through grace, he considered funerals an occasion for joy. In his early years, he taught that it was inappropriate for a Christian to express grief at a funeral. However, age and experience softened his view.[70]

Wesley also urged his ministers to use the funeral as an evangelistic opportunity. While he believed that the faithful Christian was assured of heaven, he also taught that each person must choose to follow Christ to receive such assurances. Therefore, he removed all references to the final state of the person from his burial liturgy, keeping only the scriptural references. Thus, the deceased was no longer the focus of the service but rather the community gathered.[71]

The Twentieth Century

The twentieth century would involve significant changes in society's understanding of death. With urbanization, burial practices moved from country parishes with spacious cemeteries to city churches, where cemeteries were some distance away. Also, the advent of cremation services extended the time between death and burial. Thus, the procession from the home to the church was truncated to a procession into the church when the remains arrived.

The procession from the church to the gravesite after the church service became more complex. If the cemetery or columbarium were not in or next to the church, a motorcade would accompany the body from the church to the gravesite. In the latter half of the twentieth century, these motorcades became important symbols as they progressed from the church, through the city, and to the cemetery at its outskirts.

Another significant change in the twentieth century was the rise in secularism. The church's influence in public society waned. Scientific advances called into question the reality of an afterlife. The threat of eternal damnation no longer held the sway over people's lives as it had in former times. The rise of psychology

---

68. John Wesley, *Popery Calmly Considered*, 10 and 18 respectively.
69. Westerfield Tucker, *American Methodist Worship*, 202-203; also, Wesley, "Sermon 115: Dives and Lazarus," in *The Works of John Wesley*, 4:5-18.
70. Westerfield Tucker, *American Methodist Worship*, 204.
71. Westerfield Tucker, *American Methodist Worship*, 204; and Wesley, *Sunday Service*, 156-161.

and its interest in death moved the focus of burial rites from public ceremonies to private and familial opportunities to express grief.

Medical advances significantly extended life. Life expectancies changed radically from an average of the mid-forties around 1900 to an average of sixty years in 1950 to an average of seventy years in 2020. With these medical changes came a denial of death, particularly in Eurocentric cultures. The elderly were often institutionalized instead of cared for in the home. Domestic practices at the time of death became the purview of professionals, increasing the cost of death significantly. Also, families became more mobile. Children and grandchildren might live great distances away from their elders. Thus, it would become possible for someone to be institutionalized in their later years, die, be cremated, and then be buried with no one seeing their body.

All of these changes and more led to a significant shift in the emphasis of the burial service. It moved from being a public ceremony to become a pastoral rite for the grieving family and friends. The early twentieth century saw only modest changes to the burial rite. The most significant changes occurred after Vatican Two. *Sacrosanctum Concilium* (The Constitution on the Sacred Liturgy) expressed a significant theological shift in the burial office: "The rite for the burial of the dead should express more clearly the paschal character of Christian death, and should correspond more closely to the circumstances and traditions found in various regions. This holds good also for the liturgical color to be used."[72]

This proclamation resulted in a theological return to a resurrection theology. Initially, this return might appear to support the prevailing denial of death in society. However, ecclesial traditions also sought to value the importance of grief. The "Order for Burial" from the Church of England's *Series Three* provisional liturgy expresses this shift.

> The liturgy for the dead is an Easter liturgy. It finds all its meaning in the resurrection. Because Jesus was raised from the dead, we, too, shall be raised.
>
> The liturgy, therefore, is characterized by joy. This joy, however, does not make human grief unchristian. The very love we have for each other in Christ brings deep sorrow when we are parted at death. Jesus himself wept at the grave of his friend. So, while we rejoice that one we love has entered into the nearer presence of our Lord, we sorrow in sympathy with those who mourn.[73]

Thus, both resurrection and grief remain central themes. Contemporary burial rites attempt to maintain a balance between them.

These changes in society and theology resulted in the funeral rite becoming more firmly a pastoral rite. The concern became less about the eternal destiny of the deceased, although that remained, to the expression of grief for the family

---

72. Second Vatican Council, "Constitution on the Sacred Liturgy," No. 81.
73. *The Proposed Book of Common Prayer*, 50.

and friends. Funerals would take on a much more psychological nature to them in which the grief of death would not be denied but expressed through the liturgy and the hope of resurrection would remain the focal point.[74] The following section will explore these theological themes in the contemporary church.

Theological Insights[75]

Ministry to the Dying

As discussed in chapter four, most Christian traditions sought to move away from extreme unction as the only opportunity for healing ministry. Healing was understood as a holistic ministry that could happen at any stage of illness, although usually for a severe illness, and could be repeated if the person recovered. This change recognized that modern medicine has permitted even seriously ill people to recover fully and that healing need not occur only at death.

Nonetheless, Christian traditions have retained special prayers and other liturgical rites for ministration at the time of death.[76] Of these traditions, the Roman Catholic Church and the Evangelical Lutheran Church in America have explicitly retained the *viaticum* as communion for the dying.[77] *The United Methodist Book of Worship*'s "Ministry with the Dying" section includes a rubric that "*Holy Communion may be administered.*"[78] However, it provides no additional directions about the context. Other ecclesial traditions may administer communion to the dying, but no such mention is made in the corresponding sections of their liturgical rites.

The Roman Catholic rites for the Pastoral Care of the Sick are quite explicit about the importance of *viaticum* for ministration to the dying, "The celebration of the Eucharist as viaticum, food for the passage through death to eternal life, is the sacrament proper to the dying Christian."[79] The fact that *viaticum* is to be understood as "the sacrament proper to the dying Christian" underscores the change in theological emphasis for the sacrament of anointing. The following paragraph explains this change: "The sacrament of the anointing of the sick should be celebrated at the beginning of a serious illness. Viaticum, celebrated when death is close, will then be better understood as the last sacrament of Christian life."[80] This instruction emphasizes the desire to move away from thinking

---

74. Geoffrey Rowell, *The Liturgy of Christian Burial*, 110-114.

75. Appendix F contains the rites for ministration at the time of death from the BCP, BCW, BOW, ELWPC, and RITES in tabular format for easy reference. Appendix G contains the burial rites from the BCP, BCW, BOW, ELW, and RITES in tabular format for easy reference.

76. See Appendix F for a comparative table of these prayers and rites.

77. RITES, 848 and ELWPC, 221.

78. BOW, 264.

79. RITES, 848.

80. RITES, 848.

of the sacrament of anointing as "last rites." *Viaticum* is to be the final sacrament in this tradition.

In addition to offering *viaticum* or "A Service of Word and Table," the Roman Catholic Church and the United Methodist Church offer an opportunity for the dying to reaffirm their baptismal covenant.[81] As discussed in the section below, baptism is a common theme in the burial liturgies of all Christian traditions. However, these two traditions offer this opportunity to the dying while still living. Thus, the dying may be comforted through the assurance of their baptismal faith.

The Roman Catholic *viaticum* includes an "Apostolic Pardon," either in the concluding rites if done within Mass or in the introductory rites if done outside of Mass. This pardon includes pertinent theology, "Through the holy mysteries of our redemption, may almighty God release you from all punishments in this life and in the life to come. May he open to you the gates of paradise and welcome you to everlasting joy."[82] The prayer purposefully fails to mention any explicit information about the nature of the punishments. Nonetheless, the implicit theology is one of purgatory. Since the rite of penance would be necessary to forgive a mortal sin, this "apostolic pardon" handles venial sins on one's soul. The other rites do not include any form of confession, penitential rite, or penance for ministration to the dying.[83]

For many rites that do not begin with *viaticum* or "A Service of Word and Table," opening sentences of Scripture followed by a prayer for the dying person begin the rite. The passages of Scripture and the opening prayer speak of God's comfort to the dying one. Sometimes, the prayers speak to particular circumstances, such as the end of life-sustaining treatment, sudden death, death by violence, or death of a child.[84]

As death approaches, some rites include a litany. In the Roman Catholic Church, the litany seeks the intercession of the saints. The more extended option includes saints from Mary to Saint Teresa and may include others. The shorter option includes Mary, the holy angels; John the Baptist; Joseph, Peter, and Paul; and other saints, optionally.[85] The litanies in the Book of Common Prayer and *Evangelical Worship (Pastoral Care)* do not include petitioning the saints. However, they join the Roman Catholic litany in invoking Christ's incarnation, passion, death, resurrection, ascension, and the coming of the Holy Spirit. The litanies beseech God to deliver the dying from the power of evil, pardon them from sin, grant them a place of refreshment, and bring them into joy and gladness.[86]

---

81. RITES, 852 and BOW 264.
82. RITES, 854.
83. See Appendix F.
84. See BOW 264-265, ELWPC 214, and *Enriching Our Worship 2: Ministry with the Sick or Dying Burial of a Child*, 97.
85. RITES, 863-865.
86. RITES, 864-865; ELWPC 215-216; and BCP 462-464.

At the time of death, all these rites include a commendation. These prayers trace their origins to one of Christ's final prayers, "Father, into your hands I commend my spirit (Luke 23:46)." Some rites include several options for the commendation. However, two prayers are found in nearly all the rites.

The first prayer, common to all the rites, contains a spirit of active departure. It begins with "Go forth"[87] or "Depart."[88] It is as if the priest or minister releases the spirit from the body. The prayer continues by invoking the Name of the Trinity, "In the Name of God the Father Almighty who created you; In the Name of Jesus Christ who redeemed you; In the name of the Holy Spirit who sanctifies you."[89] Thus, the imagery is one of travel. The soul is released on a journey from this world. The prayer ends that the soul may find rest with the saints in paradise.

The second prayer as an option for the commendation is common to these rites, except for *The United Methodist Book of Worship*. This prayer differs slightly from the first in its tone. The first prayer spoke to the dying, urging them to depart and find rest. This prayer speaks to Christ, "Into your hands, O merciful Savior, we commend your servant." Thus, the dying are linked with Christ. Just as Christ commended his spirit to the Father, the dying are commended to Christ and, thereby, to the Father. It continues with a request for acknowledgment, "Acknowledge, we humbly beseech you, a sheep of your own fold, a lamb of your own flock, a sinner of your own redeeming." It concludes, "Receive *him* into the arms of your mercy, into the blessed rest of everlasting peace, and into the glorious company of the saints in light. *Amen.*"[90] Each of these requests includes a tripartite epistrophe that poetically emphasizes first the relationship of the dying with Christ, "a sheep of your own fold, a lamb of your own flock, a sinner of your own redeeming" and then the destiny of the dying, "into the arms of your mercy, into the blessed rest of everlasting peace, and into the glorious company of the saints in light."[91]

The conclusion of the rites varies. The commendation concludes the service in the Anglican Book of Common Prayer and *The United Methodist Book of Worship*. The Presbyterian *Book of Common Worship*, the *Evangelical Lutheran Worship (Pastoral Care)*, and the Roman Catholic *Rites* include additional prayers for family, friends, and others and a concluding blessing. These prayers offer messages of hope and consolation that will also feature prominently in the burial rites.

---

87. RITES, 866 and ELWPC 217.
88. BCP 464, BCW 774, and BOW 265.
89. BCP 464; see also RITES, *866*; ELWPC 217; BOW 265; and BCW 774-775.
90. BCP 465; BCW 774; ELWPC 219.
91. The Roman Catholic prayer differs in that it speaks to the dying and commends them to God. It contains the same elements but lacks the poetic rhythm. RITES, 866.

Hope and Consolation

As discussed above, the theological tenor of Western Christian burial rites evolved. During the apostolic and Nicene periods, the church emphasized a theology of hope in the resurrection. This theology starkly contrasted the despair often associated with pagan funerals. However, this theological message of hope changed to fear and judgment in the Middle Ages due to concerns regarding purgatory. While the reformers rejected the doctrine of purgatory and the stipendiary Masses associated with it, the overall tenor of the burial service remained bleak. Contemporary burial services have further evolved. The joint themes of hope and consolation feature prominently in Western Christian burial services today.

For example, the traditional anthem accompanying the body's procession at the start of the burial service in the Book of Common Prayer begins, "I am Resurrection and I am Life, says the Lord. Whoever has faith in me shall have life, even though he die. And everyone who has life, and has committed himself to me in faith, shall not die for ever."[92] This anthem invokes Christ's self-declaration from John 11:25-26, "I am the resurrection and the life. Those who believe in me, even though they die, will live, and everyone who lives and believes in me will never die. Do you believe this?" Thus, the gathered assembly is immediately reminded that Christians in death are united with Christ and his resurrection.

Similarly, the *Book of Common Worship*'s opening prayer states the hope of the resurrection forthrightly, "We gather today in the sure and certain hope of the resurrection."[93] One of the opening prayers of the Roman Catholic burial service also declares, "Almighty God and Father, it is our certain faith that your Son, who died on the cross was raised from the dead, the first fruits of all who have fallen asleep."[94] This prayer invokes 1 Corinthians 15:20.

The focus of this resurrection hope is always Christ. Nowhere do the prayers indicate that this hope is connected to the good merits of the deceased. One's entrance into paradise relies only on Christ and his destruction of death through his resurrection. This theology is solidly rooted in Scripture.

However, general misconceptions prevail. The average person believes that entrance into paradise is predicated on good behavior. One must have more good than evil deeds to be permitted into heaven. The robust resurrection theology in these services speaks forcefully against this unscriptural theology.

Coupled with the hope of the resurrection is God's mercy. While most contemporary burial services have rejected the medieval fear of judgment, they still

---

92. BCP 491.
93. BCW 781.
94. RITES, 976.

address the reality of sin and the need for forgiveness.[95] The Roman Catholic rite explicitly states, "O God, to whom mercy and forgiveness belong."[96] One of the opening collects in the Book of Common Prayer begins, "O God, whose mercies cannot be numbered,"[97] and one of the opening prayers in *Evangelical Lutheran Worship* starts, "Blessed be the God and Father of our Lord Jesus Christ, the source of all mercy."[98]

These calls for mercy are multivalent. Are they asking for mercy for the deceased or the grieving? Often, that distinction is unclear. Theologies regarding the availability of mercy and forgiveness after death differ among ecclesial traditions. The Roman Catholic Church has a clear theology that mercy and forgiveness are available after death for those who have committed venial sins and, therefore, find themselves in purgatory. In contrast, *The Westminster Confession of Faith* states, "They whom God hath accepted in his Beloved, effectually called and sanctified by his Spirit, can neither totally nor finally fall away from the state of grace: but shall certainly persevere therein to the end, and be eternally saved."[99] In these cases, God's mercy is meant for the assembly.

In Roman Catholic theology, invoking God's mercy and forgiveness would include the deceased because the eternal destiny of the deceased is known only to God. In the Calvinist theology expressed in *The Westminster Confession*, the eternal destiny of the deceased is known if they are one of the elect. Thus, there would be no need for invoking God's mercy and forgiveness for the deceased, only for the grieving. Ecclesial traditions may fall at different places between these two theological positions.[100] Thus, the multivalence of the liturgical rites permits worshippers to enter into these services with different theological understandings of how God's mercy works for the deceased.

While the hope of the resurrection is the central theological theme of contemporary Christian burial services, a theology of consolation also features prominently. *Evangelical Lutheran Worship* begins one of its opening prayers, "Blessed be the God and Father of our Lord Jesus Christ, the source of all mercy and the God of all consolation, who comforts us in all our sorrows so that we can comfort others in their sorrows with the consolation we ourselves have received from God."[101] *The United Methodist Book of Worship* explicitly names the grief of those gathered, "We come together in grief, acknowledging our human loss. May

---

95. One exception to the move away from judgment is the opening anthem of the Rite One committal service and the same anthem as an option at the beginning of the Rite Two burial service in the Book of Common Prayer, which includes phrases such as "O Lord, who by our sins are justly angered," "deliver us not into the bitterness of eternal death," and "O worthy and eternal Judge, do not let the pains of death turn us away from you at our last hour." BCP 492, for Rite One, BCP 484.

96. RITES, 976.

97. BCP 493.

98. ELW 279.

99. *Book of Confessions*, 231 (Westminster Confession 6.094).

100. Unfortunately, the scope of this work does not permit further elaboration.

101. ELW 279.

God grant us grace, that in pain we may find comfort, in sorrow hope, in death resurrection."[102]

These prayers attest to the theology of consolation. Consolation is not only a profoundly pastoral response to death, it is also theological. That theology is rooted in the hope of the resurrection, but it acknowledges the pain of separation. A theology that focuses solely on the resurrection fails to affirm grief as the primary human response to the death of loved ones. A resurrection theology unbalanced with a consolation theology risks superficiality. It could too quickly be a forced theology in which fake smiles and unauthentic optimism cover over the real pain of loss.

A theology of consolation recognizes God as the source of consolation. God's nature is to comfort those who sorrow as "the God of all consolation."[103] This theology moves away from God as a judge toward God as a comforter. It is an imminent theology. God is not distant and removed from the pain of sorrow but abiding with the sorrowful. Thus, consolation ties the resurrection theology to the present day rather than only being about the future.

This theology of consolation is also dynamic. The purpose of consolation is not to remain fixed in sorrow. As the Book of Common Prayer states, "In your boundless compassion, console us who mourn. Give us faith to see in death the gate of eternal life, so that in quiet confidence we may continue our course on earth, until, by your call, we are united with those who have gone before."[104] The purpose of consolation is to have the strength to "continue our course on earth." Recognizing that people's journeys through grief can vary widely, the ultimate purpose of consolation is not to become static in grief but to continue in life.

Also, God offers the gift of consolation to the grieved not only to be received but also to be given to others. *Evangelical Lutheran Worship* poignantly proclaims "that we can comfort others in their sorrows with the consolation we ourselves have received from God."[105] The grace of consolation is meant to be given as much as to be received.

Hope and consolation work in tandem. The hope of the resurrection provides a foundation for faith that death is not the final answer. This hope is grounded in Christ's resurrection, so one's good deeds and sins are not the primary focus. Beseeching God's mercy recognizes the reality of sin and the reality of forgiveness. Consolation draws on the hope of the resurrection while also keeping it real. Grief, sorrow, and loss are authentic human experiences God attends through the gift of consolation. That dynamic gift allows the grieved to continue living and offering comfort to others.

---

102. BOW 222.
103. ELW 279.
104. BCP 493.
105. ELW 279.

Baptism and Death

"Do you not know that all of us who have been baptized into Christ Jesus were baptized into his death? Therefore we have been buried with him by baptism into death, so that, just as Christ was raised from the dead by the glory of the Father, so we too might walk in newness of life. For if we have been united with him in a death like his, we will certainly be united with him in a resurrection like his (Rom 6:3-5)." Paul makes a direct connection between baptism and death. As discussed above, Christ's death and resurrection are the foundation for the burial theology. Baptism is the key to the Christian's connection with Christ's death and resurrection through identity with Christ.[106] Thus, baptism links Christ and his resurrection with Christians and their resurrection.

Unsurprisingly, baptismal theology features prominently in the burial services of every Christian tradition. *Evangelical Lutheran Worship* and the *Book of Common Worship* have an explicit section in their burial rites called "Thanksgiving for Baptism." These sections reference Romans 6:3-5 and Galatians 3:27 "As many of you as were baptized into Christ have clothed yourselves with Christ." A Trinitarian acclamation then follows it.

Other rites without a specific section also make explicit reference to baptism. The Book of Common Prayer invokes baptism by introducing and using the Apostles' Creed: "In assurance of eternal life given at Baptism, let us proclaim our faith and say."[107] The Apostles' Creed is the baptismal creed recognized ecumenically. The prayers of the people or general intercessions from the Book of Common Prayer and the Roman Catholic *Rites* reference the deceased's baptism and subsequent nourishment at the eucharistic table.[108]

Symbols play an important role in connecting the burial service with baptismal theology. Of course, water is the primary symbol of baptism. Many ecclesial traditions use asperging after a baptism or during the reaffirmation of baptismal vows. Asperging involves sprinkling water on the heads of the congregants using hyssop or other tree branches or devices known as an aspergillum, the lever, with an aspersorium, the bucket, as depicted in Figure 5.1. In burial rites, the coffin or cremains may be asperged to symbolize the waters of baptism.[109] These aspersions, either in the reaffirmation of baptismal vows or in burial rites, should never be interpreted as a rebaptism. Most ecclesial traditions recognize baptism as a one-time event.[110] The asperging is solely a symbol of baptism.

---

106. See chapter one for more details.

107. BCP 496.

108. BCP 497 and RITES, 978. The BCP indicates that these prayers are optional, likely in case of the funeral of a non-baptized person. While RITES does not indicate that this portion of the prayer is optional, it does have a prayer for "A deceased non-Christian married to a Catholic," RITES, 1082.

109. See RITES, 975 and BCW 781.

110. See chapter one for more details.

Another important symbol of baptism is the white baptismal gown in which the newly baptized is clothed.[111] It references Galatians 3:27 "As many of you as were baptized into Christ have clothed yourselves with Christ." In the burial rite, the white funeral pall symbolizes the white garment of baptism. It is draped over the casket when it arrives at the church before the procession.[112]

Figure 5.1: The aspergent shell and aspersorium at Mission San Carlos Borromeo, Monterey, USA (California Historical Society, Public Domain; https://picryl.com/media/aspergent-shell-and-aspersorium-mission-san-carlos-borromeo-monterey-ca1907-12638e)

The Paschal or Easter Candle is another primary symbol of baptism. It is first lit at the Easter Vigil and represents the light of Christ that has broken through the darkness of sin and death through the power of the resurrection—the ancient hymn known as the *Exultet* is sung as the candle is processed into the church. Congregants will light their candles from the Paschal Candle, filling the space with light. It will often be kept lit through the fifty days of Easter.[113]

The Easter Vigil is the customary time for baptism from the most ancient rites of the church. Thus, the Paschal Candle lit at the beginning of the service remains lit for the baptisms or reaffirmations of baptisms occurring during that service. For baptisms outside of Eastertide, the Paschal Candle may be lit to hearken back to that primary experience.[114] Some traditions also have special days of the year beyond the Easter Vigil, such as Pentecost, All Saints' Day, and the Feast of the Baptism of Our Lord (First Sunday in Epiphany), when baptisms or the

---

111. See OBC 69; ELW 231; BOW 150; and BCW 411.
112. RITES, 975; BCP 490; ELW 280; BCW 781; BOW 218.
113. See BCP 285-287; ELW 266-267; BCW 290-293; BOW 437-441; *The Roman Missal: English Translation according to the Third Typical Edition*, 344-363.
114. See BCP 313; BOW 139; BOW 412.

Renewal of Baptismal Vows are strongly encouraged.[115] The Paschal Candle will often be lit on these days as well. Thus, it is fitting for the Paschal Candle to also be present during the burial rites as another symbol of baptism.[116]

These words and symbols form a strong connection between baptism and death. Working multivalently, they point to the deceased and the congregation. They remind everyone of their connection to Christ through baptism and, therefore, to Christ's resurrection.

One area in which the church's theology has evolved most significantly concerns the death of an unbaptized person. Historically, the church offered no official rites for the death of an unbaptized person, whether an adult or an infant. The medieval theology of judgment offered little assistance to the loved ones of the unbaptized deceased.

Influenced by the theologies of hope and consolation, contemporary burial rites provide some response to the burial of an unbaptized person. However, the responses vary. The Roman Catholic Church's "Order of Christian Funerals" provides a prayer for "A child who died before baptism" and special readings for "Funerals for Children who Died before Baptism."[117] The prayer includes a commendation, "You are the author and sustainer of our lives, O God, you are our final home. We commend to you N., our child." Such a commendation is grounded in the hope of the resurrection.

Other ecclesial traditions also offer special rites for the burial of a child. Contemporary situations are also addressed, such as miscarriages and stillbirths. For example, *Evangelical Lutheran Worship (Pastoral Care)* includes an entire service for "When a Child Dies Before or At Birth."[118] These prayers emphasize the parent(s)' great sorrow and the hope of the resurrection. *The United Methodist Book of Worship* also includes a burial rite, "At the Service for a Child." The Presbyterian *Book of Common Worship* offers a prayer, "At the Death of a Child," and the Anglican Book of Common Prayer offers a prayer, "At the Burial of a Child."[119] While they do not specifically reference the nature of the child's death, they offer the hope of the resurrection. The Anglican supplemental volume *Enriching Our Worship 2* includes an entire rite for the "Burial of a Child" with prayers for "The Death of an Infant," "For a Miscarriage," "For a Stillbirth or Child Who Dies Soon after Birth."[120]

The theological presumption for the death of an unbaptized infant is that the parents intended the child to be baptized. The death of an unbaptized adult presents additional theological challenges. Not all ecclesial traditions offer a rite in this circumstance. Those traditions that offer such a rite vary in their response.

---

115. BCP 312.
116. See RITES, 162 and ELWPC 252.
117. RITES, 1026 and 1059, respectively.
118. ELWPC 260-266.
119. BCW 255-257, BOW 822, and BCP 494 respectively.
120. *Enriching Our Worship 2*, 131-142.

The Anglican supplemental resource *Enriching Our Worship 3* offers a rite entitled "Burial of One who does not Profess the Christian Faith."[121] This rite provides consolation and offers an implicit theology of resurrection. The prayers only reference God without mentioning Christ or the Holy Spirit. The commendation is theologically important, "Into your hands, Immortal One, we commend N. Of your infinite goodness, wisdom, and power, work in *her* the wonderful purpose of your perfect will, for your mercies' sake. *Amen.*"[122] The prayer includes no trinitarian reference, but it implies an afterlife in that the departed is commended to the Immortal One. Unlike a Christian commendation, it does not refer to Christ's resurrection. Presumably, these omissions are to respect the non-Christian faith or lack of faith of the deceased while providing comfort to the bereaved.

The United Methodist Book of Common Worship prayer "When Faith is Uncertain," the Presbyterian *Book of Worship*'s "At the Service for a Person who did not Profess the Christian Faith," and the Anglican "Burial of One Who Does Not Profess the Christian Faith" in the *Book of Occasional Services* take a different approach.[123] These prayers are focused on the bereaved, presumably Christian, as the prayers conclude with "through Jesus Christ, our Savior/Lord." They ask God for consolation and recognize God's mercy and grace. However, they do not refer to the eternal destiny of the deceased.

Committal

Because the Christian faith takes the body seriously through its theologies of incarnation and resurrection, the final resting place for the deceased also has theological importance. Some ecclesial traditions will bless the place of burial. The Roman Catholic *Rites* and the Anglican Book of Common Prayer offer a prayer of blessing or consecration for a grave that has not been previously consecrated for Christian burial.[124]

These prayers reference Christ's burial as the theological rationale for such consecrations. They connect Christ's burial and subsequent resurrection with the one to be buried and the hope of their resurrection. The Roman Catholic prayer points to the symbolism of the grave explicitly, "Lord Jesus Christ, by your own three days in the tomb, you hallowed the graves of all who believe in you and so made the grave a sign of hope that promises resurrection even as it claims our mortal bodies." Like the baptismal symbols of water, white garments, and light in the funeral service, the grave also points to the hope of Christ's resurrection.

---

121. *Enriching Our Worship 3: Burial Rites for Adults together with a Rite for the Burial of a Child*, 66-69.

122. *Enriching Our Worship 3*, 68.

123. BCW 823, BOW 261-263, and *The Book of Occasional Services 2022*, 234-236, respectively.

124. RITES, 995 and BCP 503, respectively.

The committal services include the themes of hope and consolation that permeate the preceding funeral services. One common theme among most services is the prayer associated with the burial itself.

> In sure and certain hope of the resurrection to eternal life through our Lord Jesus Christ, we commend to Almighty God our brother N., and we commit his body to the ground; earth to earth, ashes to ashes, dust to dust. The Lord bless him and keep him, the Lord make his face to shine upon him and be gracious to him, the Lord lift up his countenance upon him and give him peace. Amen.[125]

Again, the hope of the resurrection features prominently in this prayer. It includes a commendation. Some services will have a commendation prayer separate from the committal prayer. The commendation prayer may also be said at the funeral if the committal does not occur immediately afterward.

The traditional phrase "earth to earth, ashes to ashes, dust to dust" may often be accompanied by throwing dirt on the coffin or cremains. This prayer recognizes that the body is not the final abode. It references the creation story of Genesis, in which God makes humankind from the dust of the earth. Thus, the body's creation is an act of God's will. These words speak of the cycle of life.

However, this cycle of life is not the end of the story. A traditional final prayer often concludes the service, "Rest eternal grant to him, O Lord; And let light perpetual shine upon him. May his soul, and the souls of all the departed, through the mercy of God, rest in peace. Amen."[126] This prayer reminds the bereaved of the hope of resurrection as the final note of the service. Death is not the end. God's mercy offers peace to all.

Remembering the Dead

From its earliest days, the church has remembered those who have died. The death of the martyrs was particularly poignant. They were marked with annual visits to the gravesite. Eventually, these commemorations developed into the commemoration of saints. The medieval concern for praying for the dead included intercessions to the saints on behalf of deceased loved ones. These intercessions became so entangled with the doctrine of purgatory and stipendiary Masses that many reformers forbade them.

Ecclesial traditions today take diverse approaches to the remembrance of the dead. Some traditions offer a service of remembrance for a certain number of days after or on the anniversary of the death.[127] All Saints' Day on November 1 and, for some traditions, All Souls Day on November 2 are opportunities to remember those who have died.

---

125. BCP 501. Similar prayers are found in RITES, 997, ELW 284, and BOW 245-246.
126. BCP 502 and also in RITES, 1002.
127. See ELWPC, 267-272 and *Enriching Our Worship 3*, 87-88.

Where ecclesial traditions differ most significantly is intercessions involving the dead. These intercessions can take three approaches: intercessions *for* the dead, intercessions *to* the dead, and intercessions *with* the dead. Most ecclesial traditions from the reformations eschew intercessions *for* the dead. Because they have rejected the doctrine of purgatory, they feel no need to intercede with God for the dead because the dead are in their final resting place.

Many ecclesial traditions from the reformations will also reject intercessions *to* the dead. These intercessions ask the saints to pray for the departed. It is important to note that this is not an act of worship. Christians only worship the Triune God, not the saints. Thus, they are not praying to the saints so much as asking the saints to pray for them or their loved ones. This distinction is notable in the Litany of the Saints, "pray for him/her."[128]

Intercession with the saints is a theological option that could bridge this ecumenical divide. Hebrews 12:1a states, "Therefore, since we are surrounded by so great a cloud of witnesses, let us also lay aside every weight and the sin that clings so closely." The author of Hebrews evokes an image in which the faithful departed are active witnesses to the living and seek to be an encouragement to them. Thus, just as one prayed with a fellow Christian in life, one could also pray with a fellow Christian after life.

The intention is not to affect the eternal destiny of the departed but to remain in prayerful communion with them. The *Apology of the Augsburg Confession* summarizes this thought well, "We know that the ancients spoke of prayer for the dead. We do not prohibit this, but we do reject the transfer, *ex opere operato*, of the Lord's Supper to the dead."[129] The reformers' concern was the use of Masses in a transactional way. The relational nature of prayer need not end with death. The communion of the saints remains forever.

Cultural Connections

As discussed above, burial rites have a tripartite structure to them. The first part of the rite is domestic and involves the final days before death and then the preparation of the body after death. The second part involves the rites done at the church, and the third part occurs at the gravesite. This same cycle of home, church, and gravesite is important not only for the burial but also for remembering the dead. Rituals occur in each of these places on those occasions as well.

This tripartite structure predates Christianity. Thus, Christianity has inculturated these practices. Because of the power that death holds over the human experience, tensions can develop when traditions and rituals surrounding death are not honored. Therefore, special attention to cultural differences is paramount when pastoring people through the death of a loved one.

---

128. RITES, 863-865.
129. *The Book of Concord*, 275-276 (*Apology of the Augsburg Confession*, §94).

This section includes cultural practices from around the world. However, these practices can differ significantly among and within cultural groups. Therefore, wise pastors will use them to prompt further inquiry rather than as monolithic examples.

Practices at the Time of Death

For many cultures, the days before and during death are critical. As death approaches, close family members gather. If the dying person is at home rather than in the hospital or other care facility, family members care for the person. Being surrounded by family as death approaches brings comfort to the dying. After death, family members often care for the corpse.

Among the Shona people, the women are the primary caregivers for the dying. At the time of death, these women must cry out loudly, a practice known as *mariro*. This wailing informs the rest of the community that a death has occurred in the home. Community members will arrive to express their condolences to the bereaved. The bereaved respond with "*Matambudziko*," which means "we have experienced suffering."[130]

Similarly, Latine cultures will gather family as the death of a loved one approaches. Family members may kiss their loved ones (*un beso para que muera en paz de Dios*). They may recite the Lord's Prayer, the creed, the *Salve Regina*, or even the seven last words of Christ as sources of comfort for the dying. The belief is that the dying person needs their family to assist them with accepting their impending death (*la ayuda de otros*). When death occurs, close family members may grieve expressively. This expressiveness is an act of ritual solidarity with the deceased. It is as if the family takes on the pain of death to ease the deceased's passage. The community will then begin arriving to express their condolences.[131]

In Taiwanese culture, the response can differ dramatically. The close family will gather with the one who is dying. However, when the death occurs, the family notifies the surrounding community so that they stay away. The traditional belief is that the deceased's spirit may linger for up to seven days after death. If non-family members enter the domicile, the spirit may accompany them back home instead of finding their final rest. Thus, close family members may not visit other family members for seven to forty-nine days after the death. They will also put a large piece of white paper on their door and small pieces of red paper on their neighbors' doors to signify that a death has occurred. Children will wear white robes, and grandchildren will wear white robes with red paper, meant to be a blessing.[132]

---

130. Chitakure, *African Traditional Religion Encounters Christianity*, 61-62.
131. Empereur and Fernández, *La Vida Sacra*, 266-268.
132. John Yieh, personal conversation.

For some cultures, domestic rituals include washing the body, which is done in the home. For the Shona people, the body is returned to the family if someone dies away from home. It is often kept in the kitchen, considered the home's most sacred room. Before the wake, the family members of the same gender will wash the body. Then, the body will be clothed, which for Christians may include their guild regalia.[133]

Before the popularization of embalmment, Mexican-American families would also prepare the body for the wake. They might place the body on the kitchen table with white sheets or use a board across chairs. They would place four white candles in a cruciform pattern. Blocks of ice would be used to preserve the body.[134]

The wake is a vital service before the funeral in many cultures. It may occur in the home, the church, or the funeral home. It is when extended family, friends, and community members visit the family to express their condolences. In contemporary times, the body has been embalmed and is present in the casket. A strong preference for a casket funeral rather than cremation continues in many cultures.

For Latines, the wake, or *velorio*, is one of the primary domestic rituals. It often involves the recitation of the rosary. Sometimes, a family member with experience as a prayer leader, known as a *rezador(a)*, will lead the recitation. At other times, it may be the priest or a deacon. Women from the community will prepare food for the bereaved and bring it all during the day of the wake.[135]

The wake can last from twenty-four hours to several days in Liberian communities. Mirrors will be covered in the home. Family members will wear black. The body is often present because of the desire to view it. However, for emigres, the cost of shipping the body back home can be exorbitant, so cremation is becoming an alternative. The wake involves many eulogies describing the life and faith of the deceased. However, as wakes become less popular and more condensed, eulogies have begun to enter the church's funeral service instead.[136]

Wakes are also significant in the African-American experience in the United States. Collins and Doolittle describe the end-of-life practices for an African-American woman in Kentucky. In this case, the wake occurred the evening before the funeral. It included an open casket to allow a viewing of the body. Prominent family members sat near the body to greet those viewing it. Guests would offer remembrances, many of which focused on her faith. At times, they would erupt into laughter, recalling the joyous moments of her life.[137]

---

133. Chitakure, *African Traditional Religion Encounters Christianity*, 62.

134. Norma Williams, *The Mexican American Family: Tradition and Change*, 35.

135. Empereur and Fernández, *La Vida Sacra*, 273-274.

136. John Harmon, personal conversation.

137. Wanda L. Collins and Amy Doolittle, "Personal Reflections of Funeral Rituals and Spirituality in a Kentucky African American Family," 960.

These practices would prepare the body and the family for the funeral service that would often occur on the following day. These funeral services may include cultural elements through music, but the ecclesial tradition determines much of their content. While important to the families, these services often do not include as many cultural practices as domestic and gravesite services before and after the funeral.

Gravesite Practices

As mentioned above, many cultures continue to prefer full-body burials to cremations, although the latter practice is growing. One of the significant costs associated with funerals is the casket and the limousines to transport it to the church and the gravesite. Lotta and Doolittle report that the cost of a funeral for African Americans can be as high as $8000 or more.[138] John Harmon commented that funerals for people of the African diaspora can be even more expensive than weddings.[139]

With full-casket funerals comes pallbearers. However, this role is not just logistical. In many cultures, the pallbearers are usually prominent family or community members. Honorary pallbearers may be family members who were close to the deceased but are physically unable to carry the casket. They still have a place of honor in the funeral procession.

For the Shona people, another position of honor is being the first to mark the grave, called *kutema ruhahu*. A close family member performs this responsibility on the morning of the funeral. After the first mark is made, the other men in the village assist with digging the grave. Once the grave is prepared, the body is taken from the house on a stretcher or carried by pallbearers and brought to the gravesite. As the coffin approaches the gravesite, the pallbearers lower it to the ground three times to allow the dead person's spirit to rest. Women, known as *varoora*, precede the coffin. They sweep the path before the coffin and bring water pots for the gravesite. They may also lay down cloths when the coffin touches the ground along its route.[140]

In many cultures, a final committal service will be held as the coffin is lowered into the grave. A common practice is for family members and other attendees to throw dirt on the coffin, usually at the words "dust to dust, ashes to ashes." In Latine cultures, women may express emotions on behalf of the bereaved family. A crucifix may be given to the family involved in the *Levantacruz* ceremony after the *Novenario*. Others may make the sign of the cross as they pass by.

In Taiwan, the somberness and orderliness of Christian funerals, compared to the Daoist services that often involved very public displays of grief, have

---

138. This cost is as of the article's publication in 2006; Collins and Doolittle, "Personal Reflections of Funeral Rituals," 965.

139. John Harmon, personal communication.

140. Chitakure, *African Traditional Religion Encounters Christianity*, 63.

attracted people to become Christians. Christian graveyards are often well kept as the family will visit their deceased loved one's resting place. On the other hand, traditional burial sites may often be unkempt because of the fear that spirits may still abide at them.[141]

For some cultures, the committal service at the gravesite marks the conclusion of the funeral services. However, additional practices will follow for other cultures immediately after the service and as anniversary remembrances.

Post-Burial Practices

While the committal may end the formal funeral rituals of the church, additional ritual practices continue immediately following the committal and, sometimes, for months to come. These rituals usually occur in the home and involve fewer and closer family members as time passes. Modern life has often curtailed these practices.

Immediately after the burial, the Shona people gather in the home and cut their hair to signify mourning. Women will often wear a black dress, and men will pin black cloth to their clothes to signify mourning. They will not cut their new hair or celebrate festive occasions, such as weddings, until the cleansing ceremony (*kurova guva/kugadzira*). Relatives who could not attend the funeral are expected to come when they can. They greet the mourning family and place a rock on the grave as a sign of respect to the deceased. On the day of the burial, some Shona groups will announce the *nayaradzo*, a Christian ceremony to pray for the deceased and comfort the mourners. The ritual *masuka foshora*, which means "cleaning of the shovels," occurs then and involves those who dug the grave. The final ritual is the cleansing ceremony when the deceased's spirit is welcomed as an ancestor.[142]

Liberians and other West Africans perform similar rituals. Immediately after the service, the repast will occur, which involves eating lots of food in celebration of the life of the deceased. Then, the family will enter a stage of mourning known as "sitting on the mat." It begins after the service when the family will gather in their home, sit on a mat, cut their hair, and mingle the locks with prayers as a sign of their unity during grief. During full mourning, the family wears only black. This period can last about six to twelve months. Then, the family may enter into "second mourning," wearing black and white. This period can last an additional twelve to eighteen months. Family members may also wear black armbands or ribbons to symbolize that they are in mourning.[143]

Ethiopians also observe periods of mourning. They will attend additional services three days, forty days, six months, and one year after the death. It is the custom to give food to the poor at these observances in the name of the dead.

---

141. John Yieh, personal conversation.
142. Chitakure, *African Traditional Religion Encounters Christianity*, 64-65.
143. John Harmon, personal conversation.

These traditions are observed more fully by Ethiopian Orthodox Tewahedo Church members than by Ethiopian Protestants.[144]

Latine communities will complete the last two of the tripartite rituals after the burial. The first part was the *Velorio,* or wake, the day before the burial. After the service, the family will host a repast in which much food and celebration occurs as the deceased is remembered.

Traditional Catholic families will then begin the *Novenario,* which is a nine-day series of prayers. As with the *Velorio,* a *rezandero/a* will lead the prayers, usually consisting of the rosary and the litany for the dead. The final day of the *Novenario* concludes with the *Levantacruz,* or "raising of the cross." This service includes a Mass, usually performed in the home. The cross that was given at the burial is marked with the birth and death dates of the deceased. It is then "enthroned" in a sacred place in the home. The *Levantacruz* may be celebrated on the anniversaries of the death as well.[145]

Remembering the Ancestors

The custom of remembering the dead has ancient roots. The desire to mark moments after the death of a loved one evolved into annual celebrations. These customs continue into the present in various ways. Sometimes, they involve domestic rituals with just the family. Sometimes, they occur in the church and involve the entire community. Because these customs often pre-dated Christianity, they have also caused tension as Christianity attempts to inculturate them while maintaining its theological foundation. Traditions within Christianity have also viewed these customs disparately due to differing theologies.

Two feast days developed in the Middle Ages around commemorating the dead. All Saints Day commemorated the faithful departed, known as the "Church triumphant." These persons were known to be in heaven due to their virtuous lives. They included the apostles and a host of others designated by the church as saints. All Souls Day commemorated the faithful departed, known as the "Church penitent." These were the souls believed to be in purgatory. They included the "average" Christian and, thus, had a more personal connection.

Because of the theological disputes surrounding purgatory and stipendiary Masses during the Reformations, some Protestant traditions stopped celebrating All Souls Day. They argued that all baptized Christians were saints. Notably, Martin Luther sent his famous *Ninety-five Theses* to his bishop in Wittenberg on October 31, 1517, the day before All Saints' Day, commemorated today as Reformation Day among some ecclesial traditions.

---

144. Rode Molla, personal conversation.

145. Francis and Pérez-Rodríguez, *Primero Dios,* 126-143. Samples of these three rituals are included.

With grand festivities, some Latine communities celebrate All Souls Day, El Día de Los Muertos (The Day of the Dead). People will dress up in costumes with skulls and skeletons. However, instead of being macabre, these costumes take on an almost ridiculous nature, as if they are making fun of death. The origin of these festivities is unclear. They may come from indigenous traditions or have developed as a reversal of the grimness of death. Also, the graves in cemeteries are adorned with flowers. People will have picnics in the cemetery. This practice hearkens back to the ancient Roman *refrigerium*.

The Day of the Dead celebrations are not always confined to November 2nd. Sometimes, they can form a triduum from October 31st to November 2nd, akin to the triduum of Maundy Thursday, Good Friday, and the Easter Vigil, celebrated in the spring. Sometimes, they can also last a whole week or beyond.

One of the customs from Mexico that has spread among the Latine diaspora in the United States is the *ofrenda* or *altarcitos*. These are altars usually set up in one's home, but the practice of setting them up in churches is growing. Depending on the altar's location, family and community members will place pictures of deceased loved ones on it. They will include food, especially *pan de muerto* (bread of the dead), candles, flowers, and other special mementos.[146]

Figure 5.2: A Día de los Muertos parade (Poloide93, CC BY-SA 4.0 <https://creativecommons.org/licenses/by-sa/4.0>, via Wikimedia Commons)

---

146. Empereur and Fernández, *La Vida Sacra*, 278-280.

These celebrations have a strong theological foundation to them. These acts of remembrance have an anamnestic quality similar to the Eucharist. Many ecclesial traditions believe Christ is present in the Eucharist, not through a mysterious, ghostly act but through anamnesis, a ritual remembering. Similarly, deceased loved ones are made present, not in a macabre, ghoulish manner, but through these rituals of remembrance.

Also, these celebrations recognize the power of the resurrection. By making fun of death, the participants are not being masochistic. Instead, they claim the power of life over death through the resurrection. The suffering of death does not claim the final victory. Life prevails.

Finally, community is central to these celebrations. The celebrations involve the entire community as children gather with parents and grandparents in the cemeteries to remember their ancestors. While some rituals may be performed in the home, they involve the family. Death and grief can be isolating. These celebrations remind people of the support they have in their families and the broader community through the grief of death.[147]

El Día de Los Muertos celebrations exemplify *mestizaje*, the combination of Spanish Catholicism and indigenous beliefs. Spanish Catholics brought the commemoration of All Saints and All Souls Days. These ecclesial traditions were inculturated with rituals and practices from popular religion. Many of these practices do not involve clergy but are led by family and community leaders. They illustrate how church and domestic practices can combine fruitfully.

Another example of a practice of remembering the deceased in Taiwan and other Asian countries is ancestor worship. Ancestor worship has its roots in the animism of folk religions among the Taiwanese and other Asian communities. The rituals associated with it are complex and can vary significantly from community to community.[148]

The practice's origins are grounded in the animistic belief that the spirits of the deceased reside in another world. This other world is not a paradise, as the ancestor spirits can get hungry. If they become angry due to neglect, they can cause mischief in this world by causing diseases and calamities for the family. Therefore, the family must appease them by offering food and incense. The connection between this world and the other is an ancestor tablet on the home altar. When the family offers food and incense on this altar, their essence transfers to the other world and appeases the ancestral spirits.

As these beliefs and practices developed, they moved from occurring only in the home to public temples. As clans and lineages developed, the desire to worship the ancestors in a communal gathering place, such as the temple, grew. Eventually, this practice was not only a religious one but also a sociological one in that it maintained group solidarity among the clan members.

---

147. Empereur and Fernández, *La Vida Sacra*, 280-281.
148. Lim Guek Eng, "Christianity Encounters Ancestor Worship in Taiwan," 47.

Ancestor worship also involves the tombs. One practice is a tomb-sweeping festival called Ching Ming or Tomb Sweeping Day in April. Family members are expected to visit the tombs to clean them. Paper money may be hung from the tombs as gifts to the ancestors. Also, the selection of a tomb is carefully considered based on the weather patterns and other natural phenomena to allow for the most auspicious burial possible.[149]

Ancestor worship has permeated much of Taiwanese society. One of its many influences impacts familial life. Men are expected to get married and have children as a way of appeasing their ancestors. They are also expected to carry on the necessary familial rituals that will comfort their ancestors and prevent them from becoming hungry ghosts. Annually, the family will invite the ancestor spirits to come home from their abodes in the temple or tombs at New Year's. After the family rituals, the spirits are invited to return to their original dwellings.[150]

Taiwanese conversion to Christianity can significantly impact family dynamics due to ancestor worship. Many Christian ecclesial traditions, especially the more conservative ones found in Taiwan, reject ancestor worship as a form of idolatry. Therefore, if the convert is a man, his family may become concerned that he will not fulfill his filial duty to maintain the rituals for the ancestors, especially at the time of death.

Lim Guek Eng offers some proposals for inculturating practices related to ancestral worship with Christianity. Eradicating ancestral tablets from the home may be very distressing. Alternatively, Eng suggests that Christian families replace the ancestral tablet in their home altar with a tablet inscribed with a cross. They may also replace the names of the ancestors with Scripture verses, such as Acts 16:31, 'Believe on the Lord Jesus Christ and you shall be saved, you and your household'; or Joshua 24:15, 'But as for me and my house, we will serve the Lord'; or 'Honour your father and mother, that it may be well with you, and that you may live long on the earth' (Ex 20:12; Deut 5:16; Eph 6:2, 3). The family may also gather regularly for prayer meetings as a substitute for the ancestral rituals.

Eng also offers alternatives for ancestor worship in the temple. She suggests constructing a Christian Memorial if significant numbers of villagers become Christians. On All Souls Day or the Chinese New Year, services could be conducted at the memorial that allows people to remember their dead.[151]

In its *Additional Liturgy Book*, the Taiwan Episcopal Church has a service named *Jing zû* or, roughly translated, Liturgy of Ancestor Remembrance or Commemoration. This liturgy is very similar to the burial rite. It includes Confucian teaching on ancestors nourishing the living, but it is clear that no worship occurs. As part of the liturgy, candles are set up on a separate table from the altar with

---

149. Eng, "Christianity Encounters Ancestor Worship in Taiwan," 47.
150. Eng, "Christianity Encounters Ancestor Worship in Taiwan," 48.
151. Eng, "Christianity Encounters Ancestor Worship in Taiwan," 53.

a cross. People come forward and place the names of their ancestors on the table and light a candle. Some churches may have an incense burner instead of candles; people will add incense to it as they come forward. This liturgy usually occurs on the Sunday before the Chinese New Year's Eve.[152]

Many ecclesial traditions have regularized funeral services with cultural elements limited to music selections and the surrounding art and architecture. However, domestic and gravesite rituals can be fulsome opportunities for cultural expression. Furthermore, remembering the dead can have strong cultural connections. The degree to which pastors are involved in these additional rituals will vary. Nonetheless, wise pastors will be aware of them and support them as inculturated expressions of the Gospel.

Pastoral Perspectives

Preparing for Death

A pastor's primary responsibility is to take care of the spiritual needs of their congregation. One of the most poignant spiritual needs is preparing to die. Of course, a pastor should make every attempt to be present near or at the moment of death. However, preparing for death needs to be a lifelong endeavor. Arguably, all pastoral responsibilities could be reduced to this priority. How are one's congregants prepared to meet death?

Pastors ministering in congregations in Western societies may face challenges addressing death with their congregations. Western societies, particularly the United States, have attempted to remove death from conscious consideration. Care for the sick and elderly typically occurs in institutions rather than at home. While medical facilities may be necessary for providing appropriate care, institutionalization of the sick and elderly can also be about institutionalizing death. Sickness and eventual death become an issue to be handled by professionals rather than care handled by the family and church.

Pastors can help congregations prepare for death by speaking about it. Preaching on death is essential. Of course, such preaching should discuss the hope of the resurrection. However, preaching that only discusses resurrection fails to address the grief, suffering, and even fear that death can cause. One can simultaneously have firm hope in the resurrection and anxiety about death. Pastors approach this existential tension best by addressing both aspects rather than focusing solely on hope or anxiety.

Children and youth also need to discuss death in age-appropriate ways. The death of a family member can impact them significantly, even if they do not know the person well. Classmates may get sick with a terminal illness. Suicide is a tragic reality, especially among adolescents. And the increase in

---

152. Taiwan Episcopal Church, *Additional Liturgy Book*, n.p. Translation and information about customs provided by Chia-Lin Wang.

school shootings and other forms of violence can make the risk of death very personal.

Younger and older people need a place to discuss death. The church can and should be such a safe place. However, pastors must approach this topic with great sensitivity. The temptation to avoid the realities of death with superficial quotations from scripture or attempts to remain "upbeat" should be avoided. Regular conversations in Sunday School, youth groups, and adult formation can help congregants prepare for death.

Another practical way of assisting congregants in preparing for death is to have a series on end-of-life planning. Many adults have not considered end-of-life planning. Sometimes, they avoid it because they consider it too depressing or macabre. Frequently, they allow other priorities to take precedence. Churches offer an excellent service to individuals and their families by discussing end-of-life planning.

October is a traditional month for end-of-life planning discussions, leading into the Feasts of All Saints and All Souls. Pastors may want a legal professional to come and offer guidance on document preparation. Five Wishes (https://www.fivewishes.org) is a well-known organization that offers guided assistance to individuals and families for end-of-life planning.

Funeral planning is an integral part of this process. One of the greatest gifts someone can offer their family is to have their funeral already planned. It allows family members to have clarity about their wishes and focus on other necessary details. Pastors can assist congregants in making wise choices about their funeral plans.[153]

Selecting a final resting place for one's remains is also essential. Some churches may have cemeteries or columbariums where congregants can be buried or their remains stored. If a church does not have these resources, pastors can offer referrals to cemeteries and funeral homes at which advanced planning can be arranged. Wise pastors will have several options available to meet the financial needs of their congregants.

Congregants may ask churches to store copies of these documents for them. This service can be a gift to families, as tracking down documents after a death can be challenging. Having the funeral arrangements on file is especially helpful since families expect the church's assistance in planning the service. Of course, such documents must be stored either in a physical location that is impervious to fire, such as a safe, or a digital location that is regularly backed up.

Finally, pastors must remember that not all congregants have family members to assist them. Some congregants may have remained single and have no spouse or children. Some congregants may be estranged from their families. And some congregants may have outlived their families. Churches can be especially helpful in such circumstances.

---

153. See the discussion below on funeral customaries.

Figure 5.3: The cases of the columbarium of the Père-Lachaise cemetery (Pierre-Yves Beaudouin / Wikimedia Commons / CC BY-SA 4.0 / https://fr.m.wikipedia.org/wiki/Fichier:P%C3%A8re-Lachaise_-_Division_87_-_Columbarium_40252-40306.jpg)

At the Time of Death

One of the most critical pastoral moments occurs near or during death. However, discerning the imminence of death can be challenging. Sometimes, death is sudden and tragic. Pastors must immediately make themselves available to the family in such situations if desired. Pastors can be a vital resource for a family as they absorb the shock of the tragic end of their beloved's life.

However, death can also linger. Medical advances have extended the lives of terminally ill patients well beyond what was inconceivable only a few years ago. Pastors also play an essential role in supporting families as they may need to make decisions about life-sustaining treatment. Advanced preparations can lift the burden of such important decisions, especially when emotions are high. However, such preparations may not exist, or other contingencies may have occurred. By being a non-anxious presence, pastors can give family members the support they need to make these important decisions without unduly influencing them.

A pastor should not impose their personal views during these times. While ecclesial traditions may have differing teachings on end-of-life care, the pastor's primary responsibility is to provide spiritual support. Nonetheless, the dying person or their family members may pose challenging questions to pastors. Pastors also should not avoid these questions but be prepared to answer from their theological tradition.

As death approaches, one of the critical spiritual tasks is gathering with one's family.[154] If time and physical stamina permit, the pastor may encourage the dying person to meet with their children or other significant family members for a final blessing. Genesis 49 offers the account of Jacob blessing his sons at his death. This moment can be very poignant in the life of the family. If tensions exist between the dying person and other family members, this moment could offer reconciliation. This final blessing can allow the dying person peace in letting go and provide the family with needed comfort.

When death is imminent, the pastor should come to the home, hospital, or other healthcare facility to offer the final prayers and rituals. If possible, the family should be present, and the dying person should be conscious. However, this service is essential even if the person is unconscious or unable to respond.

The person may want to offer a confession, in which case the pastor should excuse the family and offer as much privacy as the physical circumstances permit. Hearing the words of forgiveness can be very important for someone approaching death. They may also want communion. If possible, the family should join. Even if the person cannot receive the bread, the pastor could commune them with a drop or two of wine. If the circumstances do not permit any consumption of food or liquids, the pastor can assure the person of the benefits of spiritual communion or communion of desire.

The pastor should lead the commendation prayer at the time of death, if possible. However, if the pastor is not present at the time of death, they can offer the commendation prayer anyway. It can provide great comfort to the dying and their family.

After the death, the pastor should use discernment about their continued presence. In most cases, the pastor should excuse themselves, allowing the health care professionals to handle the body and the family to begin their arrangements. The pastor may wish to offer care if a family member appears distressed. However, emotional expressivity does mean one is in distress. Pastors must employ wise discernment.

Other people may also need pastoral care if the death was particularly tragic. Members of the health care facility could use pastoral care if such resources are not available to them. Church or wider community members may also need pastoral care, especially if the death resulted from a community tragedy.

Pastors may also need pastoral care—deaths, especially tragic deaths, impact pastors as much as others. Even expected and peaceful death can take their spiritual toll on pastors. Utilizing therapists, spiritual directors, and self-care practices is vital for pastors, too.

---

154. This material comes from a personal conversation with John Harmon.

At the Funeral and Burial

Pastors receive news about the death of the congregants in varied ways. As discussed above, they sometimes provide pastoral care for the deceased and their family up to and at the time of death. Perhaps the deceased had prepared all the necessary documents for their death and notified the family. The deceased ensured that their wishes were made known, and the family could gather before death for a final blessing and to participate in the rites at the time of death. Such well-prepared endings occur but are rare.

More often, pastors receive a phone call or email from a member of the deceased's family informing them of the death and requesting a funeral. The pastor may not have met the deceased if they moved away from the area, perhaps to receive care closer to family members. The family may not be actively involved in a church or even Christians. Members of the family may have been estranged from the deceased and each other and are only communicating now due to the death. These dynamics require pastoral sensitivity.

First, a pastor needs to establish the primary contact for the funeral. While such a task may appear simple, it can become complex if family dynamics are also complex. The person to notify the pastor of the death may be the primary contact. However, that designation should not be assumed but asked forthrightly. Planning funeral arrangements can be a way in which grief or family dynamics play out in unhelpful ways. If the pastor becomes triangulated among family members, the best resort may be to communicate with the estate executor as the primary contact.

After establishing the primary contact, the pastor will want to gather information to plan the funeral. A funeral customary can be helpful in this endeavor. Congregants can use it for their advanced planning, and families can use it to make decisions if such advanced planning is not done or needs to be modified. A pastor should check the physical or digital files to see if the deceased has completed a customary. If not, the pastor can use the customary to discuss the plans with the family.

The customary includes a list of suggested scripture lessons for the service. Including a one-sentence summary of the reading is often helpful, as biblical literacy varies. The church's musician can provide a list of appropriate hymns. How much families know about the deceased's scriptural and musical interests can vary greatly, so pastors should be ready to offer guidance. For example, suppose a customary was prepared by the deceased many years before their death. In that case, they may have left instructions for elaborate music such as Duruflé or Fauré's Requiems, which require significant musical resources. If the church does not have those resources and none were left in the will for the service or if the expected attendance will be small, then a pastor may need to encourage a family member to make other choices for the service. A completed customary is a guide, not a binding document.

The customary should also articulate the church's policies regarding music. Many churches require that the music director give final approval for music selections and may wish to be involved with the family in selecting the music. Policies regarding the use of recorded or secular music, family members as soloists or instrumentalists, and other considerations are best handled by clarifying them in the customary. A written policy feels less personal than a verbal decision. However, not all circumstances can be forethought. Therefore, music directors must also have good pastoral skills when guiding family members in making appropriate decisions for the service. If an honorarium is expected for the musicians, that information should be presented as the preparations are made.

The customary can include an information sheet for planning the funeral. One of the most critical pieces of information is the date and time of the service. Establishing the date and time for the service can be challenging for families as they may be living some distance from each other and have to coordinate their schedules. The availability of the church, the music director, and others must also be considered before agreeing to a date. Confirming the service only when the date has been settled is wise.

The disposal of the remains also needs to be clarified. Will there be a coffin or cremains? If a coffin will be present, who will be the pallbearers? Can they all physically carry the coffin? If the church's architectural arrangement or accessibility poses any challenges for a coffin, those challenges should be discussed. The funeral home can be of great assistance with these logistical details. Therefore, obtaining their contact information is paramount.

If cremains will be present, how will they arrive? Will they be sent by the funeral home or brought by a family member? One of the greatest pastoral gifts to family members can be offering to receive and store cremains until the service, especially if there will be a considerable time between the death and the service. However, such an offer presumes that the church has a safe place to store the cremains, such as near the altar or in a side chapel, and that the cremains are adequately marked. It is not unusual for multiple cremains to accumulate as scheduling funerals can take considerable time.

Other details are essential. Will there be a wake before the service? Will it be at the church, family, or funeral home? Is the pastor expected at the wake? How many people are expected at the service? Are flowers desired? If so, does the church require the use of their flower arrangements, or does the family need to contact a florist? Having a referral to a florist who knows the church's layout would be wise. Will there be a reception at the church after the service? If so, catering policies should be clearly articulated in the customary.

Eulogies can be complicated. On the one hand, eulogies can allow family members and friends to remember the deceased. They can be a part of the grieving process and allow families to resolve issues and let go. On the other hand, eulogies can direct the attention solely to the deceased, creating paragons of virtue instead of authentic memories. If the deceased was a prominent community member, eulogies can be politicized.

Therefore, it is crucial to establish a policy regarding eulogies beforehand. Some churches permit eulogies at the wake or the reception but not during the funeral service. They argue that the funeral's primary focus should be on Christ's resurrection, not the deceased's good deeds. Other churches will permit eulogies but under certain conditions. For example, they may limit the number of eulogies. They may require the persons offering the eulogy to write them down and submit them beforehand. Otherwise, eulogies can fill excessive time in the service and become its focal point.

An open invitation to offer a eulogy during the service is very unwise. Sometimes, people, including family members, can take those opportunities to air unresolved grievances with the deceased. People having little or no relationship with the family may use this time to address an audience. Or, no one may choose to speak at all, which can be awkward.

If eulogies are permitted in the service, it is wise for the pastor's sermon always to follow them. That can allow the pastor to redirect the attention to the primary focus of the funeral service, the hope of Christ's resurrection. It also ensures that a pastoral word is the last word.

When planning the service, the time of the committal must also be determined. Will it occur immediately after the service, after the reception, or later? If the church has a cemetery or columbarium, does the deceased have a site or niche? If not, where will the deceased's remains be brought? The funeral home can arrange transportation to the cemetery if a coffin is used. It can provide logistical support for the family members and others from the service who wish to attend the committal. However, sometimes, the family determines that only they and close friends are permitted to attend the committal.

If the committal is to occur at a later date, where will it occur? Sometimes, the committal may occur in a location some distance away from the funeral service, out of state, or even out of the country. Does the family expect the pastor to be present, and can the pastor be present? If not, does the family expect the pastor to make arrangements with another clergyperson in that area? Will the deceased receive a military burial? If so, those arrangements must be made with the appropriate government officials. The pastor may or may not be able to be present depending on their protocols. It is not unusual for a committal to occur weeks or even months after the service. Also, the committal may have already occurred before the service due to these same logistical challenges.

Grief and Remembrances

Grief is complex and takes time. People will process their grief in myriad ways. Pastors should avoid discussing "stages of grief" with the bereaved. Grief does not follow a linear process. Understanding that grief can take different forms, such as anger, avoidance, and depression, can help offer support. However, expecting the bereaved to act per a pre-determined grief process is unrealistic and can be harmful.

The nature of the death can complicate grief. A sudden, tragic death can be especially difficult. The death of a child is always challenging. Deaths that involve violence may also involve the criminal justice system and, therefore, may require extended attention. Suicides can impact a family for the rest of their lives. However, even the peaceful death of a nonagenarian can be challenging. All grief is complex.

Suppose the bereaved displays unhealthy behaviors such as extended periods of isolation, failure to eat or maintain hygiene, suicidal ideations, or other symptoms of depression. The pastor should refer them to a mental health professional in that case. However, expressions of emotion such as crying, deep sobs, and even yelling can be a healthy part of the grieving process. Similarly, emotional stoicism does not necessarily mean that one is suppressing emotions. Emotional expressivity varies by individual and over time. It is not unusual for the logistical challenges of death, funeral preparation, and estate execution to require such attention that little energy is left for emotional expression.

Therefore, if possible, pastors must maintain contact with the bereaved at specific periods after the funeral. A few days to a week after the funeral and when the extended family has left can be a time when grief catches up with them. A month, six months, and, especially, the anniversary of the death are also essential touchpoints for pastoral presence. A simple phone call or card can be enough for them to know that their pastor is present and praying for them.

Grief can have a significant impact on family dynamics. For adult children, grief can bring them back to an emotional past and may cause them to act out in ways they would typically never consider. Unresolved issues with the deceased may surface. Unresolved issues among siblings may also surface. As much as possible, the pastor wants to avoid triangulation. Depending on the past and future relationship with the family, providing substantive pastoral care may be unrealistic.

Sometimes, the most critical ministry a pastor can provide during death is presence. Family members may not desire pastoral care. Either they process their grief in other ways, or they have other sources of support. The only care some families desire from the pastor is arranging the funeral service. Yet, that service can be significant for them.

Pastors also need to attend to their grief. Tragic deaths can evoke strong emotions for pastors as well as for families. Pastors expressing emotion before, during, or after the service can be healthy for the family and the congregation to witness. However, excessive emotion can cause the family or congregation to focus on caring for the pastor. Therefore, it is unwise for pastors to lead the funeral services for their own families. They need to be pastored at those times. Also, certain deaths or family dynamics can trigger responses within the pastor that may have to do with their own grief or family issues. Discussing these responses with a therapist or pastoral counselor is wise and can allow the pastor to be present to provide pastoral care for the family. Sometimes, deaths may occur in close succession, even if they are unrelated. Attending to several deaths within a short time can also provide emotional and spiritual strain. Self-care is paramount for pastors.

As discussed above, the church offers many opportunities for remembrance. These opportunities are an essential part of the healing process. Not only do they remind the bereaved of their lost one, but they also remind them that they are not alone in their grief. Others carry grief also. They also provide opportunities to remember the hope of the resurrection. Hope and consolation are equally important in grief.

While ministering to the dying and burial practices predate Christianity, the church has offered necessary support during these times. Its theology of resurrection provides hope and consolation for the bereaved. Nonetheless, death and grief are complicated. Wise pastors balance presence, support, and comfort during these poignant time.

Questions for Discussion

1. Did any historical Christian practices around death described in this chapter seem compelling for appropriating in your context? Did any seem important to avoid and reject?

2. The chapter describes some difficulties in conducting funerals for families and congregations, including those of different traditions and beliefs. How can ministers ensure they are conducting end-of-life liturgies that are welcoming and healing for a group of diverse cultural and ecclesial backgrounds?

3. The importance of balancing a consolation theology with a resurrection theology is described in the chapter. Does your ecclesial tradition tend to emphasize one or another? What can you do as a minister to ensure your preferred side is not highlighted at the expense of the other?

4. The chapter describes the vital link between baptism and death found in many Christian funeral liturgies, which has historically made celebrating Christian death rituals for the unbaptized difficult. As a practitioner, how might you draw from different contemporary ecclesial traditions described in the chapter in handling such a situation with pastoral sensitivity and theological seriousness?

5. As the chapter describes, Christian ministry around death does not end with the funeral. As a practitioner, how might you continue liturgically and pastorally accompanying the bereaved beyond the funeral?

6. Does anything about how your broader societal context handles death make addressing death and dying as a minister difficult? How might you proactively prepare those under your care for the deaths of themselves and their loved ones in such a context?

Additional Resources

Carter, Marian. *Dying to Live: A Theological and Practical Workbook on Death, Dying and Bereavement.* London: SCM Press, 2014.
Written by an Anglican priest, this book provides a pastoral guide to all elements of ministry involving death and dying with scriptural, pastoral, and theological reflection on various case studies. Chapters four and five explicitly deal with liturgy, and the book includes a helpful, practical resource list for ministers.

Five Wishes. www.fivewishes.org
This organization provides excellent resources for end-of-life planning. Pastors may wish to use these resources if they offer a formational event for end-of-life planning.

Kelley, Melissa. *Grief: Contemporary Theory and the Practice of Ministry.* Minneapolis: Fortress Press, 2010.
This book attempts to bridge the gap between secular theories of grief and ministerial practice. Though not centrally concerned with liturgy, the book significantly enriches any practitioner's understanding of grief and grieving, making one's ministry much more sensitive to the complex and diverse ways people mourn death.

Paxton, Frederick. *Christianizing Death: The Creation of a Ritual Process in Early Medieval Europe.* Ithaca: Cornell University Press, 1990.
This book explores the rituals and later liturgical consolidations in Christian liturgies of death and dying between the 6th and 10th centuries. Academic in tone and approach, this book gives a wealth of historical information to help understand the ritual development from early to medieval Christian observations of death.

Richard Rutherford, *The Death of a Christian: The Order of Christian Funerals*, rev. ed., vol 7, Studies in the Reformed Rites of the Catholic Church. Collegeville, MN: The Liturgical Press, 1990.
This book explains the theology and practice of post-Vatican II Roman Catholic funeral liturgies. Though most relevant for those ministering in Roman Catholic contexts, it also contains a historical and theological overview of Christian funerals relevant to any ecclesial tradition.

Sheppy, Paul. *Death Liturgy and Ritual.* 2 Vols. 2nd Edition. New York: Routledge, 2017.
This book, written by an English Baptist minister, gives a wide-ranging theological overview of Christian funeral liturgies. Volume 1 is a more philosophical analysis of Christian theologies and practices of death and dying, and Volume 2 includes the author's commentaries on many different Christian traditions' death liturgies and rituals.

Appendices

Appendix A
Baptismal Rites

BCP	BCW	BOW	ELW	OBC
		Introduction to the Service		
Presentation and Examination of the Candidates	Presentation [includes examination]	Presentation of Candidates	Presentation	Reception of the Children
[*Liturgy of the Word occurred previously*]	[*Liturgy of the Word occurred previously*]	[*Liturgy of the Word occurred previously*]	[*Liturgy of the Word occurred previously*]	Biblical Readings & Homily
The Baptismal Covenant	Profession of Faith	Renunciation of Sin and Profession of Faith	Profession of Faith	[*Occurs right before the baptism*]
Prayers for the Candidates				Prayer of the Faithful
				Prayer of Exorcism and Anointing before Baptism
Thanksgiving over the Water	Thanksgiving over the Water	Thanksgiving over the Water	Thanksgiving at the Font	Blessing of Water and Invocation of God over the Water
				Renunciation of Sin and Profession of Faith
The Baptism	The Baptism	Baptism	Baptism	Baptism

BCP	BCW	BOW	ELW	OBC
\multicolumn{5}{c}{*The post-baptismal acts differ in order. They have been aligned together with the numbers indicating their order.*}				
1) Consignation and optional Chrismation	3) Consignation and Chrismation	2) Consignation and optional Chrismation (optional)	3) Consignation and optional Chrismation	1) Anointing after Baptism
	1) Receiving a White Garment	3) Receiving a White Garment	1) Optional Reception of Baptismal Garment	2) Clothing with a White Garment
2) Offering of a Lighted Candle	4) Receiving a Lighted Candle (occurs after the welcome)	4) Receiving a Lighted Candle		3) Handing of a Lighted Candle
	2) Handlaying	1) Handlaying	2) Handlaying	
				4) Ephphatha (optional)
		5) Receiving a Certificate of Baptism		
Welcoming the Baptized	Welcome	Welcome	Welcome	
[Service normally continues with communion]	[Service normally continues with communion]	[Service normally continues with communion]	[Service normally continues with communion]	Lord's Prayer Blessing and Dismissal

BCP 4301-308; BCW 407-413; BOW 130-139; ELW 227-231; *Order of Baptism of Children* 29-51.

Appendix B
Rites of Affirmation

BCP*	BCW	BOW**	ELW	OCN
		Introduction		Homily or Address
Presentation and Examination of Candidates	Presentation	Presentation of Candidates	Presentation	
The Baptismal Covenant	Profession of Faith	Renunciation of Sin and Profession of Faith	Profession of Faith	The Renewal of Baptismal Promises
			Affirmation in the Presence of the Assembly	
Prayers for the Candidates				
		Thanksgiving over the Water [For reaffirmations also]		
		[Candidates may touch the water, scoop it, use it on their heads, hands, or faces, but no rebaptism.]		
				Celebration of Reception‡
				Invitation‡
				Profession of Faith
				Act of Reception
For Confirmation with Episcopal Handlaying	Laying on of Hands with Optional Chrismation	Prayer by the Pastor with Handlaying	Blessing [No distinction made for types of affirmation]	The Laying on of Hands with Anointing with Chrism

BCP*	BCW	BOW**	ELW	OCN
		Invitation for the Congregation to Use the Water, including Asperging		
For Reception with Implied Episcopal Handlaying		Reception into the United Methodist Church		
For Reaffirmation With Implied Episcopal Handlaying				
				Celebrant's Sign of Welcome‡
Concluding Prayer	Welcome	Commendation and Welcome	Concluding Acclamation	The Universal Prayer
[*Service normatively continues with communion*]	Peace of Christ [*Service does not explicitly state that communion follows.*]	[*Service normatively continues with communion*]	[*Service normatively continues with communion*]	[*Service normatively continues with communion*]

BCP 413-419; BCW 420-423; BOW 131-143; ELW 234-237; OCN 19-35.

* Confirmations, receptions, and reaffirmations may also occur within the baptismal rite; see BCP 309-310.

** Confirmations and reaffirmations occur within the baptismal rite.

‡ The rite of Reception within Mass is separate from confirmation and found in RITES 279-283.

Appendix C
Marriage Rites

BCP	BCW	BOW	ELW	OCM
	Opening Sentences			
Congregational Address	Greeting	Greeting	Greeting	Congregational Address
			Declaration of Intention	
	Prayer of the Day		Prayer of the Day	
	Presentation [optional]			
	Declarations of Intent	Declaration of Intent		
	Affirmations	Response of the Families		
Marital Charge				
Declaration of Consent				
		Prayer		
Ministry of the Word	Ministry of the Word	Ministry of the Word	Ministry of the Word	Liturgy of the Word
		Intercessory Prayer		
				Address to the Couple
				Questions before the Consent
Exchange of Vows	Exchange of Vows	Exchange of Vows	Exchange of Vows	The Consent/ Exchange of Vows
				The Reception of the Consent

BCP	BCW	BOW	ELW	OCM
Blessing & Exchange of the Rings	Blessing & Exchange of the Rings	Blessing & Exchange of the Rings	Exchange of Rings (no blessing)	Blessing & Exchange of the Rings
				Blessing & Giving of the *Arras*
	Prayer			
Announcement of Marriage	Announcement of Marriage	Declaration of Marriage	Acclamation	
Prayers				
Blessing of the Marriage		Blessing of the Marriage	Marriage Blessing	
			Prayers of Intercession	
Exchange of Peace	Exchange of Peace		Exchange of Peace	
				Universal Prayer
Communion [optional]	Communion [optional]	Communion [optional]	Communion [optional]	Communion (if with Mass)
	Charge and Blessing		Blessing	
				Blessing & Placing of the *Lazo* or Veil
				Nuptial Blessing
		Prayer of Thanksgiving		
			Dismissal	Conclusion

BCP 422-432; BCW 690-700; BOW 179-198; ELW 286-291; *Order of Celebrating Matrimony* 21-39.

Appendix D
Rites of Reconciliation

BCP*	BCW	BOW	ELW	OPN
Individual Confession				
Reception of the Penitent	*No individual rite is provided.*	*No individual rite is provided.*	Reception of the Penitent	The Reception of the Penitent
Optional Reading of Scripture (Form Two)				The Reading of the Word of God (Optional)
Confession			Confession	The Confession of Sins and the Acceptance of Satisfaction
The priest offers counsel.			*The pastor offers counsel.*	*The priest offers counsel.*
Priest Asks Penitent for Repentance and Forgiveness of Others (Form Two)			Forgiveness	
Absolution				The Prayer of the Penitent and the Absolution
Dismissal			Greeting of Peace	The Proclamation of Praise of God and the Dismissal of the Penitent

BCP*	BCW	BOW	ELW	OPN
Corporate Confession				
[*Offers general confessions and absolutions in several services.*]	[*Offers general confessions and absolutions in several services.*]	[*Offers general confessions and absolutions in several services.*]		Liturgical Song
			Gathering	Greeting
				Prayer
			Word	The Celebration of the Word of God with Homily
			Confession	General Confession of Sins
			Forgiveness	General Absolution with Deacon or Minister or Individual Absolutions at Stations with Priests
				Proclamation of Praise for God's Mercy
			Exchange of Peace	Concluding Prayer and Thanksgiving

BCP 447-452; ELW 238-242(Corporate) and 243-244 (Individual); *Order of Penance* 31-33 (Individual) and 37-65 (Several Penitents with Individual or General Absolution).
*Two forms are provided. Differences are indicated in parentheses.

Appendix E
Rites of Public Healing

BCP	BCW	BOW	ELW	RITES
				Reception of the Sick
	Opening Sentences	Greeting		Opening Prayer
Ministry of the Word	Scripture Verses			Liturgy of the Word
	Hymn or Spiritual Song	Hymn of Praise		
General Confession (optional)	Confession and Pardon			
Absolution or Declaration of Forgiveness (optional)				
	Prayer for Illumination	Opening Prayer		
	Scripture	Scripture	Introduction	
	Sermon	Sermon		
		[Affirmation of Faith]		
		Confession and Pardon		
		The Peace		
	Hymn, Psalm, or Spiritual Song			
	Offering of Our Lives	[Offering]		
	Intercessions for Healing		Prayers of Intercession	Litany
		[Holy Communion]		

228

BCP	BCW	BOW	ELW	RITES
[Blessing of Oil by Priest]		[Thanksgiving over the Oil]		
		[Hymn of Healing]		
Laying on of Hands and Anointing	Laying on of Hands [and Anointing with Oil]	Prayers for Healing and Wholeness with Anointing and/or Laying on of Hands	Laying on of Hands with Optional Anointing	Laying on of Hands
				Prayer over the Oil
				Anointing
Concluding Prayer	Prayer	Prayer after Anointing and/or Laying on of Hands	Concluding Prayer	Prayer after Anointing
		[Sharing of Thanksgiving]		
	Hymn or Spiritual Song	Hymn		
	Blessing	Dismissal with Blessing	Blessing	
			Peace	
Holy Communion			[*The service can continue with communion.*]	Liturgy of the Eucharist

BCP 453-457; BCW 733-740; BOW 657-669; ELW 276-278; RITES (Anointing within Mass), 831-835.

Appendix F
Rites for Ministration at the Time of Death

BCP	BCW	BOW	ELWPC	RITES
		Holy Communion		Celebration of the Viaticum
		Baptismal Covenant		Baptismal Profession of Faith
	Opening Sentences		Scripture Readings	Scripture Readings
A Prayer for a Person Near Death	Prayer	Prayer	Greeting & Prayer	
		Prayer when life-support system is withdrawn		
Litany at the Time of Death			Litany	Litany of the Saints
A Commendation at the Time of Death	Commendation	A Commendation at the Time of Death	Commendation	Prayer of Commendation
				Prayer after Death
	Prayer for Family & Friends		Concluding Prayers	Prayer for the Family & Friends
	Blessing		Blessing	

BCP 422-432; BCW 773-776; BOW 264-270; ELWPC, 211-220; RITES, 852-871.

Appendix G
Burial

BCP*	BCW	BOW	ELW	Rites
Opening Anthem		Gathering	Gathering	
		The Word of Grace		
	Greeting	Greeting		Greeting
				[Placing of Pall, Entrance Procession, Placing of Christian Symbols]
	Thanksgiving for Baptism		Thanksgiving for Baptism	
	[Hymn]	Hymn or Song		
	Opening Sentences		Greeting	
Collect	Prayer	Prayer	Prayer of the Day	Opening Prayer
	Hymn or Spiritual Song			
	Confession and Pardon			
The Liturgy of the Word	Word	Proclamation and Response	Readings	Readings
Homily	Sermon	Sermon	Sermon	Homily
		Naming		
		Witness		
		Hymn or Song	Hymn of the Day	
Apostles' Creed	Affirmation of Faith	Creed or Affirmation of Faith	Creed	

231

BCP*	BCW	BOW	ELW	Rites
	Hymn or Spiritual Song			
	[Expressions of Gratitude for the Deceased]			
Prayers of the People	Prayer of Thanksgiving, Intercession, and Supplication		Prayers of Intercession	General Intercessions
	Hymn, Psalm, or Spiritual Song			
	Communion		[Communion]	Liturgy of the Eucharist
Concluding Prayer [when no communion]				
[Communion]				
The Commendation	Commendation	Commendation	Commendation	Final Commendation
		Prayer of Thanksgiving		
		The Lord's Prayer		
		Hymn		
	Blessing	Dismissal with Blessing	Exchange of Peace	
The Committal	The Committal	A Service of Committal	Committal	Rite of Committal

BCP 491-502; BCW 780-798; BOW 221-238 and 242-248 (A Service of Committal); ELW 279-285; *Rites*, 975-984 and 995-1002 (Rite of Committal).
*A traditional version known as Rite One is available in BCP 469-489. The elements are essentially the same.

Bibliography

Liturgical Sources

The Episcopal Church. *Book of Common Prayer and Administration of the Sacraments and Other Rites and Ceremonies of the Church, together with the Psalter or Psalms of David.* New York: Church Publishing, 1979.
———. *The Book of Occasional Services 2022.* New York: Church Publishing, 2022.
———. *Enriching Our Worship 1: Morning and Evening Prayer, The Great Litany, and The Holy Eucharist.* New York: Church Publishing Incorporated, 1998.
———. *Enriching Our Worship 2: Ministry with the Sick or Dying Burial of a Child.* New York: Church Publishing, 2000.
———. *Enriching Our Worship 3: Burial Rites for Adults together with a Rite for the Burial of a Child.* New York: Church Publishing, 2007.
Evangelical Lutheran Church in America. *Evangelical Lutheran Worship.* Minneapolis: Augsburg Fortress, 2006.
———. *Evangelical Lutheran Worship, Pastoral Care.* Minneapolis: Augsburg Fortress, 2008.
Presbyterian Church (U.S.A.). *Book of Common Worship.* Louisville: Westminster John Knox Press, 2018.
The United Methodist Church. *The United Methodist Book of Worship.* Nashville: United Methodist Publishing House, 1992.
United States Conference of Catholic Bishops. *The Order of Baptism of Children, Second Typical Edition.* New Jersey: Catholic Publishing Corp., 2020.
———. *The Order of Celebrating Matrimony, Second Typical Edition* New Jersey: Catholic Publishing Corp., 2016.
———. *The Order of Confirmation, Typical Edition*, Washington, D.C.: United States Conference of Catholic Bishops, 2016.
———. *The Order of Penance, Typical Edition*, New Jersey: Catholic Publishing Corp., 2023.
———. *The Rites of the Catholic Church.* 2 vols. Collegeville: Liturgical Press, 1990-1991.
———. *The Roman Missal: English Translation according to the Third Typical Edition.* Collegeville, MN: Liturgical Press, 2011.

Secondary Sources

Alexopoulos. Stefanos A. and Maxwell E. Johnson. *Introduction to Eastern Christian Liturgies* Collegeville, MN: Liturgical Press, 2022.
Augustine. *Confessions.* Translated by Sarah Ruden. New York, NY: The Modern Library, 2017.
———. "*De cura pro mortuis gerenda.*" in *Corpus Scriptorum Ecclesiasticorum Latinorum*, vol. 41, 629-630. Vindobonae: F. Tempsky, 1900; Reprint, New York: Johnson Reprint, 1979.
———. "Enchiridion." In *The Library of Christian Classics*, vol. 7, *Augustine: Confessions and Enchiridion*, translated and edited by Albert C. Outler, 337-412. Philadelphia: The Westminster Press, 1955.
———. *A Treatise on the Merits and Forgiveness of Sins, and on the Baptism of Infants.* Translated by Peter Holmes and Robert Ernest Wallis, revised by Benjamin B. Warfield, updated by A.M. Overett. Savage, MN: Lighthouse Publishing, 2018.
Austin, Gerard. *Anointing with the Spirit: The Rite of Confirmation: The Use of Oil and Chrism.* Studies in the Reformed Rites of the Catholic Church, vol. 2. Collegeville, MN: Liturgical Press, 1985.
Avis, Paul ed. *The Oxford Handbook of Ecclesiology.* Oxford Handbooks. Oxford: online edition, Oxford Academic, 10 July 2018.

Baldovin, John F. "Mass Intentions: The Historical Development of a Practice." *Theological Studies* 81, no. 4 (December 2020): 870-891.

Ballard, Richard G. "Lutheran Ambivalence toward Healing Ministry." Lutheran Forum 21, no. 4 (Advent 1987): 17-21.

Bevans, Stephen B. *Models of Contextual Theology*. Rev. ed. Maryknoll, NY: Orbis Books, 2002.

Bhandari, Aditi. "Uganda's anti-gay bill is the latest and worst to target LGBTQ Africans," *Reuters*, April 7, 2023. https://www.reuters.com/graphics/UGANDA-LGBT/movakykrjva.

Bloy House. "Claiming the Vision: Baptism and the Sacramental Life." YouTube video, 1:52:53. May 16, 2013. https://youtu.be/ElnxGX64YTk.

Bonhoeffer, Dietrich. *Life Together*. Minneapolis, MN: Fortress Press, 2015.

Borgen, Ole E. *John Wesley on the Sacraments: A Theological Study*. Nashville, Abingdon Press, 1972.

Boswell, John. *Same-Sex Unions in Premodern Europe*. New York: Villard Books, 1994.

Botte, Bernard. "Postbaptismal Anointing in the Ancient Patriarchate of Antioch." In *The Syrian Churches Series*, vol. 6, 63-71. Kottayam: C.M.S. Press, 1973.

Bradshaw, Paul F. *Apostolic Tradition: A New Commentary*. Collegeville, MN: Liturgical Press, 2023.

———. *The Canons of Hippolytus*. Bramcote, Nottingham: Grove Books, 1987.

Brock, Sebastian and Michael Vasey. *The Liturgical Portions of the Didascalia*. Bramcote, Nottingham: Grove Books, 1982.

Brown, Peter. *The Ransom of the Soul: Afterlife and Wealth in Early Western Christianity*. Cambridge: Harvard University Press, 2015.

Brown, Raymond. *An Introduction to the New Testament*. New York: Doubleday, 1997.

Bysted, Ane L. *The Crusade Indulgence: Spiritual Rewards and the Theology of the Crusades, c. 1095-1216*. Leiden: Brill, 2015.

Calvin, John. *Institutes of the Christian Religion*. 2 vols. Translated by Henry Beveridge. Grand Rapids, MI: Wm. B. Eerdmans Publishing, 1989.

Catholic Church and Theodore Alois Buckley. *The Catechism of the Council of Trent*. London: G. Routledge and co., 1852.

Chidester, David. *Empire of Religion: Imperialism and Comparative Religion*. Chicago: The University of Chicago Press, 2014.

"Child marriage is a violation of human rights, but is all too common." *UNICEF*, June 2023. https://data.unicef.org/topic/child-protection/child.

Chitakure, John. *African Traditional Religion Encounters Christianity*. Eugene, OR: Pickwick Publications, 2017.

Chow, Alexander. "The East Asian Rediscovery of 'Sin.'" *Studies in World Christianity* 19, no. 2 (2013): 126-140.

Chrysostom, John. Baptismal Instructions. Translated by Paul W Harkins. Westminster, MD: Newman Press, 1963.

Chupungco, Anscar J. "Liturgy and Inculturation." In *Handbook for Liturgical Studies: Fundamental Liturgy*, Vol. 2, edited by Anscar J. Chupungco, 337-375. Collegeville, MN: Liturgical Press, 1998.

Code of Canon Law, Latin-English Edition. Washington, DC: Canon Law Society of America, 1999.

Collins, Wanda L. and Amy Doolittle, "Personal Reflections of Funeral Rituals and Spirituality in a Kentucky African American Family." *Death Studies* 30 (2006): 957-969.

Constitution on the Sacred Liturgy. Vatican, December 4, 1963. https://www.vatican.va/archive/hist_councils/ii_vatican_council/documents/vat-ii_const_19631204_sacrosanctum-concilium_en.html.

Cornwall, Susannah. *Un/Familiar Theology: Reconceiving Sex, Reproduction and Generativity*. Rethinking Theologies. London: T&T Clark, 2017.

Cuming, G.J. *A History of Anglican Liturgy*, 2nd ed. London: Macmillan, 1982.

Cummings, Brian, ed. *The Book of Common Prayer: The Texts of 1549, 1559, and 1662*. Oxford: Oxford University Press, 2011.

Cyprian, "Epistle 73." In *Saint Cyprian Letters (1-81)*, translated by Rose Donna, 268-285. Washington, DC: Catholic University of America Press, 1965.
Dallen, James. *The Reconciling Community: The Rite of Penance*. Studies in the Reformed Rites of the Catholic Church, vol. 3. Collegeville, MN: The Liturgical Press, 1986.
Dionysius. *Dionysius the Pseudo-Areopagite: The Ecclesiastical Hierarchy*. Translated and annotated by Thomas L. Campbell. New York: University Press of America, 1981.
Dix, Gregory. *The Theology of Confirmation in Relation to Baptism*. Westminster: Dacre Press, 1946.
Dix, Gregory, ed. *The Treatise on the Apostolic Tradition of St. Hippolytus of Rome, Bishop and Martyr*. London: Society for Promoting Christian Knowledge, 1937.
Douglass, Katherine M. "Findings from The Confirmation Project." *Theology Today* 76, no. 1 (2019): 7-16.
Edmonson, Stephen. "Opening the Table: The Body of Christ and God's Prodigal Grace." *Anglican Theological Review* 91 (Spring 2009): 213-234.
Empereur, James. *Prophetic Anointing: God's Call to the Sick, the Elderly, and the Dying*. Wilmington, DE: Michael Glazier, 1982.
Empereur, James and Christopher Kiesling. *The Liturgy That Does Justice*. Collegeville, MN: The Liturgical Press, 1990.
Empereur, James and Eduardo Fernández. *La Vida Sacra: Contemporary Hispanic Sacramental Theology*. Lanham: Rowman & Littlefield, 2006.
Eng, Lim Guek. "Christianity Encounters Ancestor Worship in Taiwan." *Evangelical Review of Theology* 8, no. 2 (October 1984): 46-54.
Erickson, John H. "Divergencies in Pastoral Practice in the Reception of Converts." In *Orthodox Perspectives on Pastoral Praxis*, edited by Theodore Stylianopoulos, 149-178. Brookline, MA: Holy Cross Orthodox Press, 1988.
Euchologian, A Book of Common Order. Edinburgh: William Blackwood and Sons, 1890.
Evangelical Lutheran Church in America. "Table and Font: Who is Welcome?" https://download.elca.org/ELCA%20Resource%20Repository/ELCA_Table_And_Font.pdf.
Fabian, Richard. "First the Table, then the Font." The Association of Anglican Musicians, 2002. http://www.saintgregorys.org/Resources_pdfs/FirsttheTable.pdf.
"Faith Positions on Marriage Equality." *HRC Foundation*, accessed on July 20, 2023. https://www.hrc.org/resources/positions-of-faith-on-same-sex-marriage.
Ferguson, Everett. *Baptism in the Early Church: History, Theology, and Liturgy in the First Five Centuries*. Grand Rapids, MI: William B. Eerdmans Publishing Company, 2009.
Fisher, J.D.C. *Christian Initiation: Baptism in the Medieval West*. Alcuin Club Collections, no. 47. London: SPCK, 1965.
———. *Christian Initiation: The Reformation Period*. Alcuin Club Collections, No. 51. London: SPCK, 1970.
Francis, Mark R. and Arturo Pérez-Rodríguez. *Primero Dios: Hispanic Liturgical Resources*. Chicago, IL: Liturgy Training Publications, 1997.
Fry, Richard, Jeffrey S. Passel, and D'Vera Cohn. "A majority of young adults in the U.S. live with their parents for the first time since the Great Depression." *Pew Research Center*, September 4, 2020. https://www.pewresearch.org/short-reads/2020/09/04/a-majority-of-young-adults-in-the-u-s-live-with-their-parents-for-the-first-time-since-the-great-depression.
Fuller, Reginald. "Christian Initiation in the New Testament." In *Made, Not Born: New Perspectives on Christian Initiation and the Catechumenate*, 7-31. Notre Dame: University of Notre Dame Press, 1976.
Gatta, Julia and Martin L. Smith. *Go in Peace: The Art of Hearing Confessions*. New York: Morehouse Publishing, 2012.
God in Christ Reconciling: On the Way to Full Communion in Faith, Sacraments, and Mission. Report of the Joint International Commission for Dialogue between the World Methodist Council and the Catholic Church, 39. http://www.christianunity.va/content/unitacristiani/en/dialoghi/sezione-occidentale/consiglio-metodista-mondiale/dialogo/documenti-di-dialogo/god-in-christ-reconciling--on-the-way-to-full-communion-in-faith.html.

Gusmer, Charles W. *And You Visited Me: Sacramental Ministry to the Sick and Dying*. Rev. ed. Studies in the Reformed Rites of the Catholic Church, Vol. 6. Collegeville, MN: The Liturgical Press, 1990.

Haigh, Christopher. *English Reformations: Religion, Politics, and Society under the Tudors* Oxford: Oxford University Press, 1993.

Hatchett, Marion J. *Commentary on the American Prayer Book*. New York: Harper Collins, 1995.

Hatzung, Erin Swenson. "Reimagining Confirmation Ministry as a Lifelong Practice." *Word & World* 38, no. 1 (Winter 2018), 79-89.

Hejzlar, Pavel. "John Calvin and the Cessation of Miraculous Healing." *Communio Viatorum* 49, no. 1 (2007): 31-77.

Heller, Dagmar. *Baptized into Christ: A Guide to the Ecumenical Discussion on Baptism*. Geneva: World Council of Churches Publications, 2012.

Henderson, J. Frank. *Liturgies of Lament*. Chicago, IL: Liturgy Training Publications, 1994.

Herbert, Clare. *Towards a Theology of Same-Sex Marriage*. London: Jessica Kingsley Publishers, 2021.

Hugh of Saint Victor. *On the Sacraments of the Christian Faith: (De Sacramentis)*. The Mediaeval Academy of America, No. 58. Cambridge, MA: Mediaeval Academy of America, 1951.

Hunter, David G. "Augustine and the Making of Marriage in Roman North Africa." *Journal of Early Christian Studies*, 11, no. 1 (Spring 2003): 63-85.

Ignatius. "*Ad Polycarpum*." In *The Ante-Nicene Fathers*, vol. 1, edited by Alexander Roberts and James Donaldson, 93-96. Grand Rapids, MI: Wm. B. Eerdmans Publishing Company, 1956.

———. "To the Ephesians." In *The Apostolic Fathers*, vol.1, edited and translated by Bart D. Ehrman, 219-241. Cambridge, MA: Harvard University Press, 2003.

———. "To the Romans." In *The Apostolic Fathers*, vol.1, edited and translated by Bart D. Ehrman, 269-283. Cambridge, MA: Harvard University Press, 2003.

Johnson, Maxwell E. *The Prayers of Sarapion of Thmuis: A Literary, Liturgical, and Theological Analysis*. OCA 249. Rome: Pontificio Istituto Orientale, 1995.

———. *The Rites of Christian Initiation*. Rev. ed. Collegeville, MN: Liturgical Press, 2007.

Kavanagh, Aidan. "Unfinished and Unbegun Revisited: The Rite of Christian Initiation of Adults." In *Living Water, Sealing Spirit*, edited by Maxwell E. Johnson, 259-273. Collegeville, MN: The Liturgical Press, 1995.

Kolb, Robert and Timothy J. Wengert, eds. *The Book of Concord: The Confessions of the Evangelical Lutheran Church*. Minneapolis, MN: Fortress Press, 2000.

Korse, Piet. "Baby Rituals, Ritual Baths, and Baptism – A Case from Congo." In *Life and Death Matters: The Practice of Inculturation in Africa*, edited by Anthony J. Gittins, 13-18. Nettetal: Steyler Verlag, 2000.

Kramer, Stephanie. "Polygamy is rare around the world and mostly confined to a few regions." *Pew Research Center*, December 7, 2020. https://www.pewresearch.org/short-reads/2020/12/07/polygamy-is-rare-around-the-world-and-mostly-confined-to-a-few-regions.

Lancel, Serge. *Saint Augustine*. Translated by Antonia Nevill. London: SCM Press, 1999.

Langstaff, Beth. "A Case of Apostolic Discontinuity: John Calvin on the Anointing of the Sick for Healing." *Stone-Campbell Journal* 16 (Fall 2013): 217-233.

Levesque, Joseph L. "The Theology of Postbaptismal Rites in the Seventh and Eighth Century Gallican Church." *Ephemerides Liturgicae*, 95 (1981): 3-43.

Liturgical Resources 1: "I Will Bless You, and You Will Be a Blessing." Rev. ed. General Convention, 2015. https://extranet.generalconvention.org/staff/files/download/15668.

The Liturgy of John Knox: Received by the Church of Scotland in 1564. Glasgow: University Press, 1886.

Lloyd, Charles and Andrew Raines, eds. Formularies of Faith: Confessional Documents Issued by Henry VII and Thomas Cranmer. Library of Anglican Theology, No. 8. Galesburg, IL: Seminary Street Press, 2022.

Lumbala, F. Kabasele. *Celebrating Jesus Christ in Africa: Liturgy and Inculturation*. Maryknoll, NY: Orbis Books, 1998.

Luther, Martin. *Luther's Works, American Edition*. Vols. 1–30, edited by Jaroslav Pelikan. St. Louis: Concordia, 1955–76. Vols. 31–55, edited by Helmut Lehmann. Philadelphia/Minneapolis: Muhlenberg/Fortress, 1957–86.

Luther, Martin and Theodore G. Tappert. *Letters of Spiritual Counsel*. Philadelphia: Westminster Press, 1955.

Lutheran Church in America, The American Lutheran Church, and The Lutheran Church-Missouri Synod. *The Report of the Joint Commission on the Theology and Practice of Confirmation*. 1970. http://www.ctsfw.net/media/pdfs/JointCommissiononTheologyandPracticeConfirmation report1970.pdf.

Macy, G. *The Banquet's Wisdom: A Short History of the Theologies of the Lord's Supper*. New York: Paulist Press, 1992.

Mead, Margaret. "Ritual and Social Crisis." In *The Roots of Ritual*, edited by James D. Shaughnessy, 87-101. Grand Rapids, MI: William B. Eerdmans Publishing Company, 1973.

Mendenhall, George E. and Gary A. Herion. "Covenant." In *The Anchor Bible Dictionary*, vol. 1, edited by David Noel Freedman, 1179-1202. New York: Doubleday, 1992.

Milavec, Aaron. *The Didache: Text, Translation, Analysis, and Commentary*. Collegeville, MN: Liturgical Press, 2003.

Miles, Sara. *Take This Bread*. New York: Ballantine Books, 2007.

Mitchell, Nathan D. "Reforms, Protestant and Catholic." In *The Oxford History of Christian Worship*, edited by Geoffrey Wainwright and Karen B. Westerfield Tucker, 307-350. Oxford: Oxford University Press, 2006.

Mitchell, Leonel L. *Baptismal Anointing*. London: SPCK, 1966.

McGowan, Anne and Paul F. Bradshaw, *The Pilgrimage of Egeria: A New Translation of the* Itinerarium Egeriae *with Introduction and Commentary*. Collegeville, MN: Liturgical Press Academic, 2018.

Meyers, Ruth A. *Continuing the Reformation: Re-Visioning Baptism in the Episcopal Church*. New York: Church Publishing, 1997.

———. "Fresh Thoughts on Confirmation." *Anglican Theological Review* 88, no. 3 (Summer 2006): 321-340.

Needham, Belinda L., Talha Ali, et al. "Institutional Racism and Health: A Framework for Conceptualization, Measurement, and Analysis." *Journal of Racial and Ethnic Health Disparities* 10 (2023): 1997-2019.

Ofula, Kenneth. "'The River Between': Negotiating Dual Identities in the Anglican Churches of Kenya." *Studies in World Christianity* 25, no. 1 (2019): 95-113.

Osmer, Richard Robert. *Confirmation: Presbyterian Practices in Ecumenical Perspective*. Louisville, KY: Geneva Press, 1996.

Park, Andrew Sung and Susan L. Nelson, eds. *The Other Side of Sin: Woundedness from the Perspective of the Sinned-Against*. Albany, NY: State University of New York Press, 2001.

Parry, Tyler D. *Jumping the Broom: The Surprising Multicultural Origins of a Black Wedding Ritual*. Chapel Hill, NC: The University of North Carolina Press, 2020.

Paxton, Frederick S. *Christianizing Death: The Creation of a Ritual Process in Early Medieval Europe*. Ithaca, NY: Cornell University Press, 1990.

Pearson, Sharon Ely, ed. *Signed, Sealed, Delivered: Theologies of Confirmation for the 21st Century*. New York: Morehouse Publishing, 2014.

Peter Lombard. *The Sentences: Book 4: On the Doctrine of Signs*. Translated by Giulio Silano. Mediaeval Sources in Translation 48. Toronto, ON: Pontifical Institute of Mediaeval Studies, 2010.

Pfatteicher, Philip H. "Some Early and Later Fathers on the Visitation of the Sick." *Pro Ecclesia* 19, no. 2 (Spring 2010): 207-222.

Porter, H. B. "The Origin of the Medieval Rite for Anointing the Sick or Dying." *The Journal of Theological Studies* 7, no. 2 (October 1956): 211-225.

Prayer Book Studies 18: On Baptism and Confirmation. New York: Church Pension Fund, 1970.

The Proposed Book of Common Prayer. New York: Church Publishing, 1970.

Presbyterian Church (U.S.A.). *Book of Confessions, Study Edition, Revised*. Louisville, KY: Westminster John Knox Press, 2017.

Raebum, Gordon D. "The Reformation of Burial in the Protestant Churches." In *A Companion to Death, Burial, and Remembrance in Late Medieval and Early Modern Europe, c. 1300-1700*, edited by Philip Booth and Elizabeth Tingle, 156-174. Leiden: Brill, 2021.

Raj, Selva J. "The Santal Sacred Grove and Catholic Inculturation." *Journal of Ecumenical Studies* 42, no. 2 (Spring 2007): 243-252.

Repp, Arthur C. *Confirmation in the Lutheran Church*. St. Louis, MO: Concordia Publishing House, 1964.

Rowell, Geoffrey. *The Liturgy of Christian Burial: An Introductory Survey of the Historical Development of Christian Burial Rites*. London: S.P.C.K., 1977.

Rutherford, Richard. *The Death of a Christian: The Order of Christian Funerals*. Rev. Ed. vol. 7, Studies in the Reformed Rites of the Catholic Church. Collegeville, MN: The Liturgical Press, 1990.

"Same-Sex Marriage Around the World." *Pew Research Center*, June 9, 2023. https://www.pewresearch.org/religion/fact-sheet/gay-marriage-around-the-world.

Scherzer, Carl J. *The Church and Healing*. Philadelphia: Westminster Press, 1950.

Searle, Mark, and Kenneth W. Stevenson, eds. *Documents of the Marriage Liturgy*. Collegeville, MN: The Liturgical Press, 1992.

Second Vatican Council. "Dogmatic Constitution on the Church, *Lumen gentium*, 21 November, 1964." In *Vatican Council II: The Conciliar and Post Conciliar Documents*, edited by Austin Flannery. Collegeville, MN: Liturgical Press, 1975.

———. "Constitution on the Sacred Liturgy, *Sacrosanctum Concilium*, 4 December 1963." In *Vatican Council II: The Conciliar and Post Conciliar Documents*, edited by Austin Flannery. Collegeville, MN: Liturgical Press, 1975.

Smith, Martin L. *Reconciliation: Preparing for Confession in the Episcopal Church*. Cambridge, MA: Cowley Publications, 1985.

Smith, Melody K. "Presbyterian Church (U.S.A.) approves marriage amendment." *Presbyterian Church (U.S.A.)*, March 17, 2015. https://www.pcusa.org/news/2015/3/17/presbyterian-church-us-approves-marriage-amendment.

Sperry-White, Grant. *The Testamentum Domini: A Text for Students, with Introduction, Translation, and Notes*. Bramcote, Nottingham: Grove Books, 1991.

Spinks, Bryan. "A Seventeenth-Century Reformed Liturgy of Penance and Reconciliation." *Scottish Journal of Theology* 42, no. 2 (1989): 183-197.

Stamm, Mark. *Let Every Soul be Jesus' Guest*. Nashville, TN: Abingdon Press, 2006.

Stark, Rodney. *The Rise of Christianity: A Sociologist Reconsiders History*. Princeton, NJ: Princeton University Press, 1996.

Stevenson, Kenneth. *Nuptial Blessing: A Study of Christian Marriage Rites*. Oxford: Oxford University Press, 1983.

———. *To Join Together: The Rite of Marriage*. Studies in the Reformed Rites of the Catholic Church, Vol. V. New York: Pueblo Publishing Company, 1987.

Stuhlman, Byron. *Occasions of Grace: An Historical and Theological Study of the Pastoral Office and Episcopal Services in the Book of Common Prayer*. New York: Church Publishing, 1995.

"Supplemental Resources for use within the Evangelical Lutheran Worship Service of Marriage." Evangelical Lutheran Church in America. Minneapolis, MN: Augsburg Fortress Press, 2016.

Taiwan Episcopal Church. *Additional Liturgy Book*. Taiwan: n.p., n.d.

Tanner, Norman P., ed. *Decrees of the Ecumenical Councils*. Vol. 2. Washington, DC: Georgetown University Press, 1990.

Thomas Aquina. *Summa Theologica*. Vol. 3. New York: Benziger Brothers, 1948.

Tinker, George. *Missionary Conquest: The Gospel and Native American Cultural Genocide*. Minneapolis, MN: Fortress Press, 1993.

Tripp, D. H. "The Radical Reformation." In *The Study of Liturgy*, rev. ed., edited by Cheslyn Jones, Geoffrey Wainwright, Edward Yarnold, and Paul Bradshaw. London: SPCK, 1992.

Truscott, Jeffrey A. *The Reform of Baptism and Confirmation in American Lutheranism*. Drew University Studies in Liturgy, No. 11. Lanham, MD: The Scarecrow Press, 2003.

Turner, Paul. *Inseparable Love: A Commentary on The Order of Celebrating Matrimony in the Catholic Church*. Collegeville, Minnesota: Liturgical Press, 2017.
Turner, Peter. *Sources of Confirmation from the Fathers through the Reformers*. Collegeville, MN: The Liturgical Press, 1993.
The Use and Means of Grace: A Statement on the Practice of Word and Sacrament. Minneapolis, MN: The Evangelical Lutheran Church in America, 1997.
Van Buchem, L. A. *L'homélie Pseudo-Eusébienne de Pentecôte. L'origine de la confirmatio en Gaul Méridionale et l'interprétation de ce rite par Fauste de Riez*. Nijmegen: N.P., 1967.
Van Gennep, Arnold. *The Rites of Passage*. Translated by Monika B. Vizedom and Gabrielle L. Caffee. Chicago: The University of Chicago Press, 1960.
Viefhues-Bailey, Ludger H. *Between a Man and a Woman? Why Conservatives Oppose Same-Sex Marriage*. New York: Columbia University Press, 2010.
Ware, Kallistos. *The Orthodox Way*. Rev. ed. Crestwood, NY: St. Vladimir's Seminary Press, 1995.
Wesley, John. *John Wesley's Sunday Service of the Methodists in North America*. Nashville, TN: United Methodist Publishing House, 1984.
———. *Popery Calmly Considered*. Dublin: W.H. Whitestone, 1779.
———. *The Works of John Wesley*. 32 vols. Edited by Albert C. Outler. Nashville, TN: Abingdon Press, 1984.
———. *The Works of the Rev. John Wesley: With the Last Corrections of the Author*. Vol. 10. London: Wesleyan-Methodist Book-Room, 1872.
West, Edward N. "The Rites of Christian Initiation in the Early Church." In *Confirmation: History, Doctrine, and Practice*, edited by Kendig Brubaker Cully, 3-15. Greenwich, CT: Seabury Press, 1962.
Westerfield Tucker Karen B. *American Methodist Worship*. Oxford: Oxford University Press, 2001.
Whitaker, E. C. and Maxwell E Johnson. *Documents of the Baptismal Liturgy*. Rev. 3rd ed. Collegeville, MN: Liturgical Press, 2003.
White, James F. *Protestant Worship: Traditions in Transition*. Louisville, KY: Westminster John Knox Press, 1989.
Williams, Norma. *The Mexican American Family: Tradition and Change*. Dix Hills, NY: General Hall, Inc., 1990.
Willis, Geoffrey Grimshaw. *Saint Augustine and the Donatist Controversy*. Eugene, OR: Wipf and Stock Publishers, 2005.
Winkler, Gabriele. "Confirmation or Chrismation: A Study in Comparative Liturgy." *Worship* 58, no. 1 (January 1984): 2-17.
Witte, John Jr. *From Sacrament to Contract: Marriage, Religion, and Law in the Western Tradition*. Louisville, KY: Westminster John Knox Press, 1997.
Yarnold, Edward. *The Awe-Inspiring Rites of Initiation: The Origins of the R.C.I.A*. 2nd ed. Collegeville, MN: Liturgical Press, 1994.
Zizioulas, John. "Ordination—A Sacrament? An Orthodox Reply." In *The Plurality of Ministries*, edited by Hans Kung and Walter Kasper, 33-40. New York: Herder and Herder, 1972.

Index

A
Alcuin, 46-47, 238
Ambrose of Milan, 7, 9, 135
Anabaptist, 14-15, 23, 50
Anglican(s), 14-16, 53-54, 67, 93-94, 98, 120,
    140-141, 144-145, 147-148, 152, 190,
    196-197, 217, 237, 239-240
Anointed, 2-3, 5, 20, 43-44, 123, 129, 131, 157,
    172, 176
Apostolic Tradition, 5-6, 8, 42, 124-125,
    236-237
Augustine of Hippo, 8, 10-11, 21-22, 44, 46, 50,
    80-82, 89, 92, 99-101, 119, 127,135-136,
    174, 176, 181
Aquinas, Thomas, 47, 89, 132

B
Book of Common Prayer, 49-50, 55, 67, 72,
    89, 92-94, 136-138, 140, 143-144, 146,
    184-185, 187, 189-194, 196-197, 235, 237,
    240-241
Book of Common Worship, 58, 96, 143, 146,
    190-191, 194, 196-197, 235
Boswell, James, 85, 236
Bucer, Martin, 15, 48

C
Calvin, John, 15, 50, 57, 91-92, 102, 135-137,
    182-184, 192, 236, 238-239
Canonical Penance, 128-131, 145, 147
Carolingian Reform, 46, 130 -131, 179
Catechumenate, 5, 8, 17, 32-33, 38, 41, 126,
    129, 238
Catechumens, 5, 8, 11, 28, 32-33, 53, 129, 176,
    179
Charlemagne (Charles the Great), 11, 46
Chrysostom, John, 7, 22-23, 80, 101, 135, 236
Constitution on the Sacred Liturgy, 103, 187,
    237, 241
Cornwall, Susannah, 100-101, 120, 237
Council of Laodicea, 44
Council of Trent, 50-51, 93, 236
Cranmer, Thomas, 15, 49, 89, 92-93, 136-137,
    184, 239
Creed, 36, 48, 72, 200
    Apostle, 20, 194, 233
    Nicene, 10, 20, 148

D
Didache, 3-5, 27, 42, 126, 239
Dura Europos, 6-7
    Eastern Orthodox Church(s), 23, 51, 55

E
Ecumenical Movement(s), 16, 58, 61, 63
Egeria, 8, 240
Episcopal Church, 17, 54-57, 59, 62, 66, 71, 76,
    96-97, 99, 168, 207-208, 235, 240-241
Eastern Orthodox, 16, 23, 51, 55, 59
Exomologesis, 126-127

F
Fides, 81, 99
Fidelity 81, 84, 99, 101-102, 107, 119
Fuller, Reginald, 41, 238

G
Gelasian Sacramentary, 11, 44, 86
Gregory the Great, 176-177
Gusmer, Charles 123-124, 129,132-133, 168,
    171, 238

H
Hagia Sophia, 27-28
Harmon, John, 105, 201-203, 211
Hippolytus, 5, 125, 127, 236-237

I
Ignatius of Antioch, 79-80, 126, 172, 238

J
John the Baptist / Baptizer, 1-2,136, 189

K
Kimball, Lisa, 71
Knox, John, 39, 50, 120, 137, 168, 183, 235,
    239-240, 242

L
Lateran Council, 46, 90, 132
Latine, 66, 106-107, 150-151,153-156,
    200-202, 204-205
Liturgical Renewal Movement, 16-17, 24,
    51-52, 61
Lombard, Peter, 43, 37, 88-89, 97, 240

Lumbala, F. Kabasele, 104, 107-108, 150-153, 155-156, 239
Luther, Martin, 14-15, 47-49, 69, 72, 90, 92, 133-136, 140, 180-183, 204, 239
Lutheran(s), 14-16, 48, 53, 92, 182, 184
    Book of Worship (LBW), 52-53
    Church, 17, 52, 69
    Evangelical Lutheran Worship (ELW), 52, 96, 100, 139, 142-146, 190, 192-194, 196, 235, 241
    Inter-Lutheran Commission on Worship (ILCW), 52
    Joint Commission on the Theology and Practice of Confirmation, 53-54

M
Martyr, Justin, 4-5
Mead, Margaret, 169
Melancthon, Philip, 50, 134-136
Mitchell, Leonell, 45, 240

N
Novation, 127

O
Ofula, Kenneth, 67-68, 240
Ordo Romanus XI, 11-12
Ordines, 11, 177
Original Sin, 11-12, 16, 21-23, 35-38, 46, 87, 90, 96, 133, 139, 151-152, 179
Osiander, Andreas, 48

P
Park, Andrew Sung, 154, 168
Pentecost, 2, 13, 19, 43-44, 47, 195
Pentecostal, 17
Porter, H.B., 131
Prayer Book Studies, 55-56, 240
Premarital Counseling, 112-117
Proles, 81, 99, 101
Protestant(ism), 14-15, 39, 47-48, 50, 53, 68, 76, 93-94, 105, 110, 150-152, 182, 184-185, 204, 240, 242

Q
Quaker(s), 14
Quam Primum, 12, 16, 22, 26, 31, 46, 129

R
Realism, 13, 46
Refrigerium, 171, 205
Reformation(s), 14, 16, 23, 47-50, 52-56, 61, 72, 82, 88-90, 93, 120, 122, 133, 144, 180, 182, 184-185, 199, 204, 238, 240-241
Repp, Arthur, 52, 240
Rite(s), 173, 190, 194
    Anglican, 54, 67
    Burial, 169-170, 182-183, 187-188, 190-191, 194-197, 199, 207, 235, 241
    Byzantine, 60, 85
    Chrisitan Initiation for Adults (RCIA), 17, 52
    Coptic, 84
    Corporate Confession, 139, 146, 162, 228
    East Syrian, 84
    Funerary, 177
    Greco-Roman, 169
    Individual Reconciliation, 163
    Latin, 99
    Lutheran, 54
    Marriage, 78-80, 82, 84, 87, 91-95, 97, 108-109, 119-120, 225, 241
    Mozarabic, 131
    Of Passage Experiences (ROPES), 68
    Pastoral Care of the Sick, 188
    Penitential, 143, 162-163, 189
    Public Lament, 155
    Reconciliation, 121, 123, 125, 155, 227
    Roman Catholic, 47, 168, 188, 190, 194, 197
    Visitation of the Sick, 136-138, 144, 182, 184, 240
    West Syrian, 84
Ritual cleansing / washing, 1-3, 18
Roman Catholic Church, 17, 22, 48, 50-53, 55, 59-61, 65, 87, 90, 92, 94, 98-99, 102-103, 134, 139-142, 144, 147-148, 175, 179, 188-189, 192, 196

S
Sacramentary, 85, 177
    Gelasian, 11, 44, 86
    Gregorian, 86-87, 96
    Verona, 87
Sacramentum, 81, 89, 99-100
Same-sex marriage, 95-96, 110, 117, 237-238, 241-242
Santal, 68-69, 240
Sarum Manual, The, 88-89
Scholasticism, 3, 104, 130, 132
Shona People, 106, 109, 200-203
Smith, Martin, 164
St. Victor, Hugh of, 89, 132
Stevenson, Kenneth, 78-82, 85-89, 91-94, 96, 99, 120, 241
Stuhlman, Byron, 78, 85, 136, 241

T
Tabulae Matrimoniales, 78, 81-82
Talmudic, 77-78
Tertullian, 4-5, 42, 80, 126-127
Trinitarian, 3-5, 36, 117, 194, 197
Tucker, Westerfield, 14, 56-57, 93-94, 105, 186, 240, 242

V
Van Gennep, Arnold, 66, 77, 242
Vatican Two (II), 39, 93, 103-104, 148, 150, 168, 187, 217

Viaticum, 129, 171-172, 178, 182, 188-189, 231

W
Ware, Kallistos, 23, 242
Wesley, John, 56, 92, 137-138, 186, 236, 242
Winkler, Gabriele, 42-44, 242
Witte, Jr., John, 89, 90-92, 102, 104, 120, 242

Z
Zwingli, Ulrich, 14-15, 50

Milton Keynes UK
Ingram Content Group UK Ltd.
UKHW051602160624
444239UK00018B/225